C0-CBY-848

REFORMING INDIA'S EXTERNAL, FINANCIAL, AND FISCAL POLICIES

STANFORD STUDIES IN
INTERNATIONAL ECONOMICS AND DEVELOPMENT
STEPHEN H. HABER AND JOHN H. PENCAVEL, EDITORS

The process of international economic integration has both ardent advocates and energetic detractors. Over the last half-century, the dramatic expansion of international trade and capital flows has been linked with unprecedented economic advances. At the same time, many view these closer economic ties as a major complicating factor in macro-economic management, as well as a leading cause of financial crises. Moreover, nations share unevenly in global prosperity. Despite some conspicuous successes, many countries remain mired in underdevelopment and want. While supporters of integration attribute these failures mainly to deficiencies in developing countries' own policies, its opponents often attribute the failures to the self-same factors that help make some countries rich.

These live and vital issues are the focus of the Stanford Studies in International Economics and Development. This series, which will include single- and co-authored books, as well as edited collections of scholarly papers, deals with a broad spectrum of policy issues that influence the economic performance of low-income countries, including those engaged in the transition from command to market economies. The series concerns itself with the policy reforms that are urgently needed to raise the living standards of the world's poor, to enhance global cooperation and security, and to foster broader participation in the benefits engendered by growth in the global economy.

REFORMING INDIA'S EXTERNAL, FINANCIAL, AND FISCAL POLICIES

Edited by

Anne O. Krueger
and Sajjid Z. Chinoy

Stanford University Press
Stanford, California 2003

Stanford University Press
Stanford, California

Stanford Center for International Development (formerly the Center for Research on Economic Development and Policy Reform)

Printed in the United States of America on acid-free, archival-quality paper

Library of Congress Cataloging-in-Publication Data
Reforming India's external, financial, and fiscal policies / edited by Anne O. Krueger and Sajjid Z. Chinoy.
p. cm.—(Stanford studies in international economics and development)
Papers of a conference held at Stanford University, June 2001.
Includes bibliographical references and index.
ISBN 0-8047-4775-X (cloth : alk. paper)
1. Monetary policy—India—Congresses. 2. India—Economic policy—Congresses. I. Krueger, Anne O. II. Chinoy, Sajjid Z. III. Series.
HG1235 .R44 2003
330.954—dc21 2003003854

Designed by James P. Brommer
Typeset by G&S Typesetters, Inc. in 10/12.5 Bembo
Original Printing 2003

Last figure below indicates year of this printing:
12 11 10 09 08 07 06 05 04 03

Contents

Tables

Figures

List of Abbreviations

Abbreviation	Meaning
ADM	Anti-dumping measure
ATM	Automatic teller machine
BAL	Bajaj Auto Limited
Balco	Bharat Aluminum Company, Limited
BCR	Balance on current revenues
BIFR	Board for Industrial and Financial Reconstruction
BJP	Bharatiya Janata Party
BMS	Bharati Mazdoor Sangh (labor federation)
BOP	Balance of payments
BOPE	Balance of payments equilibrating
BSE	Bombay Stock Exchange
CAMEL	Capital adequacy, asset quality, management quality, earnings, liquidity
CAMELS	Capital adequacy, asset quality, management quality, earnings, liquidity, systems evaluation (India)
CENVAT	Centralized value-added tax
CIS	Commonwealth of Independent States (former Soviet republics)
CMIE	Center for Monitoring Indian Economy
CREDPR	Center for Research on Economic Development and Policy Reform
CRR	Cash reserve requirement
CSE	Calcutta Stock Exchange
CSO	Central Statistics Office

DMK	Dravida Munnetra Kazhagam (political party)
DOT	Department of Telecommunications (India)
EEC	European Economic
EMBI	Emerging Market Bond Index
E-Mfg	Extended manufacturing
EPZ	Export processing zone
FDI	Foreign direct investment
FER	Foreign exchange reserves
FIPB	Foreign Investment Promotion Board
FM	Forbes Marshall
FTZ	Free-trade zone
FY	Fiscal year
GATS	General Agreement on Services
GATT	General Agreement on Tariffs and Trade
GDP	Gross domestic product
GDR	Global depository rights
HIPC	Heavily indebted poor country
HS-ITC	Harmonized system, India Trade Classification
ICRIER	Indian Council for Research on International Economic Relations
IGIDR	Indira Gandhi Institute of Development Research
ILA	Initial loan amount
ILO	International Labor Organization
IMF	International Monetary Fund
IOSCO	International Organization of Securities Commissions
IT	Information technology
JPC	Joint Parliamentary Committee
LIBOR	London inter-bank offered rate
M2	A measure of the money supply, it includes currency, bank deposits, and personal money market accounts.
M3	A measure of the money supply, it includes currency, bank deposits, and all money market accounts. Larger in scope than M2.
MAT	Minimum alternative asset-based tax
MFA	Multifiber Arrangement
MFN	Most favored nation
MMCB	Madhavpura Mercantile Cooperative Bank
MNP	Movement of natural persons
MODVAT	Modified value-added tax
MoU	Memorandum of understanding
MTN	Multilateral tariff negotiation

NAFTA	North American Free Trade Agreement
NASDAQ	National Association of Securities Dealers Automated Quotations system
NASSCOM	National Association of Software and Service Companies
NAV	Net asset-value (price)
NBER	National Bureau of Economic Research
NBFC	Non-bank financial corporations
NCLT	National Companies Law Tribunal
NDA	National Democratic Alliance
NGO	Non-governmental organization
NIPFP	National Institute of Public Finance and Policy (India)
NPA	Non-performing asset
NPL	Non-performing loan
NRI	Non-resident Indians
NSCC	National Securities Clearing Corporation
NSDL	National Securities Depository Limited
NSE	National Stock Exchange
NTB	Non-tariff barrier
OBC	Other backward classes
OECD	Organization for Economic Cooperation and Development
PMO	Prime Minister's Office
POL	Petroleum, oil, and lubricants
PTA	Preferential Trade Agreement
PSU	Public sector undertaking, also called SOE
PVLP	Present value of (contractual) loan payments
QR	Quantitative restriction
RBI	Reserve Bank of India
Rs	Rupees
SAARC	South Asian Association for Regional Cooperation
SAPTA	South Asian Preferential Trade Agreement
SC(R)A	Securities Contracts (Regulation) Act
SEB	State electricity board
SEBI	Securities and Exchange Board of India
SEZ	Special economic zone
SICA	Sick Industrial Companies (Special Provisions) Act
SIL	Special import license
SLR	Statutory liquidity requirement
SOE	State-owned enterprise
SSI	Small-scale industry
TFP	Total factor productivity
TRAI	Telecommunications Regulatory Authority of India

TRIPS	Trade-Related Aspects of Intellectual Property Rights
UAE	United Arab Emirates
UNEP	United Nations Environment Program
UR	Uruguay Round
US-64	Mutual fund run by the Unit Trust of India
UTI	Unit Trust of India
VAT	Value-added tax
VRS	Voluntary retirement scheme
WTO	World Trade Organization

Contributors

Anne O. Krueger is the First Deputy Managing Director of the International Monetary Fund and founding director of the Center for Research on Economic Development and Policy Reform at Stanford University.

Sajjid Z. Chinoy is an associate at McKinsey and Company, and was a graduate researcher at the Center for Research on Economic Development and Policy reform while at Stanford University, where he received his Ph.D. in economics in 2001.

T. N. Srinivasan is the Samuel C. Park, Jr. Professor of Economics at Yale University and a senior research fellow at the Center for Research on Economic Development and Policy Reform at Stanford University.

Shankar Acharya is the Reserve Bank Professor at the Indian Council for Research on International Economic Relations. In the past, Dr. Acharya has also held numerous government positions, including that of Chief Economic Adviser, Ministry of Finance, Government of India.

Naushad Forbes is a director at the company of Forbes Marshall and a consulting associate professor and lecturer in the Stanford University Program in Science, Technology, and Society.

James A. Hanson is a senior financial sector policy advisor at the World Bank.

K. V. Kamath is the Managing Director and Chief Executive Officer of ICICI Bank, Ltd.

Ajay Shah is a consultant for the Department of Economic Affairs, Ministry of Finance, Government of India.

Susan Thomas is an assistant professor at the Indira Gandhi Institute of Development Research.

Ravi Narain is the Managing Director for the National Stock Exchange of India, Ltd.

Raghuram G. Rajan is the Joseph L. Gidwitz Professor of Finance at the University of Chicago Graduate School of Business.

John Echeverri-Gent is an associate professor at the University of Virginia, Charlottesville, Woodrow Wilson Department of Government and Foreign Affairs.

Sebastian Edwards is the Henry Ford II Professor of International Economics at the University of California, Los Angeles, Anderson Graduate School of Management.

Alan J. Auerbach is the Robert D. Burch Professor of Economics and Law at the University of California, Berkeley, and the director of the Robert D. Burch Center for Tax Policy and Public Finance.

Arnold C. Harberger is a professor of economics at the University of California, Los Angeles.

N. K. Singh is a member of the Planning Commission of the Government of India.

Preface

The papers in the volume are the outcome of a conference hosted by the Center for Research on Economic Development and Policy Research at Stanford University in June 2001. Much has happened since then. The events of September 11, 2001, the launch of a new multilateral trade negotiation by WTO members, and the global slowdown have all changed the context in which policy makers must operate. However, although these events may make reforms more difficult, they also make them more imperative. Since the first generation of reforms was undertaken in India in the early 1990s, slower progress has been made, giving reason for concern. In particular, the current tension between India and Pakistan is likely to impact fiscal decisions going forward, which will affect the economy as a whole. There is also wariness about further integration into the global economy, and the details of the much-needed financial reforms are undetermined. These are some of the questions addressed in this volume, which we hope will help to stimulate and guide the debate over the next set of reforms. Many of the authors of these papers have official positions, but all the views expressed in the book are personal.

The editors would like to thank the authors, discussants, and other participants, including the members of the (The) Indus Entrepreneurs (TiE). Logistical support was provided by the staffs of both CREDPR and the Stanford Institute for Economic Policy Research, and is gratefully acknowledged. Thanks are due to the deputy director of CREDPR, Nicholas Hope, and to graduate researcher Irena Asmundson for organizational help, both during the conference and in assisting this volume to press. Finally, our deepest gratitude goes to those whose generous support helped make the conference possible: especially Kanwal Rekhi, as well as Anil Godhwani, Naren Gupta, B.V. Jagadeesh, Kailash Joshi, Burton and DeeDee McMurtry, Vijay Vashee, and Stanford University.

INTRODUCTION

Anne O. Krueger and Sajjid Z. Chinoy

For more than four decades after India attained independence in 1947, Indian economic policy was governed by a philosophy that emphasized inward-oriented, state-led development. Import-substituting industrialization was deemed to be the major engine of growth and was implemented through a highly restrictive trade regime characterized by import licensing, quantitative restrictions, and high tariffs on imports. Furthermore, a substantial majority of economic activities were reserved for the public sector. Not only did state-owned enterprises (SOEs) have a substantial presence in industries such as steel, fertilizers, heavy chemicals, machine tools, and infrastructure, but, with time, they were given monopoly positions in banking and insurance and importation of bulk consumer goods, and even came to own hotels and bakeries. Alongside this public sector dominance existed a system of stringent controls on private economic activity, implemented through an investment-licensing regime that dictated choice of scale and technology for private economic activity.

By the late 1970s and 1980s it became obvious that the strategy of public sector dominance (characterized by overmanned, inefficient, and politicized SOEs) and controls over the private sector had greatly impeded economic efficiency and economic growth. Thus, starting from a very low per-capita income, India averaged an abysmally low 2 percent annual rate of growth of per-capita income between the late 1940s and 1980.

During the first three and a half decades of this period, India's fiscal and monetary policies were very conservative by the standards of other developing countries. By the mid-1980s, however, India's fiscal policy became significantly more expansionary. Although economic growth accelerated to more than 5 percent, the fiscal expansionism of the 1980s was unsustainable and resulted in a severe balance of payments crisis in 1991—as foreign debt ballooned, inflation rose to more than 13 percent (much above the politically acceptable rate in India), and reserves covered less than two weeks of imports.

In contrast to the response to earlier balance of payments crises, Indian policy makers responded to the 1991 crisis by undertaking a series of structural reforms that were meant to reverse some of the egregious aspects of existing regulation and government intervention in the economy, thus dramatically altering the incentive structure facing economic agents in India. Foreign trade and investment barriers were significantly reduced—as import licenses for most items were abolished, tariffs reduced, quantitative restrictions phased away, and foreign direct investment actively encouraged. Similarly, financial markets were liberalized significantly as interest rates were partially freed, competition was encouraged in the banking sector, and a new securities exchange—equipped with a host of institutional innovations—was established in the equity market. On the fiscal front, too, encouraging early progress was made as the central-government fiscal deficit was reduced from its level of 7.7 percent of GDP in 1990–91 to 5.5 percent in 1992–93. As India finally moved toward a market-oriented economy, real GDP growth accelerated to more than 6 percent per year during the early and mid-1990s—an unprecedented achievement in India's economic history.

During the latter half of the 1990s, however, and amid much political uncertainty, the reform process lost much of its early momentum, and by the end of the decade disquieting signs began to appear on the fiscal and financial front. By 1999–2000, the consolidated nonfinancial public sector deficit was estimated to have reached 10.8 percent of GDP. On the banking front, credit to the private sector continued to be restricted because of the need to finance public sector deficits, while non-performing assets continued to be at levels higher than international best practices. Meanwhile, the equity market was hit by a series of scandals during the latter half of the 1990s that highlighted several market defects and exposed the inadequacy of existing supervisory and regulatory measures. On the external front, import-weighted mean tariffs began to rise after 1996. This rise in mean tariffs during the latter part of the 1990s also coincided with a significant slowdown in the growth of exports compared to the first years after the reforms.

In light of the significant gains made over the 1990s, as well as the emergence of these disquieting signs at the end of the decade, it seemed appropriate to take stock of, and analyze, the current state of the economic policy reform process in India. To that end, academic specialists on India and policy reform, Indian administrators, and present and past policy makers were invited to discuss and analyze the current state of three key sectors—fiscal, financial, and external—at the second annual conference on Indian economic policy reform held at the Center for Research on Economic Development and Policy Reform at Stanford University in June 2001. The chapters in this volume are revised versions of the papers presented at the conference, and are organized around the three themes covered at the conference.

Part I of this volume focuses on India's external sector policies (i.e., policies on trade, exchange rates, and capital flows), with the aim of taking stock of reforms in this sector over the last decade, as well as analyzing the desirability of further reforms in this area. This focus on external sector reforms stems from both the fact that these reforms constituted the centerpiece of India's structural reforms in the early 1990s and also that decades of developmental experience have documented the importance of outward-oriented trade polices in enhancing growth and improving economic performance.

In Chapter 1, T. N. Srinivasan analyzes the reforms in India's trade and capital-inflow policy since 1991. Srinivasan motivates his analysis by noting that India's inward-oriented development policies in the first four decades after independence had resulted in a complete marginalization of the economy from the world economy. As Srinivasan reports, while world exports grew at nearly 8 percent per annum from 1951 to 1973, India's export growth rate lagged behind at about 2.6 percent per annum during that period. Analogously, by the start of the 1990s, India was able to attract less than 1 percent of all foreign direct investment (FDI) received by developing countries and less than 3 percent of all portfolio investment received by developing countries.

The structural economic reforms that began in the early 1990s—of which external sector reforms were the focal point—dramatically reversed previous policies. As Srinivasan reports, import licenses were abolished, quantitative restrictions on imports were completely phased out by 2001, import-weighted tariffs fell from 87 percent in 1990–91 to a low of 24.6 percent in 1996–97 (and the standard deviation of tariff levels was reduced to one fourth its original level), capital inflows, and specifically FDI, were liberalized, and the rupee was devalued, resulting in a significant nominal, and real, devaluation in the early 1990s relative to its value at the start of that decade. These reforms provided a much-needed impetus to trade flows over the next few years. From 1993 to 1996, the dollar value of merchandise exports and imports grew at an average annual rate of 20 percent, and by 1996 the share of exports in GDP had risen to 9.2 percent—a significant increase over its pre-reform level. This spurt of export growth also meant that India increased its market share vis-à-vis its competitors in its major export markets.

But Srinivasan is quick to point out that, while much has been accomplished during a decade of external sector reforms, much remains to be done. He motivates this assessment by noting that import-weighted mean tariffs began to rise from their 1996 levels and in 2000 were at a level much higher than those prevailing in China and East Asia. This rise in tariffs coincided with a significant slowdown in the growth of exports relative to the first years after the reforms.

Thus, as Srinivasan notes, while India's share of the growth of world exports increased, India's competitors, particularly China, did even better. Even in the area of FDI, where significant liberalization has occurred, India's share of FDI flows to developing countries peaked at a paltry 2 percent in the 1990s. Thus, the author concludes by observing that sustained reforms in the external sector are necessary if India is to complete the transformation to an outward-oriented economy, and that active engagement in multilateral trade negotiations would facilitate this transformation by enhancing access for India's exports and facilitating needed domestic reforms.

In his comments, Shankar Acharya broadly concurs with Srinivasan and makes the case for further reducing the mean level of import duties, and also for compressing the prevailing high dispersion in effective rates of protection. Acharya recognizes that reduction of import duties poses a strong challenge since these duties account for almost 30 percent of central-government tax revenues. With regard to foreign direct investment, Acharya believes there is a strong case for loosening many sectoral caps on foreign equity holdings—including those in civil aviation, telecommunications, banking, and agriculture. Acharya also believes it is important that political and monetary authorities encourage the development of foreign exchange markets and learn to live with increased exchange-rate volatility. The exchange rate would become more market determined and therefore able to better reflect changes in external circumstances. Acharya believes that, in addition to these direct reforms, a complementary set of reforms in labor laws, small-scale industry reservation, infrastructure, and the financial sector is critical to improving India's external sector performance.

As noted in Chapter 1, a key variable responsible for sustaining an outward-oriented trade regime is the evolution of the real exchange rate. In Chapter 2, therefore, Anne Krueger and Sajjid Chinoy analyze the evolution of India's real exchange rate since the beginning of the reform process. As these authors note, two important criteria by which to judge the real exchange rate are (1) whether it keeps foreign exchange receipts and expenditures in relative balance over the intermediate term, and (2) whether it provides a sufficient stimulus to exporters so that exports grow at a satisfactory pace. As these authors point out, the importance of an appropriate level and path of the real exchange rate is exacerbated during a country's transition to outward-oriented regimes, since these transitions (as in the case of India) involve a reduction in tariff and non-tariff barriers as well as a reliance on rapid export growth. Krueger and Chinoy therefore argue that transitions to outward-oriented regimes need to be accompanied by appropriate real devaluations, so as to pull adequate resources into the exportable sector as well as offset the impact of reduced import trade barriers on the balance of payments.

As these authors document, India's trade reforms of the early 1990s were characterized by a significant nominal depreciation of the exchange rate, which translated into a substantial real devaluation in the early 1990s. In particular, India's export-weighted multilateral real exchange rate in relation to the country's five largest export markets (the United States, Japan, Germany, the United Kingdom, and Hong Kong) depreciated almost 60 percent by 1993 relative to its level in 1990. From that point, however, there seems to have been a persistent—albeit gradual—real appreciation vis-à-vis these currencies—thus eroding some of the early gains. This pattern is also evident in India's real exchange rate in relation to the labor-abundant Asian countries—which constitute India's major competition in its export markets. India's real exchange rate vis-à-vis these countries depreciated significantly (relative to its level in 1990) until the mid-1990s. With the onset of the Asian crisis and the subsequent depreciation of most East Asian currencies, however, the rupee began to appreciate significantly in relation to these currencies. Indeed, as of September 2000, India's real exchange rate had appreciated almost 20 percent vis-à-vis the East Asian countries—relative to its value just before the crisis—thus offsetting much of the real depreciation that India had experienced in the early 1990s.

In sum, the authors note that a combination of factors has meant that much of the rupee's real depreciation of the early 1990s—which was, in part, responsible for unprecedented growth rates of exports in the early reform years—was undone by the end of the decade. Coinciding with this real appreciation from the mid-1990s has been a rather abrupt halt of the impressive export growth rates of the early reform years. More generally, Krueger and Chinoy note that India's export growth rates during the 1990s pale in comparison to those of some other developing countries (e.g., South Korea and Chile) during their transition to outward-oriented economies. The authors therefore question whether India's exchange-rate policy has succeeded in providing the kind of stimulus needed to transition to an outward-oriented economy, and whether the transition to an outward-oriented regime would not be hastened by a more depreciated level/path of the real exchange rate.

In his capacity as a prominent Indian businessman, Naushad Forbes notes that one of the reasons that there isn't a strong enough clamor by Indian industry for a more depreciated rupee is that most industrialists are still caught up in the mindset of the past, wherein they benefited from a combination of a strong rupee (making intermediate goods cheaper) and protective tariffs (protecting their final goods from foreign competition). As such, according to Forbes, they have still not developed an export-oriented mindset and the ability to search for opportunities overseas. In view of this, Forbes speculates that a 25 percent depreciation of the rupee would certainly benefit the few firms and sectors that are currently competitive in international markets. But most Indian firms would not benefit in the short run because they do not have the presence in international markets to take advantage of the depreciation. Importantly, however, Forbes notes that a credible, long-term real depreciation of the currency would be instrumental in helping alter the current inward-looking mindset, and thus have a much more widespread and fundamental impact on Indian industry and exports.

In Part II of the volume, the focus turns to the financial sector. Just as with the external sector, the financial sector was subject to considerable, if imbalanced, reforms in the early 1990s. While the equity market experienced significant institutional reform—resulting in the establishment of a new securities exchange with innovations like nationwide electronic trading and paperless settlement—reform in the banking sector lagged behind. To be sure, interest rates were liberalized, competition encouraged, and prudential norms strengthened. But, just as in the external sector, reforms in the banking sector seemed to have lost momentum and significant problems persist, including a large overhang of non-performing assets, preemption of bank credit to finance fiscal deficits via statutory and market mechanisms, and an inadequate legal and informational framework. The latter half of the 1990s was also a time when the equity market was subject to a number of scandals—highlighting the need for further reform in this sector. Thus, while India's financial sector is significantly more liberalized than it was a decade ago, all indications are that further reforms are needed in both the banking and equity sector if they are to facilitate a higher trajectory of growth rates.

The chapters in Part II provide an overview of the reforms that have taken place in the financial sector, their impact on the economy, and the challenges that lie ahead. In Chapter 3, James Hanson focuses on progress and problems in the banking sector, while in Chapter 4, Ajay Shah and Susan Thomas review the progress of and enumerate the challenges facing India's equity market.

Hanson motivates his analysis by noting that before the start of the financial sector reforms in the early 1990s, the Indian banking sector was dominated by public sector banks who were forced mainly to finance government deficits at repressed rates of interest. As the author notes, in the 1980s public sector banks accounted for more than 80 percent of all deposits, and of this, more than 50 percent of net demand and time liabilities was required (through a cash-reserve requirement and a statutory liquidity ratio) to be invested in low-yielding government securities to help finance rising public sector deficits. Furthermore, banks had to lend 40 percent of the remaining funds to "priority sectors" such as agriculture and small-scale industry—all at closely monitored interest rates—thus usurping funds from more productive opportunities in the private sector. As Hanson notes, India's financial sector had effectively become an arm of the government's fiscal policy in the pre-reform period. Consequently, banks were not judged on their profits or their ability to evaluate credit risks, exposures, or maturity mismatches but merely by whether loan allocation and interest rate regulations had been met. This lack of emphasis on prudential issues, in conjunction with the emphasis on directed credit (and the associated political interference), also meant that banks were left with a large stock of non-performing loans (NPLs).

As part of the economy-wide reforms, liberalization of the financial sector began in 1992. As the chapter by Hanson documents, interest rates began to be liberalized, the cash-reserve requirement and statutory liquidity ratio were reduced, and competition in the banking sector was encouraged. The liberalization efforts were also accompanied by a strengthening of prudential regulation and supervision as public sector banks were recapitalized, minimum capital adequacy requirements introduced, and rules for recognition of NPLs tightened. These liberalization measures had some tangible effects. As Hanson reports, on the deposit side liberalized interest rates and increased competition in the banking industry resulted in a healthy growth of bank deposits—in contrast to the stagnation of real deposit growth in the years preceding the reforms. On the lending side, increased competition in the banking industry meant that new sources of funds became available for the private sector. For instance, the growth of nonbank financial corporations made available funds for consumer credit and other nontraditional clients. Capital market finance was also liberalized and increased sharply in the 1990s as firms were able to use equity, bonds, private placements, and, in some cases, offshore borrowing to raise capital.

Although the financial market reforms have been beneficial, important problems remain. Primary among these are the problems associated with India's fiscal excesses. As Hanson notes, large fiscal deficits continue to be financed by banks—reducing the amount of credit available to the private sector and crowding out more productive investments. Despite the fact that, postliberalization, banks are *required* to hold a *smaller* fraction of their deposits in government securities, the total government debt held by banks actually absorbed a higher percentage of deposits in the 1990s than in the last half of the 1980s. This is because public sector debt has become increasingly attractive for banks to hold since, from the perspective of capital adequacy, it carries a low risk-weight, and also because the liberalization of interest rates has resulted in the government paying a much higher interest rate. Nonetheless, large public sector deficits, by crowding out more productive private investment opportunities, continue to impede the efficiency with which funds are put to use, thus reducing the gains from deposit mobilization that have come about due to financial market reforms.

According to Hanson, another important problem afflicting Indian banks is the continuation of high NPLs. Although bank portfolio NPL rates have declined somewhat since liberalization began, they continue to be much higher than international best practices. Hanson believes these NPLs reflect a poor legal framework for executing collateral, poor information on borrowers, and the continued dominance of public sector banks, where the incentives to undertake sound lending and collection are much smaller than in private sector banks. Hanson concludes by noting that reforms to increase the legal and informational framework and promote greater privatization of bank management and ownership are critically needed in India's banking sector.

In his comments, K. V. Kamath notes that technological progress has dramatically transformed the workings of the financial services sector the world over, by increasing operational efficiency and facilitating a more consumer-centric approach. He fears that one of the biggest threats facing India's financial services industry is that it is not yet leveraging this technology effectively. The urgency to do so, Kamath believes, is accentuated by the need for banks to attract more capital to help fulfill prudential guidelines. This is because banks that do not adapt to changing market dynamics will increasingly find it difficult to access the capital required to grow their businesses. He also believes there is an urgent need for Indian banks to attract a talented and lean human resources team. Thus, Kamath believes that the challenges facing Indian banks are not restricted to the conventional areas of asset quality and non-performing loans, but in fact encompass critical issues such as effective leveraging of technology and management of human resources.

In comparison to the banking sector, India's equity market has experienced considerable institutional reform over the last decade. In Chapter 4 Ajay Shah and Susan Thomas survey and analyze these reforms and also discuss the challenges that lie ahead. As part of the economy-wide reforms, security market reforms began in the early 1990s. Some of the early reforms included efforts to attract foreign portfolio investment and empower the securities market regulator —Securities and Exchange Board of India (SEBI). But, as Shah and Thomas point out, the most important reform of the equity market was the establishment of a new securities exchange, the National Stock Exchange (NSE), in 1994. The NSE was responsible for important new institutional innovations in securities trading in India. NSE practices were in contrast to the nontransparent illiquid, floor-based trading that characterized the Bombay Stock Exchange—the largest Indian exchange till that point. The NSE-induced innovations included (a) the establishment of nationwide electronic trading, which greatly increased efficiency, transparency, and market access to investors all over the country; (b) the introduction of a clearing corporation as a central counterparty, which eliminated counterparty credit risk, and thus facilitated anonymous electronic trading; and (c) the introduction of paperless settlement at the depository, which sharply reduced settlement costs and the opportunities for fraud. The authors estimate that these changes improved market liquidity tenfold.

These reforms notwithstanding, the equity market was subject to a series of crises during the latter half of the 1990s. These crises typically involved market manipulation in the secondary market and payments problems at one or more exchanges—and were highly disruptive. According to Shah and Thomas, while the factors responsible for the crises range from inappropriate regulation of the primary market to inadequate supervision of mutual funds, a particularly important market defect thought to have facilitated most of the crises was the extent of leverage allowed in spot-market trading. Leveraged market manipulation was thought to have underpinned each of the major crises, with manipulative cartels building up large leveraged positions in the secondary markets. It was only in July 2001, in response to the latest such crisis, that policy makers greatly restricted leveraged positions associated with the spot market.

Despite this latest reform, Shah and Thomas conclude that several important challenges lie ahead for policy makers. Foremost among these is designing the appropriate interface between the banking sector and securities markets. This concerns both the extent to which banks can be exposed to the equity market as well as the development of a nationwide funds transfer mechanism to support the national electronic equity trading system currently in place. As Ravi Narain notes in his comments, a key area where the banking system impinges on the security market is in the payments system. India's newer banks (designated as "clearing banks" by the National Stock Exchange) have set up an electronic funds transfer system across all their branches, which has facilitated an efficient transfer of funds from all across the country to the centralized clearing corporation. While this innovation has greatly aided risk-management systems of stock exchanges—particularly in monitoring swift collections of margins and funds for settlement—important shortcomings remain. For instance, as Narain points out in his comments, the centralized clearing corporation is still unable to move funds *between* clearing banks through an electronic system, and still needs to rely on physical checks written on the central bank. This exacerbates the system risk in the securities market, which can be mitigated only by the central bank pushing through an electronic funds transfer arrangement for the *entire* banking system.

Apart from issues of market design, Shah and Thomas note that important challenges also lie ahead in the realm of governance of the equity market. In particular, improvements in human capital and political interdependence in the case of the market regulator, SEBI, need to be an integral part of the policy agenda. As regards the role of SEBI, Raghuram Rajan notes in his comments that an important factor responsible for the recurrence of crises in India's equity market is the inability of India's stock market regulator to demonstrate sufficient "teeth" and "backbone" in finding and dealing with the guilty. As Rajan observes, developing teeth is not necessarily synonymous with promulgating new rules. This is because when rules can be evaded, adding new rules can indeed be counterproductive. The unscrupulous typically evade all rules, and buy their way out of trouble when caught. By contrast, honest businessmen follow rules to the detriment of their business. Thus, the more rules introduced, the greater the comparative advantage of being unscrupulous. Rajan therefore believes that it is not new rules that India needs, but enforcement of current ones.

In the case of accusations of market manipulation, for instance, Rajan believes that serious market participants and regulators normally have a sense who the culprit is, but that it is not easy for stock regulators to define market manipulation and thus not easy to write an enforceable rule. In this case, the way for regulators to develop teeth is to cultivate fear among transgressors that they will somehow be caught, punished, and made to lose business. In this vein, Rajan advocates that the regulator constantly collect information, lay traps, and use every means to punish manipulators. Thus, even if the culprit is caught on other (relatively more innocuous) charges or technicalities, but once caught is really made an example of (as was the case with the famous Drexel Burnham Lambert bond trader Michael Milken), regulators will be demonstrating the requisite backbone in deterring future offenders.

As the chapters in this part document, one of the notable features of the reforms in the financial sector has been the imbalanced nature of reform between the equity markets and the banking sector. While the equity market has experienced significant institutional innovations—the establishment of a new exchange with nationwide electronic trading, paperless settlement, and elimination of counterparty credit risk—resulting in a tenfold increase in liquidity, progress in the banking sector has been much more halting. While interest rates have gradually been liberalized, competition encouraged, and prudential guidelines strengthened, there continues to be a large overhang of non-performing loans stemming, in part, from an inadequate legal framework for recovering bad debts. John Echeverri-Gent attributes the disparity in reforms between the banking sector and the equity market to the level of political opposition encountered in each of these sectors. In the case of the equity market, Echeverri-Gent notes, strongest opposition came from stockbrokers. However, they number only a few thousand, because until the mid-1990s they maintained rules that placed exclusionary restrictions on new membership. Furthermore, although their influence extended to their allies in the business sector, Echeverri-Gent believes their power was limited to the equity market sector rather than national politics. Therefore, the political opposition encountered during reforms of the equity market was not formidable.

In contrast, important reforms in the banking sector faced much greater resistance because of the large size of the workforce and its organized opposition. For instance, the extent of NPLs in the banking sector is exacerbated by the current mechanisms to recover non-performing debt. As Echeverri-Gent notes, the priority given to protecting the jobs of workers from creditors makes debt recovery an inordinately time-consuming process that encourages proprietors to default on their financial obligations. However, current mechanisms have not been reformed, despite growing consensus on the issue, because of the sheer vehemence of organized labor's opposition to any reform. Thus, despite three committees being set up to propose changes, reform has still not been able to be pushed through—given the importance of organized labor in the political process and the strength of its opposition. Echeverri-Gent therefore concludes by noting that economic reformers would do well to study how different policies shape the incentives of political actors in their efforts to pilot reforms through the political process.

In the third and final part of this volume, attention turns to India's fiscal policy. There is widespread consensus that India's fiscal excesses over the last two decades have constituted an important impediment to increasing growth rates. In particular, the unsustainable fiscal expansionism of the latter half of the 1980s was responsible for the macroeconomic crisis that soon followed. As already mentioned, one of the important objectives of the reform process of the early 1990s was to reduce public sector deficits to sustainable levels. And, indeed, the central-government deficit was reduced from its level of 7.7 percent of GDP in 1990–91 to around 4 percent three years later. The momentum suddenly stopped thereafter. By 1999–2000, the consolidated public sector deficit was estimated to have been 10.8 percent of GDP, about the same level as existed just before the macroeconomic crisis of 1991—indicative of the urgent need for fiscal reform in India.

To put India's fiscal excesses in perspective, it seems important to understand how India's fiscal imbalances compare to those of other developing countries and also the extent to which fiscal imbalances, in general, affect key macroeconomic variables. Both of these questions are taken up by Sebastian Edwards in Chapter 5. Specifically, Edwards uses data on central-government fiscal deficits for 105 countries from 1970 to 1997 to understand, from a comparative point of view, the magnitude of fiscal deficits in different regions at different times, as well as the implications of these imbalances for growth and macroeconomic stability.

Edwards's results confirm the casual presumption that, over the last two decades, India's fiscal deficits have been high both from an absolute and a relative standpoint. Edwards notes that in thirteen out of seventeen years between 1980 and 1997, the central government fiscal deficit in India was among the highest 25 percent in Asia. Interestingly, South Korea's public sector deficit was never among the highest 25 percent of Asia's deficits during this period. Although the data for China are limited to a few years, in not one of them was the fiscal deficit classified as "high."

Edwards then explores the impact of fiscal policy on economic performance and macroeconomic stability. Specifically, Edwards's econometric results suggest that larger fiscal deficits increase the probability of a country facing a currency crisis (defined as a large currency depreciation and/or a significant loss in reserves), which in turn is correlated with a reduction in GDP growth. Thus, as Edwards notes, one of the mechanisms through which fiscal imbalances impede growth is by increasing the probability of a currency crisis. Edwards finds, in addition, that fiscal imbalances pose a direct impediment to GDP growth—above and beyond the currency crisis channel—although the quantitative significance of the direct impact is quite limited in his results. Finally, Edwards's results reveal that fiscal deficits significantly crowd out private investment, with an increase in the deficit of one percentage point of GDP resulting, on average, in a decline in private investment of 0.4 percent. In sum, Edwards finds India's fiscal deficits have been relatively very high, and that larger fiscal deficits, in general, are correlated with lower GDP growth and lower private investment—giving further credence to the urgent need for fiscal reform in India.

In his comments, Alan Auerbach notes that he agrees with Edwards's basic message that large fiscal deficits have a negative effect on growth, both directly and through their impact on currency crises, and that eliminating them is not to be feared from a macroeconomic perspective. However, Auerbach also emphasizes the need to appreciate the limitations inherent in using current debt and deficit measures as indicators of fiscal stability.

For overcoming these measurement problems, Auerbach recommends a more comprehensive indicator of a country's fiscal situation that takes into account assets and unfunded liabilities, which are not captured in current debt and deficit measures. Auerbach notes that replicating Edwards's cross-country regressions with these augmented fiscal indicators would constitute a valuable future exercise.

In light of India's sustained fiscal deficits over the last two decades, another issue of concern is the inflationary impact of continually financing these deficits. While India's rate of inflation rose to 13.5 percent in the midst of India's macroeconomic crisis in 1991, inflation has subsequently moderated over the 1990s despite sustained public sector deficits. Arnold Harberger rationalizes this phenomenon in his comments by noting that the link between fiscal deficits and inflation is much more subtle and uncertain than is often thought to be the case. This is because governments can, in the medium term, resort to a number of avenues to finance fiscal deficits in noninflationary ways. These include foreign aid, borrowing from abroad (either from multilateral agencies on concessional terms or from private creditors on commercial terms), borrowing from the local banking sector, and floating bonds in the local financial marketplace. Thus, governments have a variety of noninflationary "parking places" to park their deficits in the medium term. Thus, to the extent that the noninflationary "parking lot" is still not full, it is possible to have fiscal deficits for a long time without generating huge monetary and fiscal equilibria that lead to major inflationary episodes and devaluations.

To be sure, however, there are often real costs to be paid for availing oneself of the parking lot. Government borrowing from the local banking system often results in squeezing credit from the private sector with its concomitant effect of depressing the real economy. This has manifested itself most clearly in India, where high reserve requirements in the banking system—for the purpose of financing public sector deficits—have resulted in higher interest rates and constituted an important impediment to private investment. Furthermore, as Harberger notes, once the parking lot is full, and it becomes politically and economically unpopular to drain the financial system of any more resources, it is inevitable for fiscal deficits to translate into episodes of inflation and currency devaluations.

Therefore, to truly understand the severity of India's fiscal imbalances, Harberger recommends a program of serious study on the parking of India's fiscal deficits. Where are they being parked? At what cost? And how much vacant space remains to be occupied before major problems emerge? Answers to these questions are critical to determining the true extent of India's fiscal problem, and the sustainability of current policies.

Finally, India's sustained fiscal deficits over the last two decades also raise important questions about the adequacy of India's tax revenues and the need to reform India's tax structure to better meet the resource requirements of the economy. In the last chapter, N. K. Singh focuses on tax-reform efforts in India and the challenge currently facing policy makers in this area. Singh motivates his analysis by noting that, almost a decade after the start of economic reforms, India's ratio of total tax revenues to GDP in 2000 was lower than its level in 1990—thus greatly exacerbating India's fiscal plight. Key to this phenomenon is the fact that India has traditionally relied on indirect taxes (excise and customs duties) to generate the bulk of its tax revenue, and significant trade liberalization over the last decade has meant that tariff revenue has dropped correspondingly. In comparison, revenue from direct taxes (personal income and corporate) has risen relatively sluggishly, and not by enough to offset the fall in indirect tax revenue, resulting in a falling tax-to-GDP ratio.

As Singh notes, an important factor responsible for the sluggish growth of direct tax revenues is a very narrow tax base. Not only is agricultural income excluded from the tax base, but there are a host of exemptions, concessions, and loopholes that further erode an already narrow base. This is manifested in the fact that as of 1999–2000, taxpayers constituted only 2.5 percent of the total population. To exacerbate matters, tax-enforcement efforts have left much to be desired. Singh estimates that current taxpayers constitute only 40 percent of potential payers, and this can be attributed to a lax enforcement effort operating, primarily, out of severe resource constraints—technological and human—in the area of tax administration. Since the beginning of the reform process, efforts have been made to broaden both the personal income and corporate tax base—

such as broadening the criteria for citizens to file tax returns and introducing a minimum alternative tax for companies—but the authors note that the current tax base is still much too narrow and much more needs to done, particularly on the enforcement front, to increase its size.

An area where significant reform has taken place over the 1990s is in rationalizing and moderating a very high tax-rate structure. Personal income and corporate tax rates have been reduced from 56 percent and 54 percent in 1991 to 33 percent and 35 percent, respectively, in 2000. As the author points out, moderation of tax rates has made an important contribution in increasing the size of the tax base—as the number of voluntary compliers has almost doubled over the course of the decade. These gains notwithstanding, Singh concludes that much more needs to be done to broaden the direct tax base, so as to offset the effect of reduced indirect taxes and, more generally, help alleviate India's severe fiscal imbalances.

As the chapters in this volume document, there seems to be a common thread running through reform efforts in the fiscal, financial, and external sectors: that of significant reform in the early 1990s, resulting in unprecedented rates of GDP growth for several years in the early and mid-1990s, followed by a loss of momentum in the reform process during the latter half of that decade. Indeed, as various authors point out, many significant gains of the early 1990s had been undone by the end of the decade: the consolidated nonfinancial public sector deficit in 2000 was at the same alarming level as it was before the macroeconomic crisis of 1991; much of the real exchange rate depreciation attained from 1991 to 1993 had been reversed; some tariffs had been raised relative to their level in 1996; and euphoric growth rates of exports of the early reform years had disappeared. The common message from these chapters therefore seems clear: it is critical for policy makers in India to jump-start the reform process so that India can attain annual rates of GDP growth of the order of 7–8 percent—as is desperately needed to improve the living standards of a largely impoverished populace.

Part I

THE EXTERNAL SECTOR

1

INTEGRATING INDIA WITH THE WORLD ECONOMY

Progress, Problems, and Prospects

T. N. Srinivasan

Introduction

India was largely insulated from the world trading system for more than four decades after independence in 1947. Pursuit of an inward-oriented development strategy, rationalized both by a wary, almost hostile attitude toward foreign trade, technology, and investment, and by pessimism about export markets, inevitably led to India becoming marginalized in world trade. During the period of rapid growth in world exports, at nearly 7.9 percent per year on average during 1950–73 before the first oil shock, India's exports grew at a much slower rate of 2.7 percent per year, and the ratio of exports to GDP declined from a high of 7.3 percent in 1951 to its lowest level of 3 percent in 1965 and remained below 4 percent until 1973 (Srinivasan and Tendulkar 2002, ch. 2). Again when private capital flows to developing countries grew phenomenally since the mid-1980s, India was not one of the favored destinations for private foreign investors. After the collapse of the Bretton Woods system of fixed exchange rates in 1971, Indian exchange rate policies achieved significant depreciation of the rupee for some time against major currencies as the latter floated against each other. The depreciation, coupled with deliberate export promotion (or at least

* This is a revised version of a paper presented at a conference, India Economic Prospects: Advancing Policy Reforms, at CREDPR during June 1–2, 2001. I thank my discussant, Isher Ahluwalia, and participants of the conference, particularly Anne Krueger, for their valuable comments. Thanks are due to Jessica Wallack for research assistance.

† Editor's note: Since the conference at which this essay was presented, the members of the World Trade Organization did agree to launch a new round of multilateral trade negotiations when they met at the Fourth Ministerial Meeting during November 2001 in Doha, Qatar. These negotiations are currently under way.

reduction of bias against exports), led Indian exports to grow faster, on average, than world exports (in volume) since 1973. Still, in value terms, India's share in world merchandise exports, which stood at 2.2 percent in 1948, declined to 0.5 percent in 1983 and have recovered since only to 0.7 percent in 2000 (WTO 2001a, table II.2).

The origins of the severe macroeconomic and balance of payments crisis of 1991 and the institution of systemic economic reforms that followed have been analyzed by several authors (see Srinivasan and Tendulkar 2002 for a recent analysis). I will not go over this ground again, except to note that among the initial set of reforms was liberalization of international trade and, to a lesser extent, foreign investment. The extreme restrictiveness of the pre-reform regime can be seen from the fact that in 1990–91, the import-weighted average tariff for all imports was as high as 87 percent and even higher, 164 percent, on consumer goods imports (Table 1.1, page 21). In addition, several non-tariff barriers, particularly quantitative restrictions (QRs), applied to virtually all imports. Historically, India's attitude toward the inflow of foreign capital, particularly foreign direct investment (FDI), was one of suspicion, if not outright hostility. Before 1991, restrictions on FDI included limiting entry only into specified priority areas, an upper limit of 40 percent on foreign-equity participation in joint ventures, requirements of government approval on technology transfer, obligations to export part (100 percent in some cases) of output, and an increase in domestic content of production.

India insulated itself from the world economy prior to reforms, in part because of its fear of being taken advantage of if it relied on international markets for its output and input supplies. This fear extended also to its participation in multilateral institutions and negotiations on trade. India was one of 23 original contracting parties of the General Agreement on Tariffs and Trade (GATT) in 1947 and is a founding member of the World Trade Organization (WTO). Yet at the United Nations Conference on Trade and Employment in Havana during 1947–48, and also subsequently in the eight rounds of multilateral trade negotiations (MTN) under the auspices of the GATT, India led developing countries in demanding exemptions from multilateral disciplines and commitments to liberalize trade, on the grounds that opening their economies to competition from the rest of the world would retard industrialization.[1] The Fourth Ministerial Meeting of the WTO is to take place in Doha, Qatar in November 2001. It is expected to launch a new round of MTN. India is opposed to the launch of a new round until the problems encountered in the implementation of commitments undertaken as part of the Uruguay Round (UR) agreement are resolved. Even if a new round is to be launched, India would like the agenda to be confined essentially to concluding the unfinished items of the UR agenda.

In the next section I discuss the contents of and progress in the reform of trade policy since 1991. Then I turn to capital inflows, particularly FDI. The section following that is devoted to India's interests and possible negotiating positions in any future round of MTN in the WTO. And I conclude with a discussion of remaining tasks and an assessment of the chances of their being undertaken. In an appendix (coauthored by Jessica Wallack), I present a simple econometric exercise relating trends in real effective exchange rates to trends in export performance. The results confirm that the real effective exchange rate has a significant effect on export performance.

Decade of Trade Policy Reforms

The external sector reforms since 1991 have consisted of (1) devaluation of the rupee, (2) abolition of import licensing, (3) significant reductions in tariff rates and their dispersion, and (4) phased removal of QRs on imports and liberalization of restrictions on capital inflows and FDI.[2] These reforms were not introduced as a package in one fell swoop. For example, pre-reform tariff and non-tariff barriers (particularly QRs) on consumer goods imports were left in place initially in 1991 and reduced only much later.

Liberalization of Exchange Rate, Trade, and Foreign Investment Policies

The trade and exchange rate regime before 1991 granted a generally high level of protection and also made-to-measure protection for manufacturing industries. By 1988–89, 95 percent of all imported products (and 80 percent or more of manufactured products, other than basic metal and miscellaneous products) were subject to non-tariff barriers (NTBs) (World Bank 2000a, Annex table 6.3). As noted earlier, the import-weighted average tariff was 87 percent, with the highest tariff rate reaching 355 percent (Panagariya 1999). The net result was a bias against exports and agriculture in resource allocation. There was a large dispersion in tariffs as well as tariff escalation depending on the stage of processing. The structure of incentives for production, investment, and exports across products within manufacturing as well as agricultural sectors, resulting from foreign trade and domestic interventions, was chaotic. Although QRs were the dominant means for control of imports, tariffs constituted a major revenue-raising device for the central government. Revenue from import tariffs accounted for 3.6 percent of GDP in 1990–91, out of a total tax revenue of 9.5 percent of GDP (World Bank 2000a, Annex table 8.5.).

Changes in the Exchange Rate Regime

In July 1991 the rupee was devalued by 22.8 percent relative to a basket of currencies, each currency being weighted by India's exports to that country. Taking into account the withdrawal of most export subsidies at the same time, the devaluation of the real effective exchange rate for exporters was around 16.3 percent. Temporary measures, such as foreign exchange licensing, import compression, export-based imports, and a dual exchange-rate system to deal with the balance of payments crisis of 1991, were withdrawn soon thereafter. Since 1993 the rupee has been convertible for current account transactions (i.e., convertibility under Article VIII of the International Monetary Fund [IMF]). However, the exchange rate continues to be managed.

Trade Liberalization

Apart from removal of QRs, the monopoly held by government agencies on imports of 50 commodities (except petroleum and agricultural products) was abolished. Full or partial purchase and/or price preferences in government procurement in favor of indigenous producers were removed. A policy of phased reduction in maximum tariff rates was combined with a reduction in the average level, as well as in a dispersion of rates. The maximum tariff rate was reduced to 45 percent in 1997–98 from 355 percent in 1990–91, and as noted earlier, the import-weighted average tariff for the whole economy was brought down to 24.6 percent in 1996–97 from 87 percent in 1990–91. There was a reduction in the standard deviation of tariffs to one fourth its level in 1990–91 for intermediate and capital goods, and one third its level in the case of agricultural products (Table 1.1, upper panel). As of 2000–2001 there are just four major tariff categories: 35 percent, 25 percent, 15 percent, and 5 percent, although most imports attract tariffs of 35 percent and 25 percent. The numbers of exemptions (or use-based concessions) on tariff rates and of restricted or banned exports were reduced. Taxes on some mineral and agricultural exports were abolished. Until their removal on April 1, 2001, certain restrictions on agricultural exports, such as quotas and stipulation of minimum export prices, remained. The reduced applied tariff levels are well below the levels at which India had bound its tariffs at the WTO and, as such, could be raised at the discretion of the government. Indeed, the import-weighted average tariff has been gradually raised to 30.2 percent in 1999–2000 from its low of 24.6 percent in 1996–97. The rise is particularly large in the case of intermediate goods, from 21.9 percent in 1996–97 to 31.9 percent in 1999–2000 (Table 1.1, lower panel). The unweighted, or simple average tariff rates reached their minimum in 1997–98 and have since risen (Table 1.1, upper panel).

Turning to non-tariff barriers, Pursell and Sharma (1996) have estimated the shares of internationally *tradable* goods protected by QRs and other non-tariff barriers in total and sectoral tradable GDP. In the pre-reform period (about the end of 1980s), the QR-protected share was as high as 93 percent in total tradable GDP. It dropped to 66 percent by May 1995. In manufacturing, the pre-reform share of 90 percent was significantly reduced to 36 percent by May 1996,

TABLE 1.1
India's Tariff Structure, 1990–1999

Sector	Simple Average (%) (standard deviation in parentheses)								
	1990–91	1992–93	1993–94	1994–95	1995–96	1996–97	1997–98	1998–99	1999–2000
Whole economy	128 (41)	94 (34)	71 (30)	55 (25)	40.8 (19)	38.6 (19)	34.4 (14.8)	40.2 (15.3)	39.6 (14.0)
Agricultural products	106 (48)	59 (49)	39 (39)	31 (30)	25.1 (24.9)	25.6 (21.1)	24.6 (17.7)	29.6 (18.8)	29.2 (16.6)
Mining	NA	NA	71 (24)	48 (25)	30.0 (15.6)	24.8 (11.9)	24.4 (11.9)	29.4 (12.3)	26.6 (12.1)
Consumer goods	142 (33)	92 (42)	76 (36)	59 (33)	45.4 (26)	45.4 (27.1)	39.8 (20.5)	45.9 (20.7)	42.9 (18.9)
Intermediate goods	133 (42)	104 (25)	77 (22)	59 (17)	43.7 (13.5)	38.8 (13.2)	34.7 (10.3)	40.7 (11.1)	41.2 (10.5)
Capital goods	109 (32)	86 (26)	58 (24)	42 (20)	33.1 (12.4)	33.8 (12.2)	29.7 (9.4)	35.3 (10.2)	35.3 (8.2)

Sector	Import-Weighted Average (%)								
	1990–91	1992–93	1993–94	1994–95	1995–96	1996–97	1997–98	1998–99	1999–2000
Whole economy	87	64	47	33	27.2	24.6	25.4	29.7	30.2
Agricultural products	70	30	25	17	14.9	14.7	14.0	16.1	17.7
Mining	NA	NA	33	31	27.6	22.0	21.9	19.5	17.7
Consumer goods	164	144	33	48	43.1	39.0	33.8	39.3	32.1
Intermediate goods	117	55	40	31	25.0	21.9	26.1	31.5	31.9
Capital goods	97	76	50	38	28.7	28.8	24.7	30.1	32.2

SOURCE: World Bank (2000a), Annex table 6.6.

NOTE: The total customs duty is calculated as the sum of the basic customs duty, a surcharge of 10% on basic customs duty, and the special additional duty. The special additional duty is levied on the value of imports as well as the basic duty value, the surcharge value, and the additional duty value. Figures for 1997–98 include the 3% special duty imposed in September 1997. In 1990–91 and 1992–93 mining is included in intermediates.

the remaining QRs being mostly on consumer goods imports. In agriculture, however, the share of 84 percent in May 1995 happened to be only marginally lower than its pre-reform level of 94 percent.

Table 1.2 presents the reduction of non-tariff barriers between 1996 and 1999. As a signatory of the Uruguay Round agreements, India was required to eliminate QRs by year 2000. India's attempt to delay the elimination by invoking the balance of payments exception of GATT/WTO failed. On April 1, 1999, QRs restricted imports on about 1200 tariff lines. Of these, QRs on 600 lines were removed on April 1, 2000 and the rest on April 1, 2001.

In its review of India's trade policy in 1998, seven years into the reform process, WTO noted that about 32 percent of the tariff lines were then subject to

TABLE 1.2

Non-Tariff Barriers on India's Imports, 1996–1997 to 1998–1999

	As of 1.4.96		As of 1.4.97		As of 1.4.98		As of 1.4.99	
Type of NTB	No. of lines	% Share	No. of lines	% Share	No. of lines	% Share	No. of lines	% Share
Prohibited	59	0.6	59	0.6	59	0.6	59	0.6
Restricted	2984	29.6	2322	22.8	2314	22.7	1183	11.5
Canalized	127	1.2	129	1.3	129	1.3	37	0.4
SIL	765	7.6	1043	10.2	919	9.0	886	8.7
Free	6161	61.0	6649	65.1	6781	66.4	8055	78.8
Total	10096	100.0	10202	100.0	10202	100.0	10220	100.0

SOURCE: Government of India (2002), box 6.3.

NOTE: The number of tariff lines is on a ten-digit level, as per harmonized system of India Trade Classification, HS-ITC classification of export and import items. SIL denotes special licenses issued to exporters to import primarily consumer goods with high premiums in domestic markets. In effect, such licenses were incentives to export. Canalized items refer to certain imports (food grains, fertilizers) that only state trading companies are entitled to import.

(QR-based) licensing, which, for most of them, acted as import bans. The review also commented on the escalation of tariffs on the basis of the extent of processing. In 1997–98 the lowest tariffs (simple average rate of 25 percent) were on unprocessed goods, covering 12 percent of the tariff lines. A higher rate (average 35 percent) was applicable on imports of semiprocessed goods and the highest rate (average 37 percent) on imports of processed goods, covering 50 percent of the tariff lines. The escalation ensured a higher level of effective protection, as compared to the level of nominal protection in the processed manufacturing products.

Non-tariff barriers are not comparable internationally for a number of theoretical and measurement reasons. As such, one has to use the levels of (unweighted) average tariff and the maximum tariff as crude indicators of openness across countries. Table 1.3 provides comparisons of tariffs on manufactures across 11 developing countries in the 1990s. India's tariff is seen to be still comparatively high at the end of the 1990s. Pursell and Sharma (1996) present the post-UR applied and bound tariff rates for each of 13 product categories for 26 developing countries for the year 1993. They find that, first, among the 26 countries India's applied rate was the highest or second highest for all the 13 product categories. Second, India's average applied tariff rate was more than *twice* as high as the average for all the countries studied, for all the product categories. Third, India's post-UR bound rate was invariably higher, and for some products much higher, than the average of the bound rates for the other countries. Fourth, taking all the product categories put together, the average applied tariff rate of 51.6 percent for India is not only the highest, but also nearly three times as high as the average level of 19.2 percent for the countries studied.

TABLE 1.3
International Comparison of Tariff Barriers

Country	Year	Simple Mean Tariff (%)	Standard Deviation	Import-Weighted Mean Tariff (%)	Share of Tariff Lines with Tariffs above 15%
India	1990	79.0	43.6	49.6	97.0
	1999	32.5	12.3	28.5	93.1
Bangladesh	1989	106.6	79.3	88.4	98.2
	2000	21.3	13.6	21.0	51.8
China	1992	41.0	30.6	33.2	77.6
	2000	16.3	10.7	14.7	4.2
Indonesia	1989	21.9	19.7	13.0	50.3
	2000	8.4	10.8	5.2	11.2
S. Korea	1988	14.8	5.3	10.5	12.5
	1999	8.6	5.9	5.9	0.7
Malaysia	1988	17.0	15.1	9.4	46.7
	1997	9.3	33.3	6.0	24.7
Nepal	1993	21.9	17.8	15.9	58.9
	2000	17.9	20.9	17.7	18.7
Pakistan	1995	50.9	21.5	46.4	91.4
	1998	46.6	21.2	41.7	86.3
Philippines	1989	28.0	14.2	22.4	77.2
	2000	7.6	7.7	3.8	8.8
Sri Lanka	1990	28.3	24.5	26.9	51.7
	2000	9.9	9.3	7.4	22.0
Thailand	1989	38.5	19.6	33.0	72.8
	2000	16.6	14.1	10.1	45.9

SOURCE: World Bank (2002), table 6.6.

A comparison across 13 developing countries for 1994 by Chopra and associates (1995) showed that India had the second highest level of the maximum tariff (65 percent), next only to Egypt, and the highest level of average tariffs (55 percent). A more recent comparison for the year 1998 of large countries with population over 20 million, by the World Bank (2000a, 70) shows that India has the second highest average tariff rate, next only to Argentina and higher than Asian and Latin American large countries.

Liberalization of Foreign Investment

The 1991 reforms did not significantly liberalize FDI. However, a Foreign Investment Promotion Board (FIPB) was created with powers to approve FDI proposals at its discretion. This meant that the procedure for approval was not transparent. In addition, the Reserve Bank of India gave automatic approvals to FDI proposals (mainly for investment in infrastructure) that met specified conditions. Yet much of the FDI came through the FIPB, perhaps because its procedures, being nontransparent and discretionary, allowed deals that could be negotiated individually. Only in May 2001 did the government decide to allow

100 percent foreign investment in several industrial sectors. Foreign investors no longer are required to sell 26 percent equity to an Indian partner or the public. Also, limits on FDI in specific sectors were raised, from 20 percent to 49 percent in banking and 49 percent to 74 percent in Internet service providers, paging, and bandwidth. Even the defense sector, hitherto excluded even to domestic investors, was opened to private investors (domestic and foreign).

It is clear that compared to the highly restrictive trade, payments, and capital-flow regime that characterized India for more than four decades until 1991, the post-1991 regime represents a radical change and is far more liberal. Yet compared to the trade-policy regimes prevailing in its competitors in world markets, particularly in Asia, India's regime is still considerably restrictive.

Outcomes of Reforms

Some Caveats

Some caveats are in order in assessing the impact of external sector reforms on trade performance in particular and the economy in general. First of all, the liberalization of import restrictions has been selective (initially, imports of consumer goods were not liberalized at all), consisting mostly of reductions of tariffs until nearly 10 years after initial reforms, in a regime in which QRs, and not levels of tariffs, were usually the binding constraints on imports. Of course, all import restrictions, whether through tariff or non-tariff measures, penalize exports as well. Second, as can be seen from the appendix, the real effective exchange rate has a significant impact on export performance. After an initial depreciation following the devaluation of July 1991, in part because of substantial increased inflows of portfolio investment and FDI following liberalization of foreign investment, the real effective exchange rate of the rupee appreciated. The withdrawal of export subsidies at the time of devaluation also reduced the effective devaluation of the exchange rate for exporters, as compared to the nominal devaluation of the rupee. Besides, the massive depreciations of currencies in East Asia following the financial crisis of 1997 also eroded India's competitiveness in the last third of the 1990s. In this context, the Chinese devaluation of 1994 is also of significance. Finally, the external environment for India's trade turned unfavorable, particularly after the East Asian financial crisis.

Keeping these caveats firmly in mind, it is worth looking at several indicators of external sector performance, such as growth and composition of exports and imports, current account balance, foreign-capital inflows, and external debt. The broader impact on the economy can be assessed, not so much by aggregate growth performance, as by an assessment of total factor productivity growth, the reason being that trade liberalization is expected to improve the efficiency of resource use in the economy.

Merchandise Imports and Exports

It can be seen from Table 1.4 that there was a rapid growth, at an average rate of 20 percent per year, in the U.S. dollar value of both merchandise exports and imports other than petroleum, oil, and lubricants (POL) for three years, 1993–94 to 1995–96. In the subsequent three years there was a significant reduction in growth. Although the growth rate revived to 20 percent in 2000–2001, with the global economic slowdown since it is unlikely to be sustainable in the near future. Table 1.5, based on customs data,[3] presents a classification of principal imports in two broad categories distinguished in the pre-1991 policy regime: bulk imports, which were deemed essential and hence monopolized through the state-owned trading agencies, and *nonbulk imports*, which were controlled through various licenses. The share of exports in GDP reached a peak of 9.2 percent in 1995–96 from its level of 6.2 percent in 1990–91, the year before reforms. It has since come down to an average of 8.5 percent. Growth in the value of imports followed a pattern similar to that in exports, reaching a peak in 1995–96 and slackening thereafter. The share of imports in GDP reached a peak of 12.8 percent in 1996–97 from its level of 9.4 percent in the year before reforms and has averaged 12.5 percent since.

Table 1.5 also gives average imports per year (in U.S.$) for the immediate pre-reform triennium of 1988–90 and two post-reform triennia: 1994–96 and 1998–2000. The data of the pre-reform triennium already reflect in part the effects of the limited trade liberalization of the mid-1980s. As such, the growth of trade in the post-reform triennia relative to the pre-reform triennium perhaps understates the effects of reforms of 1991. Taking point-to-point compound annual growth with the midyear of the pre-reform triennium as the base, the aggregate value of imports increased at 7.4 percent per year in the first post-reform triennium and 8.5 percent in the second.

Bulk imports in Table 1.5 are classified into three broad categories: POL, constituting energy inputs indispensable for production; bulk consumption goods (consisting of agricultural commodities such as cereals, pulses, edible oil, and sugar) that were imported to meet domestic supply shortfalls; and other bulk items (mostly noncompeting raw materials and intermediates such as fertilizer). The share of bulk imports has gone down from 40.5 percent on the average in the pre-reform triennium to 37 percent during 1994–96 and has reduced further to 30 percent during 1998–2000 in incremental imports (columns 6 and 7). Although the impact of the abolition of state trading would seem apparent in the slower growth of bulk imports relative to total imports, the reason for this is not clear. After all, state monopolies need not necessarily respond to changes in policy and market prices in the same way as private monopolists, let alone as competitive traders. As such, it is not possible to say a priori what the impact of their abolition would be on bulk imports.

TABLE 1.4

Selected Indicators of External Sector

Indicator	1990–91	1991–92	1992–93	1993–94	1994–95	1995–96	1996–97	1997–98	1998–99	1999–2000	2000–2001
Growth of exports (DGCI&S)	9.2	−1.5	3.8	20.0	18.4	20.8	5.3	4.6	−5.1	10.8	21.0
Growth of imports (DGCI&S)	13.5	−19.4	12.7	6.5	23.0	28.0	6.7	6.0	2.2	17.2	1.9
Non-POL	3.4	−21.9	12.0	11.2	29.5	28.3	−0.2	15.5	8.0	3.0	−5.9
Exports/ imports (BOP %)	66.2	86.7	77.6	84.8	74.8	74.0	69.7	69.7	72.1	67.8	75.8
Import cover of FER (No. of months)	2.5	5.3	4.9	8.6	8.4	6.0	6.5	6.9	8.2	8.2	8.6
Growth rate of vol. index of total exports	11.0	7.5	6.9	15.5	13.7	31.3	7.2	−6.3	3.4	15.5	22.2
Growth rate of vol. index of total imports	4.4	4.1	23.7	16.7	24.1	26.1	−0.6	9.8	14.6	9.5	−1.0
Growth rate of vol. index of imports of machinery and transport equipment	−9.3	−3.6	34.6	25.0	130.1	15.2	−13.6	−21.3	1.6	7.9	3.6

Short-term debt/FER (%)	146.5	76.7	64.5	18.8	16.9	23.2	25.5	17.2	13.2	10.3	8.2
Debt service payments as % of current receipts	35.3	30.2	27.5	25.6	26.2	24.3	21.2	19.1	18.0	16.2	17.1
	As % of GDP_{MP}										
Exports	5.8	6.7	7.1	8.3	8.4	9.2	8.9	8.7	8.3	8.4	9.8
Imports	8.8	7.7	9.4	9.8	11.1	12.3	12.7	12.5	11.5	12.4	13.0
Trade balance	−3.2	−1.0	−2.3	−1.5	−2.8	−3.1	−3.8	−3.8	−3.2	−4.0	−3.2
Invisibles balance (net)	−0.1	0.6	0.6	1.1	1.8	1.6	2.7	2.4	2.2	3.0	2.6
Current account balance	−3.2	−0.3	−1.7	−0.4	−1.0	−1.7	−1.2	−1.4	−1.0	−1.1	−0.5
External debt	28.7	37.7	36.6	33.8	30.9	27.0	24.5	24.3	23.6	22.2	22.3
Debt service payments	2.8	3.0	2.9	3.1	3.4	3.4	3.2	2.7	2.6	2.5	2.9

SOURCES: 1. Reserve Bank of India (2001) for rows 1, 2, 2.a, and 5 to 7.

2. Government of India (2001, 2002).

NOTES: 1. FER = Foreign Exchange Reserves; GDP_{MP} = Gross Domestic Product at current market prices; DGCI&S = Directorate General of Commercial Intelligence & Statistics, Ministry of Commerce.

2. Rupee equivalents of BOP components are used to arrive at GDP ratios. Percentages and growth rates shown in the upper panel are based on U.S. dollar values — except rows 5 to 7, which are based on quantum indices published by DGCI&S.

TABLE 1.5

Average Imports of Selected Principal Commodities, Pre- and Post-Reform Triennia

(U.S. $million)

Sector No.	Commodity	1988–90[a]	1994–96[b]	1998–2000[c]	1994–96 over 1988–90[d]	1998–2000 over 1988–90[e]
(1)	(2)	(3)	(4)	(5)	(6)	(7)
I	Bulk imports	7814.9 (40.5)[f]	11,582.4 (39.2)	15,097.5 (34.6)	3767.5 (36.7)	7282.5 (29.8)
I.1	Petroleum, oil, and lubricants	3298.2 (17.1)	6402.4 (21.7)	8348.2 (19.1)	3104.2 (30.3)	5050.0 (20.7)
I.2	Bulk consumption goods	1000.2 (5.2)	813.5 (2.8)	2100.7 (4.8)	−186.7 (−1.82)	1100.5 (4.5)
I.3	Other bulk items	3516.5 (18.2)	4366.5 (14.8)	4648.5 (10.6)	850.0 (8.3)	1132.0 (4.6)
I.3.1	Fertilizers: crude and manufactured	706.5 (3.7)	1187.0 (4.0)	1193.1 (2.7)	480.5 (4.7)	486.6 (2.0)
I.3.1.1	Manufactured fertilizer	408.7 (2.1)	925.7 (3.1)	911.3 (2.1)	517.0 (5.0)	502.4 (2.1)
I.3.2	Iron and steel	1235.1 (6.4)	1134.9 (3.8)	1164.5 (2.7)	−100.2 (−1.0)	−70.6 (−0.3)
II	Nonbulk imports	11,475.8 (59.5)	17,962.9 (60.8)	28,977.6 (66.3)	6487.1 (63.3)	17,501.8 (71.7)
II.1	Capital goods	5051.6 (26.2)	8070.4 (27.3)	9310.3 (21.3)	3018.8 (29.4)	4258.7 (17.5)
II.1.1	Machine tools	176.3 (0.9)	246.7 (0.8)	343.0 (0.8)	70.4 (0.7)	166.7 (0.7)
II.1.2	Machinery except electrical and electronic	1918.6 (9.9)	2844.7 (9.6)	3142.2 (7.2)	926.1 (9.0)	1223.6 (5.0)
II.1.3	Electronic goods	N.A.	1297.6 (4.4)	2381.4 (5.5)	—	—
II.1.4	Project goods	1154.1 (6.0)	1955.9 (6.6)	1770.6 (4.1)	801.8 (7.1)	616.5 (2.5)
II.2	Mainly export-related items	3424.9 (17.8)	4653.8 (15.8)	7660.0 (17.5)	1228.9 (12.0)	4235.1 (17.4)
II.2.1	Pearls, precious and semiprecious stones	2101.4 (10.9)	2123.4 (7.2)	4159.5 (9.5)	22.0 (0.2)	2058.1 (8.4)
II.2.2	Organic and inorganic chemicals	1098.7 (5.7)	2024.4 (6.9)	2839.6 (6.5)	925.7 (9.0)	1740.9 (7.1)
II.3	Others	2999.3 (15.5)	5238.7 (17.7)	11627.3 (26.6)	2239.4 (21.8)	8628.0 (35.4)
II.3.1	Coal, coke, briquettes, etc.	265.5 (1.4)	700.1 (2.4)	1054.3 (2.4)	434.6 (4.2)	788.8 (3.2)
II.3.2	Miscellaneous "others"	1036.9 (5.4)	2747.3 (8.4)	8222.7 (18.8)	1710.4 (16.7)	7185.8 (29.4)
Total I + II		19,290.7 (100.0)	29,545.3 (100.0)	43,695.1 (100.0)	10,254.6 (100.0)	24,404.4 (100.0)

SOURCE: Reserve Bank of India (2000).

[a]Fiscal years 1987–88 to 1989–90, pre-reform triennium.

[b]Fiscal years 1993–94 to 1995–96, triennium of rapid growth.

[c]Fiscal years 1997–98 to 1999–2000, latest available triennium.

[d]Midpoint to midpoint compound annual growth rates of total exports for 1988–90 to 1994–96: 11.12% per annum over 6 years.

[e]Midpoint to midpoint compound annual growth rates of total exports for 1988–90 to 1998–2000: 9.51% per annum over 10 years.

[f]Figures in parentheses are percentages of the total (I + II).

The share of nonbulk items in incremental imports is unambiguously higher in both the post-reform triennia, in part as a consequence of the removal of QRs (except on consumer goods) and the reductions in and the rationalization of tariff rates. Nonbulk imports are classified into three broad categories: capital goods, mainly export-related import items, and a residual category of "others." In comparison with the pre-reform triennium, during the first post-reform triennium the average share of capital goods in incremental imports rose slightly to 27.3 percent, reflecting the effect of removal of most QRs on capital goods and some modest increase in investment. Real gross fixed capital formation at 1993–94 (prices) as a proportion of growing GDP averaged 25 percent during 1993–96 as compared to around 23 percent during 1988–90. The decline in the share of capital-goods imports to 21.3 percent during 1998–90 reflects a slowdown in aggregate growth and investment rates.

The third and residual category of imports—namely "others"—showed a rising and significant surge in both the post-reform triennia. The major item in this broad category was "miscellaneous 'others'" (II.3.2). This category includes many consumer goods with a high premium in domestic markets, the imports of which were on the banned or restricted lists, but were permitted to be imported under special licenses given to exporters as an export incentive measure. The other (nonconsumer) goods included are coal, coke, briquettes, and so on (II.3.1), whose small share in incremental imports had more than doubled, reflecting the steep reduction in import duty on them.

The effect of trade liberalization on exports can be seen from Table 1.6. At the aggregate level, exports rose at 11.1 percent per year in the first triennium before slowing to 9.5 percent in the later triennium that included the East Asian currency crisis. These growth rates compare favorably with the growth rate of 7.4 percent per year in the value of merchandise exports during 1980–90 (World Bank 2002, table 4.4). Manufactured products accounted for a major share of the incremental exports. Within this group, the share of traditional labor-intensive exports declined steeply in the case of leather and leather manufactures, and to a smaller extent in the case of handicrafts, and remained virtually unchanged in the case of ready-made garments. Since these products were reserved for production by small-scale industries, which either were not internationally competitive, or could not expand, even if competitive, given the reservations policy, the decline in the share of these products in incremental exports is not surprising. Liberalization in imports, along with the initial exchange-rate depreciation, raised the profitability of selling in international markets. As long as domestic constraints did not come in the way, one would expect this to be reflected in rising exports. This is seen in the case of chemical and allied products in general and that of drugs, pharmaceuticals, and finer chemicals in particular, as also in textile yarn, fabrics, made-ups and so on, and in engineering goods. The share

TABLE 1.6

Average Exports of Selected Principal Commodities, Pre- and Post-Reform Triennia

(U.S. $million)

Sector No.	Commodity	1988–90[a]	1994–96[b]	1998–2000[c]	1994–96 over 1988–90[d]	1998–2000 over 1988–90[e]
(1)	(2)	(3)	(4)	(5)	(6)	(7)
I	Primary products	3428.7	5795.7	7006.6	2367.0	3577.9
		(24.1)[f]	(21.6)	(19.0)	(18.8)	(17.0)
I.1	Agriculture and allied products	2610.2	4778.5	6052.8	2168.3	3442.6
		(18.4)	(17.8)	(17.2)	(17.3)	(16.4)
I.2	Ores and minerals	818.5	1017.2	953.8	198.7	135.3
		(5.8)	(3.8)	(2.7)	(1.6)	(0.6)
II	Manufactured products	10,092.3	20,187.3	27,270.7	10,095.0	17,178.4
		(71.0)	(75.4)	(77.3)	(80.3)	(81.6)
II.1	Leather and manufactures	1062.3	1554.1	1618.6	491.8	556.3
		(7.5)	(5.8)	(4.6)	(3.9)	(2.6)
II.2	Chemicals and allied products	857.2	1930.8	3099.7	1073.6	2242.5
		(6.0)	(7.2)	(8.8)	(8.5)	(10.7)
II.2.1	Drugs, pharma., and fine chemicals	363.0	819.9	1491.9	456.9	1128.9
		(0.3)	(3.1)	(4.2)	(3.6)	(5.4)
II.3	Engineering goods	1583.8	3645.7	4920.8	2061.9	3337.0
		(11.1)	(13.6)	(13.9)	(16.4)	(15.9)
II.4	Ready-made garments	1597.6	3181.2	4347.7	1583.6	2650.1
		(11.2)	(11.9)	(12.3)	(12.6)	(12.6)
II.5	Textile yarn, fabrics, made-ups, etc.	1123.7	2902.6	4109.2	1778.9	2985.5
		(7.9)	(10.8)	(11.6)	(14.2)	(14.2)
II.5.1	Cotton yarn, fabrics, made-ups, etc.	861.8	2115.8	3058.4	1254.0	2196.6
		(6.1)	(7.9)	(8.7)	(10.0)	(10.4)
II.6	Handicrafts	3223.8	5408.5	7356.3	2184.7	4132.5
		(22.7)	(20.2)	(20.8)	(17.4)	(19.6)
II.6.1	Gems and jewelry	2742.8	4590.4	6303.6	1847.6	3560.8
		(19.3)	(17.1)	(17.9)	(14.7)	(16.9)
III	Petroleum products and others	702.9	804.9	997.3	102.0	294.4
		(4.9)	(3.0)	(2.8)	(0.8)	(1.4)
Total (I + II + III)		14,223.9	26,787.9	35,274.6	12,564.0	21,050.7
		(100.0)	(100.0)	(100.0)	(100.0)	(100.0)

SOURCE: Reserve Bank of India (2000).

[a]Fiscal years 1987–88 to 1989–90, pre-reform triennium.

[b]Fiscal years 1993–94 to 1995–96, triennium of rapid growth.

[c]Fiscal years 1997–98 to 1999–2000, latest available triennium.

[d]Midpoint to midpoint compound annual growth rates of total exports for 1988–90 to 1994–96: 11.12% per annum over 6 years.

[e]Midpoint to midpoint compound annual growth rates of total exports for 1988-90 to 1998-2000: 9.51% per annum over 10 years.

[f]Figures in parentheses are percentages of the total (I + II + III).

of these three items (II.2, II.3, and II.5) together was on average 23 percent during the pre-reform triennium. Their share in incremental exports was 39 percent in the first triennium and 37 percent in the second.

The exports of products covered by the Multifiber Arrangement (MFA) are constrained on the demand side by quotas (albeit rising over time) in countries that are parties to MFA, and on the domestic side by supply constraints arising from small-scale industry reservation. The latter constrains exports to all markets, while the former applies only to exports to quota-constrained markets. As such, although reforms in principle should have made it more attractive to export to all markets, it is to be expected that growth of exports in quota-constrained markets would be slower. This is evident in the data. The share of ready-made garments in total exports remained unchanged at around 12 percent, and the share of cotton yarn, fabrics, (MFA) made-ups, and so on rose from 8 percent during the pre-reform triennium to 12 percent in the second post-reform triennium (Table 1.6). However, in the case of both, the share of exports going to industrialized countries with quota restrictions has gone down during the post-reform period. The decline was marginal, from a high level of 67 percent (pre-reform) to 63 percent (post-reform) for ready-made garments, but steeper from a low level of 37 percent (pre-reform) to 30 percent (post-reform) in the case of cotton yarn, fabrics, and made-ups (Table 1.7).

Finally, Table 1.8 presents the changes in the direction of trade. With the collapse of the Soviet empire, barter trade arrangements with that region col-

TABLE 1.7

Percentage Shares of Major Countries in Exports of Selected Commodities

Cotton Yarn, Fabrics, Made-ups, etc.				Ready-made Garments			
Country	1988–90[a]	1994–96	1998–00	Country	1988–90	1994–96	1998–00
Germany	7.3	6.5	4.7	Canada	2.9	3.2	4.0
Italy	5.8	4.8	4.7	France	6.1	6.8	7.3
U.K.	10.8	10.4	7.0	Germany	14.3	12.1	8.4
U.S.A.	13.3	12.4	13.6	U.K.	10.9	9.8	7.7
Quota countries	37.3	34.1	30.0	U.S.A.	29.1	30.7	32.3
Bangladesh	8.6	11.1	6.1	**Quota countries**	67.4	66.0	62.8
Hong Kong	2.2	3.4	6.9	C.I.S	10.5	2.6	4.2
Japan	4.1	4.0	3.4	Italy	4.1	3.4	3.0
South Korea	2.4	3.2	4.1	Japan	2.9	3.4	1.7
Mauritius	1.1	2.7	3.0	Netherlands	4.2	4.3	3.2
U.A.E.	3.5	3.6	3.1	U.A.E.	2.0	3.8	8.1
Others	40.9	37.9	43.4	Others	13.0	19.9	20.0
Total	100.0	100.0	100.0	Total	100.0	100.0	100.0
Total exports (U.S.$m)	861.8	2115.8	3058.4	**Total exports (U.S.$m)**	1597.6	3181.2	4347.7
Growth rate (% per annum)[b]		16.1	13.5	Growth rate (% per annum)		12.2	10.5
Share in total exports (%)[c]	6.1	7.9	8.7	Share in total exports (%)	11.2	11.9	12.3

SOURCE: Reserve Bank of India (2000).

[a]Triennia 1988–90, 1994–96, and 1998–2000 are the same as in Tables 1.5 and 1.6.

[b]Growth rates in the last line are midpoint to midpoint compound annual rates that are over 6 years for the first and over 10 years for the second post-reform triennium with pre-reform triennium base.

[c]Percentage shares relate to triennial average level of exports given in the last row.

TABLE 1.8

Direction of India's Trade, Pre- and Post-Reform Triennia

(U.S.$million)

Sector No.			1988–90	1994–96	1999–2000	Exports	Imports
(1)	(2)	(3)	(4)	(5)	(6)	(7)	(8)
I	OECD	8180	11,628	15,266	15,675	20,138	21,460
		(57.51)[a]	(60.28)	(56.99)	(53.05)	(57.09)	(49.11)
I.1	European Union	3525	6331	7179	8140	9276	10,760
		(24.78)	(32.82)	(26.80)	(27.55)	(26.30)	(24.63)
I.2	U.S.A.	2504	2114	4847	3168	7512	3662
		(17.61)	(10.96)	(18.09)	(10.72)	(21.30)	(8.38)
I.3	Australia	174	472	322	865	410	1337
		(1.23)	(2.45)	(1.20)	(2.93)	(1.16)	(3.06)
I.4	Japan	1457	1716	1994	2010	1751	2322
		(10.24)	(8.90)	(7.45)	(6.80)	(4.96)	(5.31)
II.	OPEC	890	2640	2631	6308	3699	6108
		(6.26)	(13.68)	(9.82)	(21.35)	(10.49)	(13.98)
III.	Eastern Europe	2507	1588	1133	1068	1214	995
		(17.62)	(8.23)	(4.23)	(3.62)	(3.44)	(2.28)
IV.	Developing countries	2219	3428	7321	6492	10025	8195
		(15.60)	(17.77)	(27.33)	(21.97)	(28.42)	(18.75)
IV.1	SAARC	373	80	1278	182	1568	351
		(2.62)	(0.41)	(4.77)	(0.62)	(4.44)	(0.80)
IV.2	Non-SAARC Asian countries	1491	2367	4691	4848	6114	8085
		(10.48)	(12.27)	(17.51)	(16.41)	(17.33)	(18.50)
V.	Africa	281	571	1017	915	1669	2611
		(1.98)	(2.96)	(3.80)	(3.10)	(4.73)	(5.98)
VI.	Latin America	74	410	334	547	675	724
		(0.52)	(2.13)	(1.25)	(1.85)	(1.91)	(1.66)
Total (I–VI)		14,224	19,291	26,788	29,545	35,275	43,695
		(100.00)	(100.00)	(100.00)	(100.00)	(100.00)	(100.00)

SOURCE: Reserve Bank of India (2000).
[a]Figures in parentheses are percentages of the total (I–VI).

lapsed as well. This led in the post-reform era to a declining share of Eastern Europe in both imports and exports and rising shares of East and Southeast Asian developing countries in both imports and exports. The share of the United States and European Union in exports rose and in imports declined. This decline in the share of the United States and the European Union and the increase in the share of East and Southeast Asia in imports, particularly after the East Asian financial crisis, reflect in part the exchange-rate depreciation of the currencies of the region and in part the effect of greater proximity of the region having a greater impact after India trade liberalization. As is to be expected, with political considerations precluding significant trade between India and Pakistan, which is India's largest South Asian neighbor, trade reforms had a negligible effect on the minuscule share of India's trade with South Asia.

Competitiveness of India's Exports

With rapid and sustained economic growth since the mid-1960s, real wages and labor costs rose in East Asian countries, thereby eroding their international competitiveness in the world markets for labor-intensive manufacturers. Other labor-abundant economies, such as China and India, which lagged behind East Asia in the growth of real wages, could be expected to gain market shares at the expense of East Asia, as the latter's competitiveness eroded. In India's case, its insulation from world markets before reforms inhibited it from increasing its market share. With the reforms of 1991, India is no longer as insulated as it was. On the other hand, China, having opened its economy a decade earlier than India, could be expected to have an initial relative advantage in the competition for market shares. Trade liberalization in effect creates greater opportunities for trading with the rest of the world compared to a more restrictive trade-policy regime. However, the extent to which these opportunities are translated into increased trade depends also on domestic factors, such as the quality and cost of infrastructural services (e.g., power, transport, telecommunications), that determine competitiveness of production for exports or for substituting imports.

To check whether these expectations are borne out in actual export performance, trends of market shares during the 1990s in total imports of selected products with North America (U.S.A. plus Canada) and the European Union (EU-15) for India and a few of its potential competitors are calculated (Tables 1.9 and 1.10). The product categories were chosen to represent labor-intensive manufactures in which India could be expected to be competitive. It is clear from the table that the market shares of South Korea, Taiwan, and Thailand show a declining trend. The World Bank (2002, table 2.5) reports a significant increase in labor cost per worker in manufacturing between 1980–84 and 1995–99 in these countries. Interestingly, according to the same source, there was virtually no increase in such cost in India and a substantial increase in China. Yet while India's market share virtually stagnated in the 1990s, with both its and China's market share at 1 percent or less, China's market share shows a rapidly rising trend. Of the eight products in 2000, nearly half of North American imports, and a tenth of European imports, came from China as compared to less than 12 percent and 4 percent, respectively, in 1990. Clearly, India is apparently still not competitive vis-à-vis China.

A more detailed study by Tendulkar (2000) confirms India's weak competitive position. It compared Indian export performance with that of three rapidly growing East Asian economies (China, South Korea, and Taiwan), three Southeast Asian economies (Indonesia, Thailand, and Malaysia), and two South Asian economies (Bangladesh and Pakistan). Exports were classified into five broad categories: (natural) resource-intensive (mainly processed agricultural and mineral products), intensive-intensive (light manufactures), scale-intensive (mostly

TABLE 1.9

Share of Country in Total North American Imports from the World

	North American Imports from World (%)											
Country	1990	1991	1992	1993	1994	1995	1996	1997	1998	1999	2000	1990–2000 Average
Brazil	2.03	1.86	1.92	2.19	1.80	1.47	1.49	1.30	1.08	0.94	1.15	1.57
China	11.79	15.20	18.51	21.27	22.89	23.98	25.74	27.13	27.44	26.93	25.33	22.38
Hong Kong	5.48	5.01	4.74	3.91	3.58	3.28	2.95	2.58	2.60	2.16	1.90	3.47
India	1.01	1.03	1.20	1.28	1.37	1.09	1.11	1.08	1.05	0.99	0.99	1.11
South Korea	9.47	7.71	6.05	4.76	4.04	3.46	2.63	2.35	2.72	3.43	4.03	4.60
Mexico	1.48	1.84	2.08	1.99	2.22	2.26	2.21	1.74	1.65	1.57	2.00	1.91
Malaysia	4.82	5.34	5.37	5.37	6.57	7.78	8.97	9.44	10.56	11.45	12.47	8.01
Thailand	11.48	10.57	9.13	7.28	6.40	5.59	5.35	4.76	4.58	4.23	4.20	6.69
Taiwan	1.75	2.04	2.26	2.26	2.24	2.28	1.99	1.90	1.75	1.76	1.55	1.98

SOURCE: COMTRADE Data Base (2001).

NOTE: Product categories are 764: telecom eqpt; 778: electrical machinery, NES; 842: men's outerwear, nonknit; 843: women's outerwear, nonknit; 847: textile clothing, ACCES, NES; 851: footwear; 893: articles of plastic, NES; 894: toys, sporting goods, etc. (PTS = parts; ACC and ACCES = accessories; NES = not elsewhere specified)

TABLE 1.10

Share of Country in Total EEC Imports from the World

	EEC Imports from World (%)											
Country	1990	1991	1992	1993	1994	1995	1996	1997	1998	1999	2000	1990–2000 Average
Brazil	0.34	0.35	0.31	0.36	0.27	0.21	0.17	0.19	0.16	0.16	0.16	0.24
China	3.36	4.89	5.43	6.95	6.86	6.23	6.82	7.23	6.99	7.76	9.23	6.52
Hong Kong	3.10	2.98	2.81	3.46	2.74	2.77	2.82	2.87	2.76	2.75	2.58	2.88
India	0.81	0.70	0.69	0.89	1.00	0.98	0.87	0.76	0.72	0.69	0.71	0.80
South Korea	2.43	2.60	2.26	2.34	2.52	2.51	1.80	1.37	1.17	1.55	1.75	2.03
Mexico	0.44	0.51	0.61	0.75	0.80	0.90	0.85	0.76	0.72	0.71	0.95	0.73
Malaysia	0.08	0.09	0.10	0.12	0.09	0.11	0.11	0.16	0.17	0.16	0.27	0.13
Thailand	2.77	2.78	2.26	2.20	1.86	1.74	1.67	1.71	1.57	1.55	1.60	1.97
Taiwan	0.99	1.23	1.24	1.28	1.22	1.08	1.06	0.99	0.98	0.92	0.96	1.09

SOURCE: COMTRADE Data Base (2001).

NOTE: Product categories are 764: telecom eqpt; 778: electrical machinery, NES; 842: men's outerwear, nonknit; 843: women's outerwear, nonknit; 847: textile clothing, ACCES, NES; 851: footwear; 893: articles of plastic, NES; 894: toys, sporting goods, etc. (PTS = parts; ACC and ACCES = accessories; NES = not elsewhere specified)

homogeneous) products, differentiated products (mostly machinery and transport equipment), and, finally, high-tech science-based products. These five categories together were taken to constitute extended manufacturing (E-Mfg) products. Tendulkar calculates the share of India and other countries in the increment to the annual average value of world exports between the four pre-reform years (1987–90) and the corresponding levels for four post-reform years

(1993–96) for each of the five categories. He finds that India's share in world incremental E-Mfg exports was tiny, 0.8 percent, compared to 5.8 percent for China, with other shares ranging between 1.3 percent (Indonesia) and 3.5 percent (South Korea).

In exports of traditional intensive-intensive products India fared relatively better, with a share of 3.0 percent of incremental world labor-intensive exports. Even this share was, however, exceeded by much smaller countries like Thailand (3.4 percent) and Indonesia (4.9 percent), as well as China (22.2 percent). Tendulkar also finds that traditional intensive-intensive and scale-intensive exports accounted for as much as 80 percent of India's and 65 percent of China's incremental exports. In contrast, the share of differentiated products in incremental world exports was more than half. Countries such as South Korea, Taiwan, and Malaysia and Thailand to a lesser extent have a large share of their incremental exports accounted for by differentiated products.

Although compared to the pre-reform era India's export performance has improved, and India's share of the growth in world exports has increased, India's competitors, particularly China, have done much better. It is clear that Indian exports have yet to become competitive in world markets, and, until they do so, the payoff from reforms of external sector policies (including exchange-rate policies) would be limited. It is also clear that domestic constraints raise the cost of Indian producers relative to their external competitors. In particular, the failure to reform state-owned enterprises in power, transport, and financial sectors and to improve the functioning of ports has meant that production as well as transactions costs of Indian producers have remained relatively high. Of course, an appropriate exchange rate could offset these cost disadvantages. But the exchange-rate policies could also reflect adjustment to capital inflows; that is, they are used to offset tendencies toward appreciation that, in their absence, might follow increases in capital inflows. Apparently, the authorities did not attempt such policies. In fact, the rupee appreciated until 1997–98 after the effects of the 1991 devaluation eroded and capital inflows surged.

Growth in Factory Output and Employment in Large-Scale Manufacturing

In labor-abundant economies such as India, import-substituting industrialization strategies protected capital-intensive industries. Such protection adversely affected the growth of employment in intensive-intensive manufactures and their exports, besides creating incentives for tariff-jumping foreign investment, which in turn has welfare-reducing consequences, as Brecher and Diaz-Alejandro (1977) showed long ago. In India, apart from trade protection, domestic policies, particularly labor laws that are protective of labor interests in the narrowest sense, have further ensured that the protected industries were even more capital intensive than they would have been otherwise. Clearly trade liberalization without reform of other domestic policies would have a limited effect in addressing the biases. Still, it is worth looking at the effects it has had.

During the four decades before reforms, the Indian manufacturing sector developed a dual structure, with the considerably more capital-intensive organized factory segment having a much higher average productivity and a higher wage per worker than the residual, unorganized, predominantly small-scale, nonfactory segment. According to the quinquennial National Sample Surveys of employment and unemployment, the share of (factory plus nonfactory) manufacturing employment in the total workforce increased only marginally in nearly 30 years, from 9.0 percent in 1972–73 to 11.1 percent in 1999–2000. The data from the Annual Survey of Industries show that the share of the factory segment in total manufacturing employment has remained virtually constant at around 17 percent over the same period. Thus, as much as 83 percent of manufacturing employment is still confined to a lower-productivity unorganized segment.

The considerable acceleration in GDP growth, compared to the previous three decades following selective deregulation and fiscal expansion in the 1980s, had virtually no effect on employment in the factory segment. The decade of the 1980s, therefore, has been described as one of "jobless growth," and there were concerns about the declining output elasticity of employment in the factory segment. These concerns were heightened during the post-1991 period, particularly among those who believed that wide-ranging liberalization of investment and trade policies would lead to "deindustrialization," almost certainly in the short run, but possibly in the long run as well. Their argument was, on the one hand, that the erstwhile-protected industries would contract in the face of greater competition from imports and, on the other, that investment in industries made profitable by liberalization would not come about (if liberalization was expected to be reversed) or would take time, even if it did come about.

The two important determinants of the demand for labor are clearly real output and the cost to the employer of a worker or, more precisely, the product wage of a worker. Tendulkar (2000) points out that real output (that gross real value added in manufacturing) grew faster at an average of about 9 percent per year during 1997–98 as compared to 7 percent per year during 1981–91. However, the real product wage grew more slowly, at 2.6 percent per year during the 1990s as compared to 5 percent in the 1980s.

Tendulkar (2000) finds that the *partial* elasticities of employment to output and to real product wage did not change between the 1980s and the 1990s, the former remaining at about 0.8 and the latter at about −1. Applying these elasticity estimates to the data on growth in output and real product wage yields estimates of expected employment growth of roughly 1.1 percent per year in the 1980s and 4.6 percent in the 1990s. In fact, there was no growth in employment in the 1980s and 2.9 percent growth per year in the 1990s. Clearly, there were factors other than output and real product wage that contributed to the differences between actual and exported growth in employment. Still, the *difference* between the 1990s and 1980s in expected employment growth (3.5 percent) and actual employment growth (2.9 percent) are similar in magnitude.

It is clear that trade reforms, particularly the removal of QRs on imports of intermediate and capital goods, and easing of entry barriers explain in large part the faster growth of GDP as well as manufacturing output in the 1990s. It is possible that, in spite of there being no changes in labor laws and other labor-market conditions, there was nonetheless greater flexibility in hiring so that growth in product wage moderated in the 1990s. If this is the case, trade reforms have had a significant positive effect on the growth of higher-paying and more productive jobs of the factory segment of the manufacturing sector.

Trends in Total Factor Productivity (TFP)

Before the reforms of 1991, producers were severely constrained in their operational and investment decisions. There were government controls on their choices of investment, location, technology, and inputs, particularly imported inputs. They did not face significant competitive pressures either, as domestic competition was limited because licenses for installing productive capacity were restricted to conform to targets for capacity creation in the Five-Year Plans, and import competition was severely limited by import licensing. A natural hypothesis under these conditions is that there would be little or no growth in total factor productivity (TFP) in the pre-reform era, except perhaps in the 1980s when the rigors of some of the controls were relaxed, and there would be a faster growth in TFP from the 1980s on. There is some support for this hypothesis in the data. For the manufacturing sector, Ahluwalia's (1992) estimates show that TFP *declined* at an annual rate of 0.5 percent in the two decades prior to 1980 and increased at a rate of 2.8 percent in the decade of the 1980s. However, for the economy as a whole, estimates of the IMF (2000) suggest that TFP stagnated throughout the 1960s and until 1974, and increased steadily thereafter, reaching an impressive growth of 2.5 percent in the post-reform year of 1996. Unless one postulates that for some reason the first oil shock of 1973 elicited a response that put the Indian economy on a rising TFP path, this finding is puzzling. The World Bank (2000a, 30) estimates TFP growth between 1.3 percent and 1.5 percent per year between 1979–80 and 1997–98, depending on whether the elasticity of output with respect to capital input was assumed to be 0.75 or 0.65. However, in the three years (1994–95, 1995–96, and 1996–97) of the post-reform era, when GDP growth averaged 7.5 percent per year, TFP growth accelerated to an annual rate of between 2.4 percent and 2.8 percent. However, given the well-known methodological and measurement problems associated with estimation of TFP, these estimates are to be treated as no more than indicative.

External Capital Inflows

Leaving aside grants and unrequited transfers, there are essentially three types of external capital inflows: borrowing from world capital markets, governments, and intergovernmental (multilateral) lending institutions, portfolio investment, and FDI. As long as the cost of borrowing from foreign sources is less than from domestic sources, it would be appropriate to borrow and invest in activities with returns adequate to service the debt. More generally, if capital markets are efficient, information asymmetries are absent, and if there were no restrictions on capital flows, capital would be efficiently allocated around the world. However, none of these assumptions hold in the real world. India has not embraced capital account convertibility yet.[4] As such, issues that arise from the interaction among open capital accounts, exchange rate regimes, and investor behavior, in particular the possibility of running into a financial crisis as in East Asia, are not important in the Indian context. Whether liberalization of inflows of FDI (assumed to be for the long term, and hence less volatile) and portfolio flows (relatively short term and more volatile) have increased the risk of some form of crisis of external finance, in spite of India's not having an open capital account, is arguable. Although private firms have been allowed to access foreign capital markets through American and Global Depository Receipt schemes, domestic financial intermediaries have not been allowed to borrow abroad. Thus, the government has accumulated most of India's external debt. In such a context, the relevant issues for India relate to the government's management of external debt and India's domestic environment for FDI (which is presumed to have positive effects in terms of technology transfer and greater access to world markets) in the post-reform era.

Turning to external debt and its management, until the 1980s the two major sources for external capital for India were bilateral government-to-government foreign aid and borrowing (largely concessional) from international financial institutions. Only in the 1980s did the government borrow from private sources on commercial terms, in part to finance growing fiscal deficits. Among private creditors, non-resident Indians (NRIs) were an important source of deposits in Indian banking system. In 1980–81, out of $18.3 billion of public and publicly guaranteed external debt, only $2 billion was owed to private creditors (World Bank 1990, table 4.1). But on the eve of the macroeconomic crisis of 1990–91 that led to the reforms, external debt had nearly *quadrupled* to $71.1 billion (World Bank 2000a, table A3.1a), of which as much as $23 billion was owed to private creditors. Thus, debt to private creditors had grown elevenfold in just 10 years.

NRI deposits, which were negligible in 1980–81, amounted to $14 billion in 1990–91. Short-term debt at $8.5 billion in 1990–91 was more than 2.5 times the level of net foreign exchange reserves at $2.1 billion. With greater political uncertainty, as three prime ministers followed in quick succession in 1990, when oil prices rose as the Gulf War broke out, the confidence of external lenders, particularly NRIs, in the government's ability to manage the economy eroded. NRI deposits dried up, with net inflows falling from $2.3 billion in 1989–90 to $1.6 billion in 1990–91 and to a mere $290 million in 1991–92 (World Bank 2000a, table, A 3.1 [d]). Thus India came close to having to default on its external debt.

The first two years of reforms ending in 1992–93 saw a severe fiscal contraction and a drastic import compression (gross fiscal deficit of the central government was reduced from 6.6 percent of GDP in 1990–91 to 4.8 percent in 1992–93 [Government of India 2001, table 2.1]), and imports declined by about 20 percent in 1991–92. There was a sharp reduction in the current account deficit, from 3.1 percent of GDP in 1990–91 to 0.6 percent in 1991–92. Short-term debt came down to $6.3 billion in 1992–93, and even further to $3.6 billion in 1993–94. In the meantime, net reserves had climbed to $14.5 billion in 1993–94, more than four times the level of short-term debt. Although there has been a substantial slippage in fiscal discipline since then and restrictions on imports have also been removed, still the current account deficit has remained modest (at less than 1.1 percent of GDP in 1999–2001), and debt management has continued to be sound. Short-term debt at the end of March 2000, at $4.04 billion, was only 11.5 percent net of foreign exchange reserves (Government of India 2001, 125).

The reforms of 1991 removed many of the restrictions on inflows of FDI and made India more welcoming and less hostile as a host for FDI, although FDI is still prohibited in certain sectors of the economy such as retail trade. FDI flows increased from an annual average of less than $200 million to a peak of $3.6 billion in 1997–98. It has subsequently declined to $2.2 billion in 1999–2000. The data for April–December 2000 suggest that the declining trend might be reversed (Government of India 2001, table 6.8). India's share in FDI flows to developing countries, even in the peak year of 1997–98, was only 2 percent. Several smaller Asian countries, let alone China (which received a massive $40 billion of FDI in 1999), receive much higher FDI flows than India. Thailand, in spite of its financial crisis of 1997, received $7 billion and $6 billion of FDI, respectively, in 1998 and 1999 (Government of India 2001, table 6.9).

It is clear that, as in foreign trade, liberalizing policies that relate to FDI in and of themselves would have limited effects unless other domestic policies that adversely affect the returns of investors are reformed. The ongoing dispute with Enron, the only foreign investor in India's power sector, is a case in point. The dispute probably would not have arisen if the bankrupt state electricity board of Maharashtra were not the sole buyer of power generated by Enron. Thus, the failure to reform the state monopolies in the power sector inhibits FDI into that crucial sector. Three other foreign investors from the United States, the United Kingdom, and South Korea who were planning to invest in the sector pulled out. Clearly if crucial sectors such as power, transport, ports, and communication continue to be dominated by poorly performing public enterprises, and bureaucratic controls at central and state levels are still inhibiting, external sector reforms by themselves would be inadequate to put India on a path of sustained and rapid growth.

India, WTO, and Multilateral Trade Negotiations

Five decades of development experience have shown that being open to external trade and investment flows enables a developing country to grow faster economically than otherwise, and that faster economic growth is an effective and efficient means for alleviating poverty. For developing countries to achieve more rapid growth through greater integration with the world economy, a liberal and open global trading and financial system is essential. After eight rounds of multilateral trade negotiations under the auspices of the GATT, trade barriers have been reduced substantially, and the world trading system is now far more open than it was when the GATT was concluded in 1947. The last round, the Uruguay Round (UR), created the WTO as a formal institution with a well-defined constitution to facilitate the implementation of multilateral trade agreements. It also went beyond earlier rounds in successfully negotiating an agreement to liberalize trade in services. Unfortunately it also brought into the WTO framework and disciplines matters that are at best tangentially related to trade, such as Trade-Related Aspects of Intellectual Property Rights (TRIPS) and investment measures. The attempt by some developed countries to introduce a social clause relating to labor standards against strong opposition of developing countries, including India, was the prime cause of the failure of the Third Ministerial Meeting of the WTO in Seattle in December 1999 to launch a new round of multilateral negotiations. The Fourth Ministerial Meeting is scheduled to take place in Doha, Qatar during November 9–13, 2001.

It is in India's interest, and that of developing countries, to endorse the launch of a new round of negotiations at Doha. With the world economy experiencing a significant slowdown,[5] protectionist forces would gain strength everywhere, particularly in industrialized countries, which are the dominant markets for exports and sources of investment capital for India and other developing countries. Without the prospect of a new round of negotiations toward further trade liberalization, it would not be easy to mobilize exporting interests against protectionists who might even succeed in reversing past liberalization. Yet India and many other developing countries are reluctant to support the start of a new round. The reasons for this reluctance have to be understood in order to make the case that the likely benefits from a new round far outweigh the costs of not launching one.

The lack of enthusiasm for a new round arises mostly from the dissatisfaction with the Uruguay Round agreement since its implementation process started in 1995. Of course, India and the developing countries have been contending right from the days of the Havana Conference of 1947–48 that the rules and disciplines of GATT/ WTO have been tilted against the interests of developing countries. Further, whenever the interests of developed countries were perceived to be adversely affected by the rules, they were circumvented either by waiving the rules or taking the affected trade out of the purview of GATT disciplines and negotiating a separate agreement to govern such trade. The two classic examples cited in this context are agricultural trade and the Multifiber Arrangement (MFA) governing trade in textiles and apparel. A waiver exempting agricultural trade from most of GATT disciplines was granted in the 1950s. MFA is an egregious violation of GATT's fundamental principle of nondiscrimination and its rule (leaving aside its balance of payments exception) prohibiting the use of import quotas. The UR agreement included the first steps in subjecting agricultural trade to the same disciplines that apply to trade in manufactures. It also phased out MFA over 10 years, that is, by January 1, 2005. Yet developing countries argue that neither liberalizing agricultural trade nor phasing out MFA would yield benefits commensurate with the many costly commitments the countries undertook as signatories to the agreement and which required major institutional development and creation of new institutions. In fact, given that commitments to reduce agricultural tariffs were from bound rates that were far above applied rates, on balance there was virtually no liberalization of agricultural trade in the UR agreement. Although subsidies on exports of manufactures (which some developing countries offered to their infant manufactured exports) were made WTO-inconsistent, agricultural export subsidies (which were used mainly by industrial countries, particularly the European Union) were reduced but not eliminated. It is true that the developing countries were given a longer time to implement their commitments as compared to the developed countries. Yet, as the implementation began, many developing countries found that even the longer implementation periods might not be long enough.

The developing countries also argue that they were pressured into agreeing to the inclusion of TRIPS in the UR Agreement, even though, unlike liberalization of trade in which all trading partners gain, there is no obvious mutual gain from TRIPS. Indeed, the cost of TRIPS is substantial: Maskus (2000, table 6.1) estimates a net transfer of rents on intellectual property of the order of $8.3 billion to just four developed countries (United States, Germany, France, and Italy) from the rest of the world, including poor countries. Although MFA phaseout is deemed as a "benefit" that developing countries got in return for incurring the cost of TRIPS, even this phaseout is backloaded. Nearly half of the quota restrictions of the MFA do not have to be removed until the last day of the phaseout. Besides, even after the phaseout, relatively high tariff barriers on products covered by the MFA might continue.

India and other developing countries have been urging a resolution of implementation issues as a down payment up front before the start of a new round. These issues relate "to various perceived asymmetries and imbalances in existing WTO Agreements and effective operationalization of various special and differential treatment provisions for developing countries. . . . [In response,] the General Council [of the WTO] decided on 3 May 2000 to hold Special Sessions to discuss various implementation issues and concerns raised by Members," and the Indian government claims that "the pressure mounted by India and other developing countries has succeeded in putting implementation issues firmly and squarely in the Agenda of the WTO for the first time" (Government of India 2001, 117). Subsequent meetings of the General Council on June 20, 2000 and December 15, 2000 have made further progress. As the *Financial Times* of May 17, 2001 reported, the ministers of the OECD at their conference in May 2001 stressed the importance of paying close attention to developing countries' concerns, particularly difficulties in meeting existing WTO obligations.

The reasons for India's (and developing countries') reluctance to embrace a new round appear legitimate. Yet there are far stronger reasons for India to welcome, and indeed vigorously participate in, a new round. Mattoo and Subramanian (2000) articulate some of these: active engagement in the multilateral trading system through participation would facilitate domestic reform and enhance access for India's exports; it can serve as a commitment to good policies and as a means of securing more firmly market-access rights that have already been established; and it can serve as a bulwark against regionalism. In support of the last argument, the two authors cite the trade diversion after the conclusion of the North American Free Trade Agreement (NAFTA): Mexico has gained market share relative to India in the United States and Canada in exports of clothing in particular, and manufacturing in general, since the conclusion of NAFTA. China, which did better than India in both markets, also experienced a slowdown in the growth of its imports after the conclusion of NAFTA.

The Summit of the Americas held in Quebec City, Canada in April 2001 has endorsed the formation of a hemispheric free-trade area extending from the High Arctic in the north to Tierra del Fuego in the south. It is a plausible presumption that unless a new round of multilateral negotiations is launched soon, negotiations at regional levels might succeed in dividing the world into overlapping as well as competing trade blocs. India has to recognize that if a new round is not launched soon, regional liberalization will become a serious alternative to multilateral liberalization. Although the World Bank (2000b) sees some positive aspects in regional liberalization, there is no convincing evidence that these outweigh their negative aspects, including trade diversion. The fact that the results of preferential regional liberalization in South Asia, through the South Asian Preferential Trade Agreement (SAPTA), have been very disappointing and that no other regional agreements appear to be open for India suggests that India should strongly support the launching of a new round. By forthrightly endorsing a new round of MTN, India would be in a stronger position to ensure that items in its interest are included and those against its interest are excluded from the negotiating agenda in the new round.

Agenda for a New Round: Possible Negotiating Positions for India

Of course, any agenda to command the support of both developed and developing countries will involve tradeoffs. But such tradeoffs should not lead to a serious imbalance between costs and benefits to the developing countries. With this in mind, the following are worth considering in formulating India's (and developing countries') negotiating position.

Market Access

Even after eight rounds of negotiations and reductions of trade barriers, the traditional issues of market access are still relevant. From the perspective of developing countries, these include tariff peaks and tariff escalation that still limit developing countries' access to industrialized country markets, high tariffs on imports of textiles and apparel, possible resort to safeguards and anti-dumping measures (ADMs) to restrict imports of textiles and apparel after the expiry of MFA (the European Union and the United States have unsuccessfully tried to do so even *before*), and liberalization of trade in services through commitments to extend MFN and national treatment to more and more categories of services. India's tariffs are still high in comparison to other Asian developing countries. In return for more liberal market access commitment by its partners, India could commit to reducing its tariffs.

Agriculture

Although the UR agreement broke new ground by bringing agricultural trade for the first time within the scope of international disciplines and set in motion a process for lowering border protection and trade-distorting domestic support measures, there was no significant liberalization of trade. A major factor contributing to this outcome was that the process of tariffication of preexisting protection measures became "dirty," and most countries bound their rates from which their commitments to reduce protection were defined at levels far above applied rates. India was no exception. India bound tariffs at 100 percent for new products, 150 percent for processed products, and 300 percent for edible oils (with the exception of 45 percent for soya oil). The simple average of these rates was 115 percent, while the average applied rate was 35 percent in 2000.

According to a recent report by the OECD cited in the *Financial Times*, April 11, 2001, the UR agreement has had limited impact—subsidies to producers accounted for as much as 40 percent of farm income in 30 OECD countries and for more than two thirds of farm income in Japan, South Korea, Norway, and Switzerland. The OECD report concludes that agricultural protection in rich countries is largely responsible for the stagnation at 40 percent in the share of developing countries in global agricultural trade, while their share in manufactured trade has doubled from 14 percent to 29 percent in the last two decades. India's commerce minister cited the distortions in agricultural trade due to export subsidies in the developed world as he raised India's agricultural tariffs when QRs were removed in April 1, 2001. Some poor developing countries in sub-Saharan Africa, which are net importers of food grains and other agricultural products, fear that removal of export subsidies by the European community will raise the cost of their food imports. However, the cost of enabling them to achieve the same welfare as they have now through income transfers in a distortion-free world market for agriculture would be lower than the cost of the subsidy on the food they are importing currently. In any case, since on balance Indian agriculture as a whole is disprotected (Pursell and Sharma 1996), India would gain from integration with distortion-free world agriculture. The CAIRNS group is for removal of trade distortions,[6] and India's interests lie in aligning with them in agricultural trade negotiations.

The domestic political economy of integrating India's agricultural sector with world markets is complex, given its insulation for nearly five decades and the fear that integration would result in the loss of hard-won food security. Even though integration of Indian agriculture with world markets and elimination of disprotection would benefit the agricultural sector as a whole, clearly in some agricultural commodities India would not be internationally competitive without protection and their production have to be phased out. Clearly producers of such commodities would not be able to immediately adjust. But the burden of adjustment can be eased through a phased reduction of protection, while credibly committing to their elimination at the end of a specified period of time. Not credibly committing to elimination, and worse still, guaranteeing existing protection, and increasing it, as was done recently following removal of QRs, is costly.[7]

I now turn to food security, which in political debate is often equated with self-sufficiency in the aggregate, rather than with ensuring that the poor are protected against fluctuations in food prices. One should also distinguish "self-sufficiency"—that is, producing as much food as is consumed—from "self-reliance"—that is, having adequate resources to acquire food from world markets in case of adverse shocks to domestic output. India's focus on "self-sufficiency" is derived from its searing experience in the mid-1960s when it faced a major food shortage following two consecutive years of drought. Not having enough foreign exchange resources of its own to import large volumes of food grains, India then depended on concessional food aid from the United States. President Lyndon Johnson, unhappy with India's opposition to the Vietnam War, punished India by deciding on a shipment-by-shipment basis whether India would get food aid. The perceived high political costs of import dependence led India to devote more resources to agricultural development. With the green revolution technology becoming available at about the same time, India succeeded in becoming self-sufficient in food grains. However, as long as world markets remain open, and a country has resources to buy in such markets, there would be no political cost to food imports.[8] Thus what matters from the perspective of resisting political pressure is "self-reliance" and not "self-sufficiency." Another concern among Indian policy makers is the fear that letting world prices pass through to domestic market prices through integration with world markets would increase the amplitude of domestic price fluctuations. There is virtually no empirical support for this argument. Also, by reviving well-functioning futures markets in India and accessing these abroad, price risks associated with integration, if any, could be minimized (World Bank 1999).

TRIPS

The inclusion of TRIPS in the WTO (rather than in a more appropriate institution such as the World Intellectual Property Organization) was unfortunate. The cost of TRIPS to developing countries is high. Yet any demand by India and developing countries for renegotiation of TRIPS, let alone taking it out of WTO, is unlikely to be accepted by the United States and other industrialized countries. India, with the support of other developing countries, could instead propose two amendments to TRIPS. The first would extend the period allowed to bring national patent regimes into compliance with TRIPS requirements and institute a peace clause precluding the use of WTO's Dispute Settlement Mechanism for TRIPS disputes for ten years. The second amendment would expand the scope of the compulsory licensing provisions to allow countries (mainly very poor) that have no production capacity of their own to license producers in other developing countries with such capacity to produce life-saving drugs under patents for their own use. India, Brazil, and other developing countries with production capacity for drugs and pharmaceuticals would potentially benefit from such an amendment. Once India and Pakistan pass appropriate domestic legislation for determining which rice varieties would qualify as basmati, they could apply for protection of geographical indication for basmati rice under Article 2.2 of TRIPS. India could also propose some form of patent protection for indigenous knowledge.

Anti-Dumping Measures (ADMs)

Indian exporters have been frequent targets of ADMs. For example, according to WTO (2001b, tables IV.5 and IV.6), between July 1, 1999 and June 1, 2000 products exported from India were subject to 11 anti-dumping investigations, the seventh largest in number. Unfortunately, India itself initiated 27 actions during the same year and had as many as 91 ADMs in force as of June 30, 2000, the fourth largest, after the United States (300), European Community (190), and South Africa (104). Imports from China were most frequently targeted, with 18 cases at the end of 1999. In May 2001, anti-dumping duties were imposed on imports of phosphoric acid from China, polyester film from South Korea and Indonesia, and ferrocyamide from the European Union. It would be in the best interest of the trading system as a whole, and to its developing country members in particular, if ADMs were made WTO-illegal. This is unlikely to come about. There is disagreement among the industrialized countries as to the inclusion of ADMs in the agenda for the next round. It would be in India's interest to join those who wish to tighten the conditions under which ADMs could be invoked.

Labor and Environmental Standards

The demand for expanding the mandate of the WTO to permit the use of trade-policy instruments to enforce labor and environmental standards is unlikely to fade away. The support for linking market access to enforcement of labor rights is strong among NGOs and student groups in industrialized countries. I have elsewhere (Srinivasan 1998a) analyzed the economics of linking market access with enforcement of labor standards. The fear that such linkage would be a means for offsetting the comparative advantage of India and other labor-abundant countries in labor-intensive products is not unfounded. India's continuing opposition to the inclusion of labor standards as an item in the negotiating agenda of a future round is well taken. But India could at the same time reiterate its willingness to discuss labor and environmental issues in other forums such as the ILO and UNEP.

Movement of Natural Persons

Negotiations toward further liberalization of movement of natural persons (MNP) for the purpose of supplying services were not completed at the conclusion of the UR. However, the UR agreement established a Negotiating Group on movement of natural persons (MNP), which was to have produced a final report no later than six months after the agreement that established the WTO entered into force—that is, by June 30, 1995. As of September 2001, there was no such report and no agreement yet on this important issue. India has a comparative advantage in labor-intensive services and in some skill-intensive services such as computer software. If no agreement is reached on liberalization of MNP as part of the ongoing review of the General Agreement on Services, MNP has to be on the agenda of the next round.

PTAs

As noted earlier, it is unlikely that India would be invited to join any PTAs on a regional basis. The South Asian Preferential Trade Agreement (SAPTA), of which India is a signatory, has not been a success. To prevent PTAs from becoming a permanent threat to a liberal multilateral trading system, India could propose an amendment to Article XXIV of WTO/GATT dealing with PTAs. The amendment would allow members of the WTO to enter into a PTA, as long as any concessions that they grant to each other under the PTA are extended to all other members of the WTO on an MFN basis within, say, five years of the PTA coming into force.

To sum up, India's negotiating position could consist of offers to lower and bind its tariffs and to relax FDI rules further in return for liberalization of agricultural trade and movement of natural persons and protection against its trade being diverted by PTAs. India could propose amendments to Article XXIV of GATT on PTAs and TRIPS and perhaps to Article VI on ADMs and countervailing duties. While not compromising on its stance against the inclusion of labor standards in the WTO, India could offer to discuss labor standards in the ILO and other forums.

Conclusions

Until the early 1980s, India's trade policy was geared to serve the objective of industrialization through import substitution. High tariffs, QRs, export controls, and hostility to foreign investment were the main policy instruments used. In the early 1980s, there was some relaxation of these rigid controls. In fact, by 1985, a conscious attempt was made to improve the competitiveness of Indian exports, by allowing exporters a more liberal access to the importers' goods and intermediate inputs, and by depreciation of the rupee. However, the overall development strategy was still inward oriented. Only with the reforms of 1991 did a significant shift away from this strategy toward outward orientation take place. Initially the reform involved a significant devaluation of the rupee, removal of QRs on imports (except for imports of consumer goods and agricultural products), and a reduction of tariffs across the board. The exchange rate was unified and made convertible for current account transactions in 1993. Relaxation of restrictions on inflows of foreign capital (FDI and portfolio) led to a surge in inflows (and an appreciation of the rupee) for a while. However, since 1996–97, mean tariffs have slowly increased, and the removal of QRs took place in 2000 and 2001, only after India failed in its attempt to defend them on balance of payments grounds, when challenged by the United States, before the Dispute Settlement Body of the WTO. In concluding, I will list the remaining tasks that need to be completed in the arena of external sector policies.

Tariff Barriers

As noted earlier, import-weighted mean tariffs have slowly increased from 24.6 percent in 1996–97 to 30.2 percent in 1999–2000. This level is much higher than those prevailing in China and other East Asian countries. Even after the withdrawal of the surcharge on import duties in the budget for 2001–2002, there is unlikely to be a significant reduction—in fact, it is more likely that there will be an increase in mean tariffs. The budget proposals included an increase in the rate of customs duty on tea, coffee, copra, coconut, and desiccated coconut from 35 percent to 70 percent, and on various edible vegetable oil imports from a range of 35 percent to 55 percent to a range of 75 percent to 85 percent. While removing QRs on imports on April 1, 2001, the government has raised several applied tariffs. For example, total customs duties on secondhand cars and other vehicles were raised to a whopping 180 percent. The commerce minister has promised to use all steps available under the WTO rules to protect the economy.

These proposals, if fully implemented, would mean that India would continue to have one of the most protective trade regimes in Asia. What is needed to achieve more rapid, sustained, and efficient growth is not maintaining or increasing protection levels, but to commit to reducing them significantly in a phased manner within a relatively short period of time.

Foreign Direct Investment

China successfully created special economic zones (SEZs) in 1980 and used them to attract foreign investment. India had an export processing zone (EPZ) in Kandla port on the west coast of India much earlier, and more EPZs were added later. Unlike in China, which waived restrictions on FDI, labor regulations, and other constraints on firms operating in SEZs, and also provided excellent infrastructure facilities, in India, except for duty-free access to inputs, firms operating in EPZs faced many of the same restrictions as firms elsewhere in India. Unlike the SEZs of China and EPZs in the rest of Asia, Indian EPZs did not attract any FDI. In 1999–2000, EPZs were replaced by free-trade zones (FTZs), which are to be treated as external to India's customs territory. Presumably other regulations will also be waived for firms operating in FTZs. It is too soon to tell whether FTZs will be any more successful than the EPZs they replaced in attracting FDI.

Liberalization of restrictions on FDI (most recently in May 2001), portfolio investment, broadening of the access of Indian companies to foreign-equity markets, and the easing of restrictions on commercial borrowing are major steps in the reform process.[9] The inflow of FDI is hampered more by other constraints than those arising from lack of capital account convertibility. The IMF (2000, 772) reports that, according to the January 2000 FDI Confidence Index constructed by the consulting firm A. T. Kearney, India's absolute attractiveness as an FDI destination increased compared to the previous survey in June 1999, but it still slipped from 6th to 11th on the list of preferred destinations. The latest survey of executives of Global 1000 companies finds that few have India on their list of likely investment destinations over the next one to three years. Investors, though generally sanguine about India, are still reluctant to invest because of a perception that it has done less than other emerging markets to reduce fundamental obstacles to investment. Of the executives surveyed, the majority of those with existing investments said that they were likely to add to those investments. But an even larger majority of companies without existing investment said the likelihood of their investing in India was low. The major obstacles to investment in India were bureaucratic hurdles and the slow pace of reforms.

Bureaucratic hurdles are not merely procedural hurdles and hassles in obtaining required clearance from central and state governments but also include regulations. For example, reservations of certain products for production by small-scale producers, prohibition of FDI flows into certain sectors such as retail trade, and regulations on urban land markets all inhibit and distort investment decisions. Whether the newly created regulatory agencies, such as for telecommunications and electric power, promote competition by easing entry of potentially more efficient suppliers or favor incumbent players (many of them state owned) who may be inefficient is another vital issue.

Infrastructure

Perhaps the most serious constraint on growth of exports and aggregate growth is the poor state of India's infrastructure (power, transport, ports, telecommunications, etc.). On the one hand, most infrastructure services cannot be imported, and, as such, import liberalization is of little consequence in augmenting their availability. On the other hand, without reliable and affordable infrastructural services, the opportunities opened up by trade liberalization would not be fully utilized. The attempt to attract FDI into infrastructure, particularly power, has not borne fruit primarily because of the political failure to reform the bankrupt state electricity boards.

Software

India has a comparative advantage in labor-intensive services as well as in certain skill-intensive ones such as software. The software industry is one of India's fastest growing industries in the electronics sector. Software exports grew by an impressive 43 percent per year between 1991–92 and 1996–97 and 68 percent in 1997–98. Although India is a significant player in the world software market, there are reasons to believe that India may not realize its vast potential unless major policy changes are made.

The industry's focus is currently on proprietary work for foreign organizations, which is only a small part of the world software market. It has not penetrated into the large off-the-shelf software market. India's cost advantage because its software professionals are inexpensive will be eroded as other players (e.g., China) with similar or lower costs enter the market. The benefits from an efficient software industry are not simply greater export earnings and FDI, but significant gains in the productivity of resource use in the domestic economy.

The single most urgent policy action needed for India to realize the potential of the information technology industry is to ensure that a vibrant and efficient world-class telecommunications infrastructure is in place. For example, the ability to compete for data-processing services that are being outsourced by industrialized countries would be constrained by a poorly functioning telecommunications infrastructure. The telecommunications sector was opened up to private investors in 1994. However, the policy framework for the sector and the conflict between the Department of Telecommunications (DOT) and the regulatory agency, Telecommunications Regulatory Authority of India (TRAI) as it was initially constituted, hampered progress toward an efficient telecommunications infrastructure. A national telecommunications policy was announced in 1999. The components of the DOT engaged in the provision of telecommunications services have been corporatized and made autonomous, so that its role as a service producer need no longer influence its policy-making role. Yet in practice the policy framework and regulatory decisions still seem to favor state-owned incumbents.

While exports of software from a domestic base will continue to grow provided the industry remains competitive, to be able to provide in situ services in foreign markets and to keep up with technological developments it is essential that Indian software technicians have the opportunity to work abroad without necessarily having to migrate permanently. Most of the Indian engineers entered the United States under a special category of nonimmigrant visas. But there is strong pressure to restrict the number of such visas issued. A liberal agreement (as part of the General Agreement on Services [GATS] of WTO) on movement of natural persons would facilitate such temporary migration.

I have to conclude on a somber, if not altogether pessimistic, note. Political uncertainties, particularly after the recent state elections, suggest that the reform process (privatization and disinvestment, reforms of labor and bankruptcy laws, and fiscal consolidation—including elimination of subsidies, reform of state electricity boards, etc.) is unlikely to gather steam. The bold pronouncements of the finance minister on these matters in his budget speech on February 28, 2001 are likely to remain just that. His and the commerce minister's statements on tariffs (particularly on agricultural products) are anything but reassuring about the prospects of further liberalization of the external sector.

Appendix:
Export Performance and the Real Effective Exchange Rate

T. N. Srinivasan and Jessica Wallack

The steady appreciation of the real exchange rate in the 1980s and 1990s appears to have adversely affected India's export performance. External sector policies used to promote import substitution up to the early 1980s contributed to significant overvaluation of the rupee. The steady depreciation from 1985 to 1993, along with liberalizations in the trade and exchange regimes, contributed to the growth of India's tradables sector.

Various econometric studies have found a significant relationship between export performance and the real exchange rate. Joshi and Little's (1994) estimated structural model, for example, finds that the price elasticity of the supply of exports is about 0.7 in the short run and 1.1 in the long run. Price elasticity of the demand for exports was found to be approximately 1.1 in the short run and about 3.0 in the long run. They find that real exchange depreciations in the 1970s and the late 1980s were associated with rapid export growth, while slower export growth occurred during periods of appreciation such as the 1960s and 1980s. Srinivasan's (1998b) analysis of India's exports over 1963–94 also finds that real exchange-rate appreciation negatively affects export performance. His results also suggest that increases in GDP and in overall world exports have, in part, offset the negative effect of real exchange-rate appreciation.

This appendix extends the analysis of the relationship between the real exchange rate and export competitiveness to 1998. It is important to include this later post-reform period in order to discern whether the real exchange-rate appreciation since 1993 has had roughly similar effects on India's export performance.

In what follows we reestimate the relationship between exports and the real exchange rate using a larger data set that runs from 1960–1998. We use two measures of export performance: the logarithms of dollar value of total Indian exports and India's exports as a share of total world exports. The figures for Indian exports are obtained from various editions of the Indian Ministry of Finance's *Economic Survey*, while world exports are from table A of the United Nations' *International Trade Statistics Yearbook*. According to Joshi and Little, the ratio of the incentive-adjusted exchange rate to the real exchange rate in 1988 was 0.95. We assumed a constant level of export incentives until reforms began in 1991 and then reduced the weighting factor linearly (add .01 each year) until 1995.[10] Data on real GDP come from the Government of India (2000) and are the series calculated at factor prices.

The real exchange rate, exports, and real GDP appear to grow at exponential rates, and the transformation to logs produces series that follow an approximately linear trend captured by a time trend. These series are not stationary in logs: in keeping with the visual impression of a trend, an augmented Dickey-Fuller test, evaluated at conventional significance levels of 5 percent, does not reject the null of a unit root in the log GDP, log exchange rates, and log export series. We find little evidence of a cointegrating relationship between the log of the real exchange rate and the log of total exports or export shares.

We thus present two versions of the original analysis. The first regressions, presented in Tables 1.A.1 and 1.A.2 are as in Srinivasan (1998b), where the nonstationarity in the original series is addressed by regression on a time trend and lagged values. This appears to be an appropriate specification for the regressions with the log of value of exports (in U.S.$) as the dependent variable. The error terms are stationary, and there is little evidence of autocorrelation. This method is not as helpful for the regressions using India's share of world exports as the dependent variable: the residuals are mildly serially correlated, and we narrowly reject the null hypothesis of a unit root in the residuals.

The second set of regressions, presented in Tables 1.B.1 and 1.B.2, modify the original regression to account for the nonstationarity by using first differences. The explanatory power of this regression, as in most first-difference regressions, is quite low. However, given the problems with nonstationarity in the original regression, this is our preferred specification for the analysis of the relationship between share of exports and the real effective exchange rate. The coefficients on the real effective exchange rate and GDP are of the expected sign, though not statistically significant at conventional levels.

Our results are similar to Srinivasan (1998b). The real effective exchange rate is still negatively, though not significantly, related to the log of India's export share, and coefficients in both the levels and first-difference regressions are of similar magnitude to those found in the analysis of 1963–1994 data. The log

TABLE 1.A.1
Regression Results for Log of India's Export Share

Dependent Variable		
Constant	−0.302	−12.436
	(−0.33)	(−5.45)
Log of real effective exchange rate	−0.128	−0.209
	(−0.67)	(−1.49)
Log of real GDP		0.971
		(5.55)
Time trend	−0.005	−0.059
	(−0.79)	(−5.48)
Log of lagged export share	0.805	0.381
	(8.98)	(3.81)
Adj-R^2	0.85	0.92
Number of observations	37	37

NOTE: *t* statistics are in parentheses.

TABLE 1.A.2
Regression Results for Log of Total Exports

Dependent Variable		
Constant	−0.222	−4.574
	(−0.16)	(−2.18)
Log of real effective exchange rate	−0.298	−0.352
	(−2.46)	(−3.11)
Log of real GDP	0.200	0.502
	(2.09)	(3.45)
Log of world exports	0.231	0.371
	(4.63)	(5.25)
Time trend		−0.027
		(−2.60)
Log of lagged Indian exports	0.554	0.514
	(6.24)	(6.19)
Adj-R^2	0.996	0.996
Number of observations	37	37

NOTE: *t* statistics are in parentheses.

of real GDP is, as before, positive, statistically significant, and of the same magnitude as in Srinivasan (1998b). The relationship between the real effective exchange rate and the log of total value of exports is stronger: the coefficients are negative, highly statistically significant, and nearly identical to those presented in Srinivasan (1998b). The elasticity of export supply to the real exchange rate does not appear to have changed significantly in the 1990s.

TABLE 1.B.1

Regression Results for Log of India's Export Share (First Differences)

Dependent Variable		
Constant	−0.020	−0.050
	(−1.10)	(−2.02)
D log of real effective exchange rate	−0.398	−0.414
	(−1.35)	(−1.44)
D log of real GDP		0.608
		(1.74)
Adj-R^2	0.02	0.07
Number of observations	37	37

NOTE: *t* statistics are in parentheses.

TABLE 1.B.2

Regression Results for Log of Total Exports (First Differences)

Dependent Variable	
Constant	−0.019
	(−1.01)
D log of real effective exchange rate	−0.292
	(−1.84)
D log of real GDP	0.610
	(3.07)
D log of world exports	0.700
	(6.37)
Adj-R^2	0.52
Number of observations	37

NOTE: *t* statistics are in parentheses.

Notes

1. The Havana Conference adopted a charter for an International Trade Organization (ITO) into which GATT was to be incorporated. But the ITO did not come into being, mainly, though not only, because its charter was not ratified by the United States.

2. This and the next section draw extensively from chapter 4 of Srinivasan and Tendulkar (2002).

3. Balance of payments data in Table 1.4 have always differed from customs data of Table 1.5 for various well-known and understood reasons.

4. Vijay Joshi (2001) argues that capital controls were crucial in insulating India, particularly from the East Asian crisis and more generally from volatile capital flows of the 1990s. He recommends that India continue its cautious approach to capital account con-

vertibility in the near future. Certainly given the current parlous state of India's financial sector (particularly state-owned commercial banks), this is a sound recommendation.

5. The terrorist attack on the World Trade Center in New York on September 11, 2001, has made global economic prospects very uncertain.

6. The group is named after Cairns, the town in Australia where it first met. It includes, as of March 2001, Argentina, Australia, Bolivia, Brazil, Canada, Chile, Cambodia, Costa Rica, Fiji, Guatemala, Indonesia, Malaysia, New Zealand, Paraguay, the Philippines, South Africa, Thailand, and Uruguay.

7. Commentators on India's commitments as a signatory of the UR agreement on agriculture tend to ignore the fact that given its current levels of domestic support and export subsidies, India is already in compliance with the agriculture agreement. Besides, applied tariff levels are far below bound levels, and, as such, market-access commitments are also not serious constraints.

8. This is illustrated by the failure of the grain embargo imposed by President Carter on the Soviet Union to punish it for its invasion of Afghanistan. With enough resources then available, the Soviet Union found willing sellers of grain in Argentina and Australia. The embargo failed to achieve its goal.

9. These steps are important from the perspective of eventual convertibility of the rupee on the capital account. The parlous state of the domestic financial sector precludes the rupee being made convertible on the capital account anytime soon.

10. Joining these two series is somewhat problematic, as the RER series that Joshi and Little use is weighted using the 10 most important countries in India's exports during 1979–81, while the RBI is weighted using 36 countries using trade statistics over 1975–91. The two series are not markedly different at the joining point, however, most likely because the exports to the top 10 countries are a large proportion of the exports to the 36 countries used in the RBI weighting scheme.

References

Ahluwalia, I. J. 1992. Structural adjustment and productivity growth in India. *Productivity* 33 (2): 201–8.

Brecher, R. A., and C. Diaz-Alejandro. 1977. Tariffs, foreign capital, and immiserizing growth. *Journal of International Economics* 7 (4): 317–22.

Chopra, A., C. Collyns, R. Hemming, and K. Parker, with W. Chu and O. Fratzscher. 1995. *India's economic reforms and growth.* Occasional Paper 134. Washington, D.C.: IMF.

COMTRADE Data Base. 2001. New York: United Nations, Statistical Office.

Government of India. 2000. *Economic survey 1999–2000.* New Delhi: Ministry of Finance.

———. 2001. *Economic survey 2000–01.* New Delhi: Ministry of Finance.

———. 2002. *Economic survey 2001–2002.* New Delhi: Ministry of Finance.

International Monetary Fund (IMF). 1998. *India: Selected issues.* Staff Country Report No. 98/112. Washington, D.C.: IMF.

———. 2000. *India: Recent economic developments*. Staff Country Report No. 00/155. Washington, D.C.: IMF.

Joshi, V. 2001. Capital controls and the national advantage: India in the 1990s and beyond. *Oxford Development Studies* 29 (3).

Joshi, V., and I. M. D. Little. 1994. *India: Macroeconomics and political economy 1964–1991*. Washington, D.C.: World Bank.

Maskus, K. 2000. *Intellectual property rights in the global economy*. Washington, D.C.: Institute for International Economics.

Mattoo, A., and A. Subramanian. 2000. *India and the multilateral trading system post-Seattle: Defensive or proactive?* Washington, D.C.: World Bank (processed).

Panagariya, A. 1999. *The WTO trade policy review of India 1998*. College Park, Md.: University of Maryland (processed).

Pursell, G., and A. Sharma. 1996. *Indian trade policies since the 1991/92 reforms*. Washington, D.C.: World Bank (mimeo).

Reserve Bank of India. 2000. *Annual report 1999–2000*. Mumbai: Reserve Bank of India.

———. 2001. *Handbook of statistics on Indian economy*. Mumbai: Reserve Bank of India.

Srinivasan, T. N. 1998a. Trade and human rights. In *Constituent interests and U.S. trade policies*, edited by A. Deardorff and R. Stern. Ann Arbor: University of Michigan Press.

———. 1998b. India's export performance: A comparative analysis. Chapter 9 in *India's economic reforms and development: Essays for Manmohan Singh*, edited by I. J. Ahluwalia and I. M. D. Little. New Delhi: Oxford University Press.

Srinivasan, T. N., and S. D. Tendulkar. 2002. *Reintegrating India with the world economy*. New Delhi: Indian Council for Research on International Economic Relations, and Washington, D.C.: Institute for International Economics.

Tendulkar, S. 2000. *Indian export and economic growth performance in Asian perspective*. Working Paper 54. New Delhi: Indian Council for Research on International Economic Relations.

World Bank. 1990. *India: Country economic memorandum*. Washington, D.C.: World Bank.

———. 1999. *Managing price risks in India's liberalized agriculture: Can futures markets help?* Report No. 15453-IN. Washington, D.C.: World Bank.

———. 2000a. *India: Policies to reduce poverty and accelerate sustainable development*. Report No. 19471-IN. Washington, D.C.: World Bank.

———. 2000b. *Trade blocs*. New York: Oxford University Press.

———. 2002. *World development indicators*. Washington, D.C.: World Bank.

World Trade Organization (WTO). 2001a. *International trade statistics 2001*. Geneva: WTO.

———. 2001b. *Annual report 2001*. Geneva: WTO.

Comment
Opening the Economy: Further Reforms

Shankar Acharya

The external sector of the Indian economy was the focal point of the economic crisis of 1991. Some of the most far-reaching reforms were focused on restoring the health of the external sector. They included the transition to a market-determined exchange rate, major reductions in customs tariffs, phased elimination of quantitative restrictions on imports, decisive opening up to foreign direct and portfolio investment, strict controls on short-term external debt, and the deliberate buildup of foreign exchange reserves.

Together with deregulation of industry and fiscal stabilization, these external sector reforms yielded exceptionally good results by the mid-1990s. Export growth soared to 20 percent in three successive years, inward remittances quadrupled to $8 billion by 1994–95, foreign investment rose from negligible amounts to over $6 billion by 1996–97, foreign exchange reserves climbed steeply from the precarious levels of 1991 to over $26 billion by the end of 1996–97, and the debt-service ratio was halved over the decade.

The pace of reforms as well as the gains from reform have slowed markedly since the mid-1990s. This is an opportune moment to take stock of the new initiatives necessary to strengthen India's external sector performance. I will group my suggestions under five broad categories of trade policy, industrial policy, exchange rate and convertibility, foreign direct investment, and tourism.

Foreign Trade Policy

Despite the major reductions between 1991 and 1997, India's import duties remain among the highest in the world. For all the well-known economic reasons, it would be desirable to reduce the average level of customs tariffs quite substantially. Successive Indian finance ministers have promised to reduce customs tariffs to East Asian levels in three to five years (from the time of their budget pronouncements). The budget speech of February 2001 states the intention of moving "progressively within three years to reduce the number of rates to the minimum with a peak rate of 20 percent." Unfortunately, this increase in precision of intent has been somewhat weakened by the recent rise in the number of tariffs above the current "peak" rate of 35 percent.

It will not be easy to fulfill the above commitment given that custom revenues still account for almost 30 percent of the central government gross tax revenues. In theory, a decline in these revenues can be compensated for through an increase in revenues from direct taxes and taxes on domestic trade. However, in practice, this desirable transition may be constrained by weakness of political will and constitutional impediments to the introduction of a full-fledged value-added tax regime in India.

Quite apart from reducing the general level of import duties, it is necessary to reduce their present dispersion and thereby compress the existing high dispersion of effective rates of protection.

Another major priority for trade policy reform is to phase out the significant extent of quantitative restrictions on agricultural exports that exist today. This process could gain impetus from more determined multilateral liberalization of global trade in agricultural products.

Finally, there is a very large agenda of necessary reforms in customs procedures at ports and airports in India.

Industrial Policy

India's rigid labor laws reduce the growth of employment and weaken the competitiveness of Indian industry. The February 2001 budget speech broke new ground by promising labor law reform. Translating intention into practice will test both political will and skill.

Second, the policy of reservation of a wide range of products for small-scale industries (SSI) has severely retarded the growth of output, employment, and exports in India's manufacturing sector and has probably hurt the long-term interests of the SSI sector. Here, too, February's budget speech has announced dereservation of 14 key items in leather, shoes, and toys. Implementation is awaited.

Reform of bankruptcy laws and other exit procedures remains very important for enhancing productivity and competitiveness of Indian industry, not to mention the health of the financial sector. Here, too, the present government has moved the reform process forward, but a great deal more remains to be done.

Exchange Rate and Convertibility

In recent years India's exchange rate and payments policies have been quite successful. The combination of a reasonably flexible exchange rate, strict control of short-term external borrowing, and ample foreign exchange reserves, backed by timely monetary policy, has served India well, including in the rigorous test of the Asian crisis of 1997–98. Looking ahead, three things are necessary. First, the political and monetary authorities must learn to live with greater volatility in a market-determined exchange rate system. The propensity for central bank interventions to manage the rate needs to be moderated. Second, the authorities should nurture the development of the foreign exchange markets, instead of constraining them through a variety of administrative measures. Third, there should be a gradual expansion of convertibility of the capital account for resident individuals and firms. These measures will all enhance market determination of the exchange rate and improve its role in guiding economic adjustments to changes in external circumstances.

Foreign Direct Investment

First, many of the reforms noted above (e.g., labor laws and bankruptcy provisions) will not only induce greater domestic industrial investment and productivity, but will also attract more foreign direct investment. Second, India has been notably unsuccessful in attracting the "export platform" type of foreign direct investment, especially in comparison with East Asian countries like China, Thailand, and Malaysia. The key here is to reduce the anti-export bias in the foreign trade policy regime along the lines mentioned earlier. Third, there is a strong case for loosening the existing sectoral caps on foreign equity holding in areas such as civil aviation, telecommunications, banking, and agriculture. Finally, there has to be far greater effort to tackle the problems of high bureaucratic hurdles and transaction costs.

Tourism

The potential for growth of tourism earnings is enormous. Actual achievements have been quite limited. Among the priorities that need to be tackled are elimination of the existing bottlenecks in civil aviation (stemming largely from a desire to protect national airlines), expansion in the number of authorized "money changers" and other tourism-specific infrastructure, and, of course, improvement in general infrastructure in roads, railways, and power.

Needless to say, the performance of India's external sector will also depend crucially on reforms and productivity increases in the woefully weak infrastructure sectors and the financial sector. Improvements in these areas are essential for spurring economy-wide investment and growth, as well as enhancing external sector competitiveness.

2

INDIAN EXCHANGE RATE POLICY

❖

Anne O. Krueger and Sajjid Z. Chinoy

A great deal has been learned over the past half century about appropriate economic policy for achieving rapid economic development, both through the successes of the rapidly growing countries, such as South Korea, and through the less satisfactory performance of other countries, such as many in sub-Saharan Africa.

Among those lessons, the crucial role played by policies fostering an open economy is perhaps the most important.[1] Those countries that have followed inward-oriented trade policies, with protection through both tariffs and nontariff barriers, have experienced innumerable difficulties and, at best, have undergone slowdowns in the rate of economic growth. By contrast, those countries that have greatly reduced their tariffs, eliminated quantitative restrictions, and otherwise fostered an outward-oriented trade regime have experienced significantly better economic performance.

To be sure, economic performance varies among the outward-oriented economies depending on the rest of the economic policy regime, but an outward-oriented trade policy greatly restricts policy makers and often prevents the adoption of policies inimical to growth. When other policies have also been conducive to growth, the results have often been spectacular. This has been true not only among some East and Southeast Asian countries, but also in a number of other countries, including Chile (since 1986), Turkey (1980–86), and Brazil (1968–74). In between the very successful episodes and the countries with very poor economic performance are countries that have opened up—even without supportive domestic policies—and have generally experienced an improvement in economic performance, at least over a period of half a decade or more.

While other policies enable countries to achieve maximum gains from outward-oriented trade policies, one of the critical findings from experience is that an outward-oriented trade policy cannot succeed unless the underlying exchange-rate policy is appropriate. There are two reasons for this: (1) there is no outward orientation if there are high and differential tariffs and other trade barriers that protect domestic import-competing industries, and yet in the absence of other mechanisms (a floating exchange rate or use of domestic monetary and fiscal policy) for equating foreign exchange expenditures and receipts, increasing protection (through increased tariffs and import surcharges or more restrictive quantitative licensing of imports) is the only available response when countries' current account balances are negative and foreign exchange reserves are diminishing; and (2) an unpredictable exchange-rate regime serves as a strong disincentive for exporters and hence results in failure to provide incentives for an outward-oriented trade strategy. Stated in another way, an appropriate exchange-rate policy to support an outward-oriented trade strategy must do two things: (1) It must provide a realistic and stable incentive for actual and potential exporters, which means that the relative price of import-competing goods cannot be significantly different from the relative price in world markets (and hence protection must be low); and (2) it must simultaneously serve to bring the demand for foreign exchange into at least rough balance with foreign exchange earnings (from goods, services, workers' remittances, and other sources) so that the authorities can permit free importation and exportation.

The critical role of exchange-rate policy, and what it must accomplish, is examined in the first section below. The second section then examines the behavior of the Indian exchange rate in light of these considerations. A final section concludes.

The Exchange Rate as a Key Policy Variable

Many things are continuous: the fiscal deficit can—at least in the short run—be of any size; economic growth can take place at any (positive or negative) rate; and monetary policy can be more or less inflationary. But it is difficult, if not impossible, to have a half-open economy. There are a number of reasons for this, but the key one is that money is fungible: if there are some prohibited, or severely limited, transactions that would be highly profitable, there will be individuals (both domestic and foreign) who will find ways of transforming proceeds from liberalized transactions into the goods, services, or assets that are prohibited. This can happen in a large number of ways: engaging in complex transactions, under- or overvaluation of goods entering or leaving the country, smuggling and the like. Once profitable opportunities exist and individuals seize on them, the authorities are normally pressured either to control (through licensing, which usually means quantitative restrictions) or to liberalize (which means removing most remaining restrictions).

Since one of the key functions any government must fulfill is to maintain its international creditworthiness, liberalization of the great majority of transactions requires that there be another means for balancing the supply of foreign exchange with the demand.[2] That means is the exchange rate. If a liberalized trade regime is to be maintained, the exchange rate must somehow be managed so that the supply of foreign exchange (originating from export earnings, capital inflows, tourism, etc.) roughly balances the demand for foreign exchange (for imports, tourism, etc.).[3]

However, the exchange rate itself is a "nominal" variable. If all goods were traded, and there were no barriers to trade, domestic prices and foreign prices would rise or fall at the same rate. In fact, however, there are many goods and services—usually referred to as "home" or "nontradable" goods, whose prices respond to domestic demand and supply conditions because of the high price of transporting them. When a nominal exchange rate is fixed, but aggregate demand in the domestic economy shifts up rapidly, due, for example, to a large fiscal deficit, the prices of tradable goods remain unchanged and the current account deficit increases. But the prices of nontradables (construction, retail and wholesale trade, domestic transportation, and the like) will rise.[4]

Recognizing that it is the relative prices of tradables and nontradables (as well as the domestic relative price of import-competing to exportable goods as contrasted with their international prices) that matter in affecting both resource allocation between tradable and nontradable goods and for maintaining an appropriate balance between foreign exchange expenditures and receipts, it is important to examine the behavior of the real exchange rate. Ideally, the real exchange rate would be measured by estimating the relative price of tradable and nontradable goods. In practice, the consumer price index is heavily weighted by nontradable goods. Economists therefore estimate the real exchange rate for most purposes as the nominal exchange rate relative to the consumer price index contrasted with some base period. Thus, if the nominal exchange rate (i.e., the price of foreign exchange) rose by 10 percent in a given period, while the consumer price index rose by 20 percent, economists would regard the real exchange rate as having *appreciated* by 10 percent (approximately) in real terms.

It will later be seen that there are several meaningful real exchange rate measures, depending on the purpose at hand. And, in considering the real exchange rate, account must also be taken of the changes in prices in other countries.[5]

Concern is with the real exchange rate because the role of the exchange rate is to link the domestic economy with the rest of the world. When domestic prices rise relatively more than the exchange rate depreciates, domestic producers of exportables and import-competing goods find that their costs (both of factors of production and of raw materials, intermediate goods, and domestic infrastructure items such as transport and power) have risen relative to the prices at which they must compete with foreign-made goods.[6]

Indeed, more generally, the relative attractiveness of producing "tradable goods"—import-competing and exportable goods—relative to producing "home goods" (construction, infrastructure such as transport and communications, and other items where transport costs in terms of either time or money are sufficiently high so that foreign producers cannot enter the domestic market) increases as the price of foreign exchange, that is, the exchange rate, rises relative to the domestic price level. Specifically, if the exchange rate depreciates proportionately more than the domestic price level rises, producers find the relative profitability of producing tradables rises relative to the profitability of producing domestic goods.[7]

But, typically, domestic producers incur current expenses in order to sell goods and receive revenue in the future. What is of concern to them in making their decisions is not only the prevailing real exchange rate (i.e., the price at which they can expect to sell the tradable good, if it is produced, relative to the costs of production), but the real exchange rate that is likely to prevail in the foreseeable future. This is all the more true when decisions to add to productive capacity are taken, but it is true even for existing production.[8]

Hence, even more than with other aspects of economic policy, what matters is not only the existing nominal and real exchange rate, but expectations as to the future path of the nominal exchange rate and the domestic price level. If policy makers can achieve coherence in domestic macroeconomic and exchange-rate policy, then they can simultaneously determine exchange rate and domestic macroeconomic outcomes. When, however, domestic macroeconomic policy is determined in significant part by unalterable (at least in the short run) fiscal stances, exchange-rate policy must be determined taking the underlying course of domestic economic activity and prices more or less as a given. In many circumstances, failure to recognize this has led to a "failed devaluation" in the sense that producers have anticipated that, despite a recent increase in the price of foreign exchange to a new fixed level that significantly increased the current profitability of producing for export, the real exchange rate would appreciate in future months. When that has happened, they have understandably failed to adjust their production plans, and it appears that the devaluation was unsuccessful: what was really unsuccessful was that there was no change in underlying macroeconomic policy and no recognition of that fact in determining exchange-rate policy.[9]

Thus far, the discussion has been couched in terms of the real exchange rate. When there are rates of domestic inflation well above the world rate, the key factor undermining foreign trade is the erosion of the real value of domestic currency receipts for exports and the decreasing domestic relative price of imports.

A key question, however, is what the real exchange rate *should* be, and what factors may result in changes in it over time. There are two concepts of the real exchange rate that are important: (1) the real exchange rate that will leave foreign exchange receipts and expenditures more or less in balance over the intermediate term; and (2) the real (and prospective real) exchange rate that will provide sufficient incentives to exporters so that exports grow at a satisfactory rate as the economy embarks upon an outward-oriented trade strategy.

Each of these notions is important in interpreting an exchange-rate regime such as India has. Here each is considered in turn. The first, or "balance of payments equilibrating" (BOPE) exchange rate, depends on a number of factors. It is easiest to consider what, in addition to inflation, might change the BOPE over time, assuming that the real exchange rate initially was one that led to balance between expenditures and receipts.

A first, and obvious, change that would affect the BOPE rate is a country's terms of trade. When, for example, the price of oil rises sharply for an oil-importing country, the real BOPE must increase (i.e., the currency must depreciate in real terms), as additional resources must be induced to be allocated to exportable production, in order to cover the increased import bill (and to induce domestic production of oil and consumption and production shifts toward other energy sources). For oil exporters, of course, the opposite is true. The same effect can also be the result of an increase in competition from foreign suppliers of the goods in which a country has a comparative advantage. After the Asian financial crisis in 1997, for example, the depreciations of the baht, rupiah, won, and Philippine peso resulted in an improved competitive position for exporters from those countries. Countries with comparative advantage in the same range of goods that did not achieve an adjustment in their currency left their exporters in a deteriorating competitive position.

A second change that can affect the BOPE is shifts in expenditure patterns. If, for example, a government raises taxes (reducing expenditures on home goods) and increases investment expenditures on capital goods that are mostly imported, the demand for foreign exchange will shift upward. The result is much the same as a deterioration in the terms of trade: more foreign exchange must be earned in order to balance the increased expenditures on imported goods.

A third change that can affect the BOPE is a shift in the trade regime itself. Significant reductions in tariffs or non-tariff barriers (NTBs) normally lead to an increased demand for foreign exchange in order to purchase more imported goods, as the domestic price of imports and import-competing goods naturally falls and consumers (commercial and private) shift their purchases toward these goods. This is, of course, desirable as it shifts resources toward exportable production. However, both because the removal of tariffs and NTBs lowers the domestic prices of importables without increasing the price of exportables, as well as because of the increased demand for imports, an increased real price of foreign exchange is necessary to restore balance.[10]

The factors to be considered in evaluating the exchange-rate regime from the viewpoint of achieving balance in foreign payments and expenditures are then straightforward to summarize. They are

1. the domestic rate of inflation
2. a change in the terms of trade facing the country
3. the extent to which foreign competitors' positions are improved
4. shifts in the composition of demand away from or toward exportables and import-competing goods
5. the degree to which import tariffs and NTBs are being removed

However, as noted earlier, the factors that are relevant for evaluation of an exchange rate regime include not only its effectiveness in bringing about balance between foreign exchange receipts and expenditures, but also its impact on economic growth. This is of crucial importance during periods when countries are shifting from inward-oriented to more outward-oriented trade regimes. The real exchange rate is the chief factor in pulling resources into exports.[11] While the real exchange rate is an outcome of policies determining the nominal exchange rate and the rate of inflation, the inflation rate is usually itself the result of monetary policies of the previous year or two. As such, when the authorities determine (or let the market determine) the nominal exchange rate, they are affecting the real exchange rate in the short run.

Outward-oriented trade strategies have successfully stimulated rapid growth of production of exportables in countries where the policies have been set to maintain an attractive real exchange rate for exporters. During its transition to an outward-oriented trade strategy, South Korea averaged almost 40 percent average annual growth in the dollar value of exports (from 1963 to 1973), while real GDP grew at around 13 percent annually. For Chile, the comparable figures were 17 percent for exports and 8 percent for real GDP (1986 to 1991). In the early 1980s for Turkey once tariffs were lowered and quantitative restrictions on imports removed, exports grew at an average annual rate of over 20 percent (despite the worldwide recession), and real GDP growth accelerated to around 8 percent annually in the mid-1980s.[12]

Thus, the second test for the real exchange rate, especially during periods of transition, is whether it is serving as a sufficient "pull" of resources into exportable industries. In general, the rapid expansion of export production comes about from nontraditional industries, although primary commodity exports also increase significantly.[13]

The final issue to be considered, before analyzing India's exchange rate policy, is the way in which the authorities handle exchange rate determination. Since the 19th century, it has been recognized that countries have to maintain balance in their international accounts. They can fix a nominal exchange rate and then adjust monetary and fiscal policy to achieve balance between payments and receipts; or they can use monetary and fiscal policy for domestic purposes (such as price-level stability) and then permit the exchange rate to find its own level as dictated by supply and demand in the international market—a floating-rate regime.[14]

An extreme case of a fixed exchange rate is a currency board, or even more extreme, dollarization. In the latter case, countries abandon any monetary unit of their own and use the money of another country (typically the United States, which is why it is referred to as dollarization). In the case of a currency board, money is issued, or withdrawn from circulation, only as there is foreign exchange backing. At the present time, Argentina has a (somewhat flexible) currency board, while Panama and Ecuador have dollarized and Estonia uses the deutsche mark as its currency. Since this "irrevocable fix" does not seem a likely option for India, no more is said about it here.

Until the 1990s, conventional wisdom was that countries could peg their nominal exchange rates, but then alter them through devaluation if such an action was needed. This led to recurrent real appreciations followed by currency crises and depreciations in many countries.[15] After the Asian financial crises of the 1990s, however, many observers and analysts have become convinced that the "fixed but adjustable" exchange rate pegs of the 1960s and 1970s are no longer viable options for countries. This "hollowing out of the middle" option would suggest that countries need to choose between the two extremes.

However, in reality, many countries are announcing that they have a floating exchange rate but are in fact intervening in their foreign-exchange market to "guide" the rate. While such "guidance" allows more flexibility than the previous regimes of fixed pegs did, it nonetheless still leaves the door open for crises. It may be noted, for example, that both South Korea and Indonesia were not pegging their currencies at the time of their financial exchange-rate crises, but were intervening in the foreign exchange market to "guide" the exchange rate.[16]

For considerable periods of time, however, the authorities can intervene in the foreign exchange market and adjust monetary and fiscal policy to achieve their exchange-rate targets, or objectives. When they believe that the exchange rate will otherwise appreciate to an unwarranted extent, they can buy foreign exchange and sell domestic currency, thus shifting the demand for foreign exchange upward and the supply of foreign exchange downward. Likewise, when they are concerned about incipient depreciation, they can pursue the opposite policy. And, of course, monetary policy can be eased (inducing depreciation) or tightened (inducing appreciation).

Since domestic price levels tend to adjust fairly slowly, while adjustment in the foreign exchange market is more rapid, intervention by the authorities can, in the short run, alter the real exchange rate. Observation of the behavior of the Indian exchange rate, and the statements of the authorities, strongly suggests that policy makers do intervene in order to achieve exchange-rate targets. While the rate is permitted to fluctuate within a range, efforts are made to prevent depreciation or appreciation outside of that range.[17]

The Indian Exchange Rate: Is the Level Appropriate?

Because there are restrictions on capital account transactions, there is more leeway for the Reserve Bank of India to "guide" the exchange rate than there is in countries with more open capital accounts. But that does not address the question as to whether guidance has been to an exchange rate most suited to India's needs. In this section, we consider that question.

In countries that have had open economies (on both trade and capital account) for a period of time at a fixed or floating exchange rate, analysts have an observation as to what a realistic exchange rate might be. Then, when a change (such as the terms of trade) occurs, the task for the analyst is relatively straightforward: the impact of the terms of trade change on the appropriate real exchange rate can be analyzed. However, when the exchange rate has been controlled and there is no base period against which to judge the appropriateness of the real exchange rate, the task is much harder.

As stated above, however, two important criteria by which to judge the appropriateness of India's real exchange rate are (1) how the exchange rate is pulling resources into exportable industries; and (2) how well the exchange rate permits the demand and supply for foreign exchange to come into balance—particularly in light of India's significant trade liberalization over the last decade—without the need for unusual borrowing from abroad, running down of reserves, or tightening of monetary policy.

In India's case, there is no question that the real exchange rate was induced to depreciate toward the end of the 1980s, and more considerably during the economic reforms of the early 1990s. This is in stark contrast to the path of the real exchange rate in the previous two decades—as is illustrated by India's real exchange rate vis-à-vis the dollar in Figure 2.1.[18] The more interesting question to consider, therefore, is the evolution of the real exchange rate since the early 1990s and to ask if the degree of real depreciation has been appropriate.

For India, there are several considerations in determining the appropriate concept of the real exchange rate. On one hand, a natural comparison is with price levels in India's export destinations, her main trading partners. The top five, listed in descending order from largest value of exports, are the United States, Japan, Germany, the United Kingdom, and Hong Kong. Figure 2.2 maps India's export-weighted multilateral real exchange rate vis-à-vis these destinations from 1990 to 1998.[19] As is evident, India experienced a large real depreciation in the early years of the decade, and by 1993 the exchange rate had

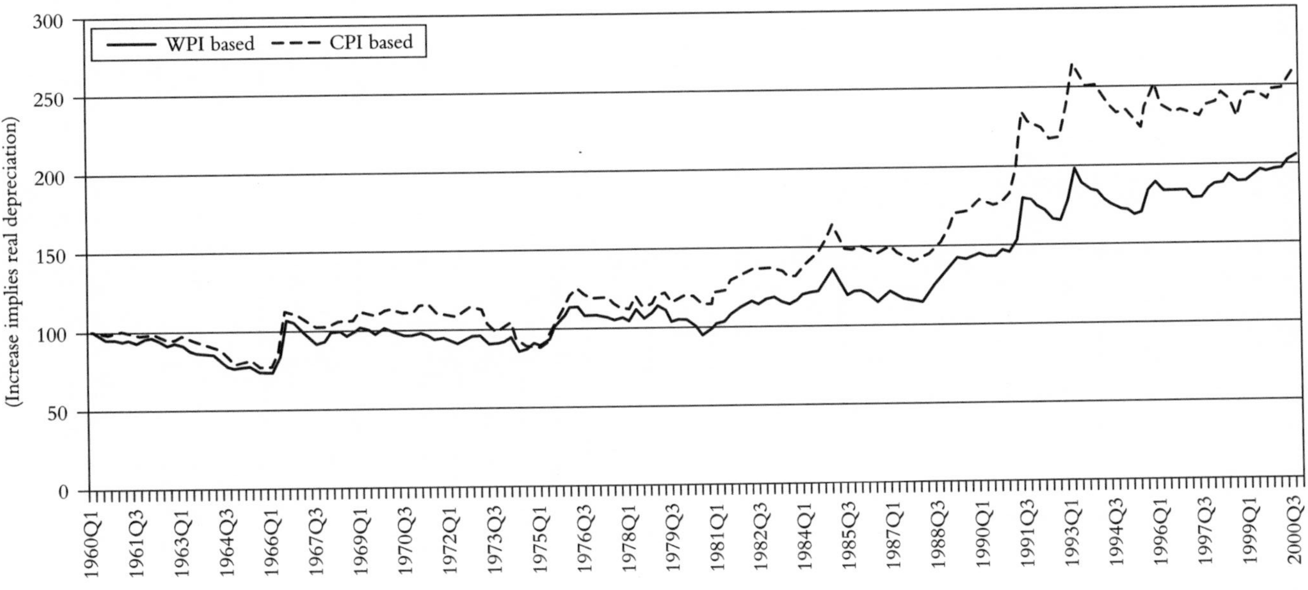

Figure 2.1. India's Real Exchange Rate vis-à-vis the United States, 1960–2000

SOURCE: International Monetary Fund (2002a).

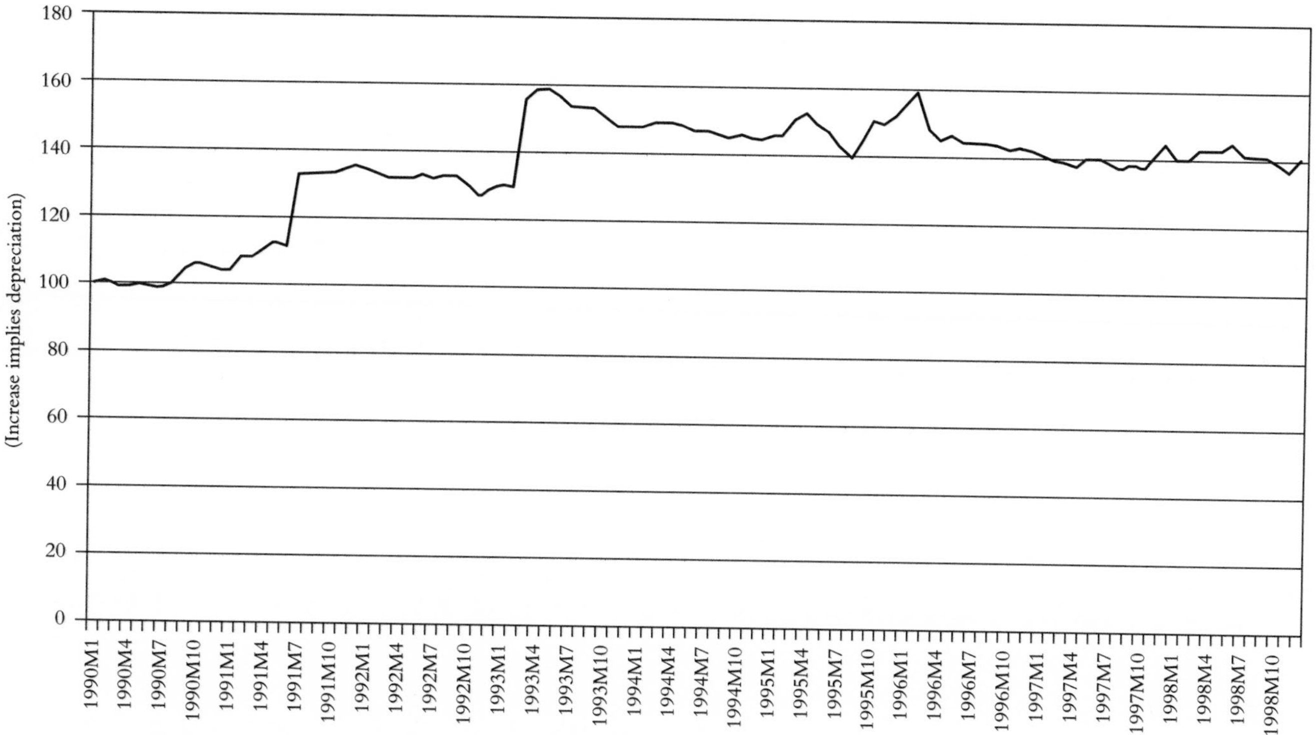

Figure 2.2. Export-Weighted Average of India's CPI-Based Real Exchange Rate vis-à-vis Its Five Largest Export Markets, 1990–1998

Countries (weights): U.S. (.43), Japan (.16), Germany (.15), U.K. (.14), Hong Kong (.12).

SOURCE: International Monetary Fund (2002a, b).

depreciated almost 60 percent in real terms relative to its level in 1990. From that high, however, there seems to have been a gradual—but persistent—real appreciation (excepting the blip in 1996) through 1998.[20] To be sure, by the end of 1998 the rupee had depreciated almost 40 percent in real terms against these currencies, but the real appreciation toward the latter half of the decade seems to have eroded some of the early gains. Figure 2.3 maps the Indian real exchange rate for the remainder of the decade, but substitutes the Euro area for Germany in the list of export destinations.[21] As this figure illustrates, the appreciation of the late 1990s extended up until May 2000 (at which point the exchange rate had appreciated more than 6 percent in real terms over its value at the start of 1999) before depreciating somewhat over the next few months. Still, by September 2000, the rupee had appreciated a further 4 percent in real terms vis-à-vis these currencies over its January 1999 level.

Figures 2.4, 2.5, and 2.6 map India's bilateral real exchange rate vis-à-vis the United States, Japan, and Germany, respectively (India's three largest export markets over the 1990s), from January 1990 to September 2000. As all three graphs show, there was a significant real depreciation in two steps in the early 1990 during the reform period. Since 1993, the real exchange rate between the rupee and the dollar has been approximately constant when measured in terms of consumer prices, and slightly depreciating (less than 5 percent) when measured in wholesale prices. With respect to Japan, the two real depreciations of the rupee also show up. But, after 1995, the rupee appreciated in real terms until the end of 1998, and since then has regained only part of the earlier level. This reflects, of course, in large part the path of the Japanese yen versus the U.S. dollar. However, the rate with respect to the German mark reflects the situation vis-à-vis much of Europe: there has been significant real appreciation since 1996.

These estimates of the real exchange rate are all based on the behavior of domestic prices in India's major export markets relative to India's prices, relative to nominal exchange rate behavior. But, as indicated above, the terms of trade also affect how the equilibrium real exchange rate should behave, both for purposes of equilibrating the balance of payments and for purposes of providing incentives for exporters to expand as the economy opens up. To examine this question, the appropriate comparisons are with India's major competitors. These are other labor-abundant Asian countries. Figure 2.7 therefore provides estimates of India's trade-weighted real exchange rate vis-à-vis six East Asian countries from January 1980 to September 2000: Indonesia, South Korea, Malaysia, the Philippines, Singapore, and Thailand.[22]

As can be seen, the real exchange rate remained approximately constant vis-à-vis these countries for much of the 1980s before beginning to depreciate rather substantially till the mid-1990s. Indeed, in June 1997, just before the onset of the East Asian financial crisis, India's exchange rate had depreciated about

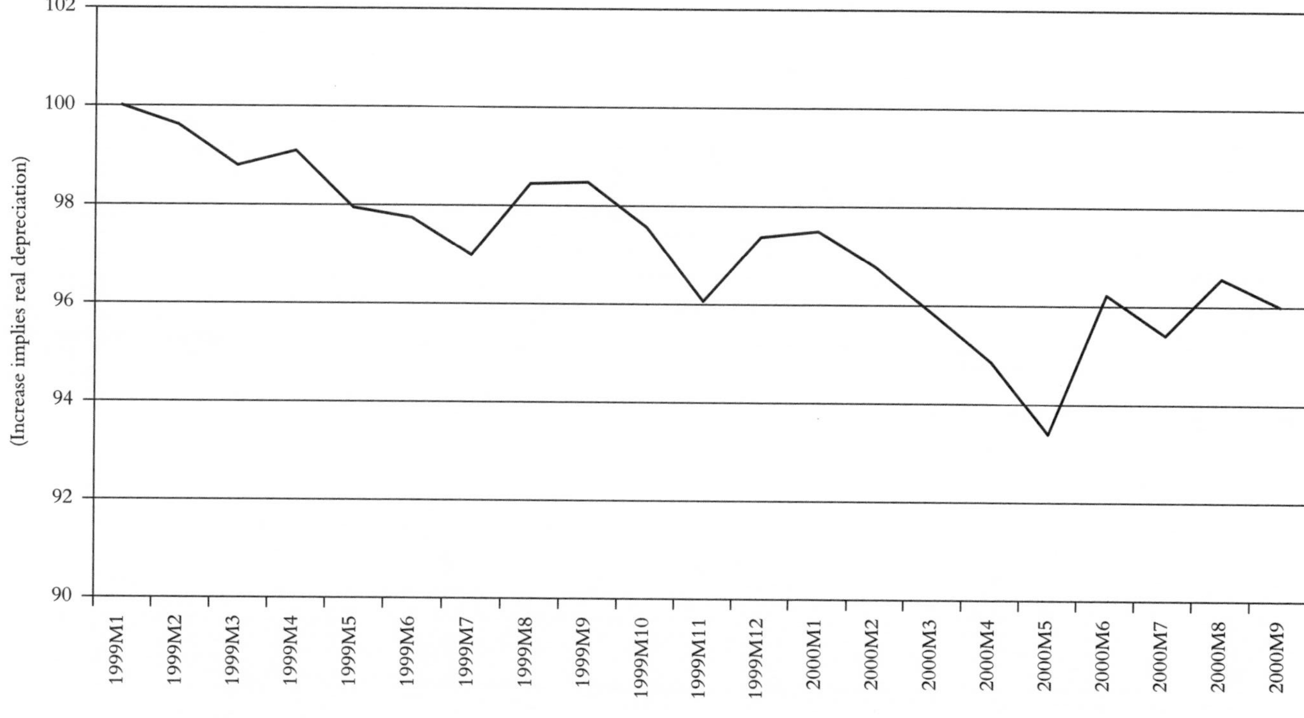

Figure 2.3. Export-Weighted Average of India's CPI-Based Real Exchange Rate vis-à-vis Its Five Largest Export Markets, 1999–2000

Countries (weights): U.S. (.39), Euro area (.33), U.K. (.10), Japan (.09), Hong Kong (.09).

SOURCE: International Monetary Fund (2002a, b).

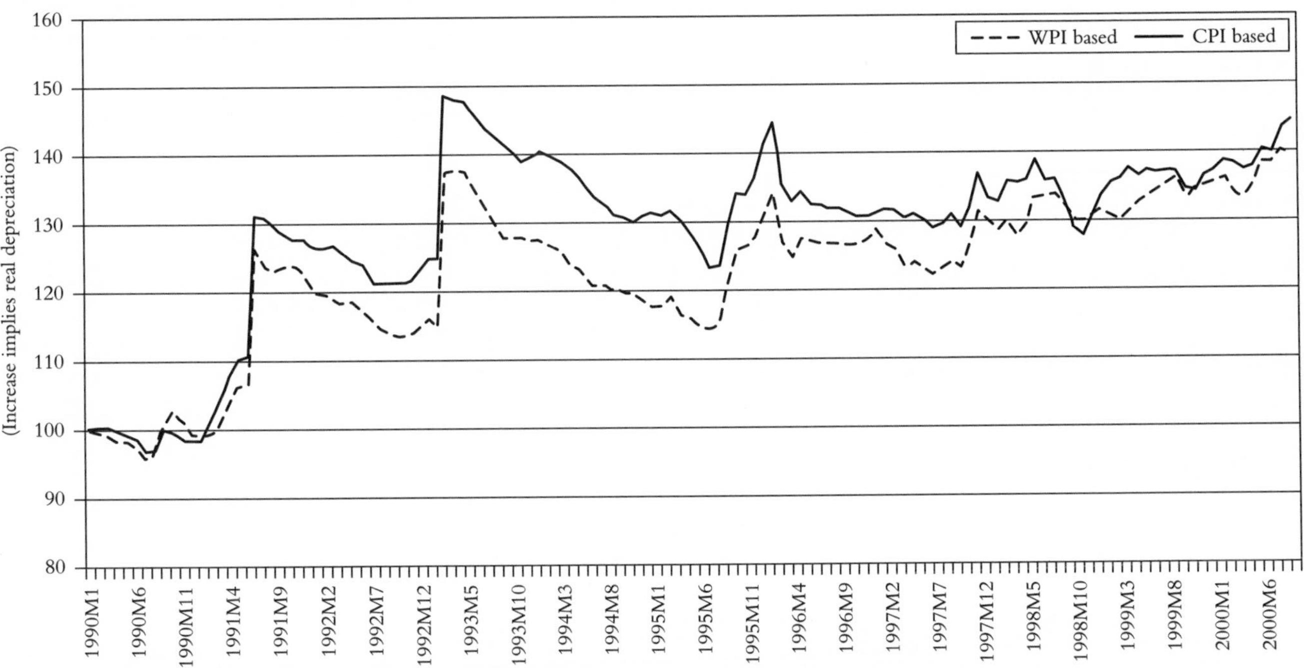

Figure 2.4. India's Real Exchange Rate vis-à-vis the United States, January 1990 to September 2000

SOURCE: International Monetary Fund (2002a).

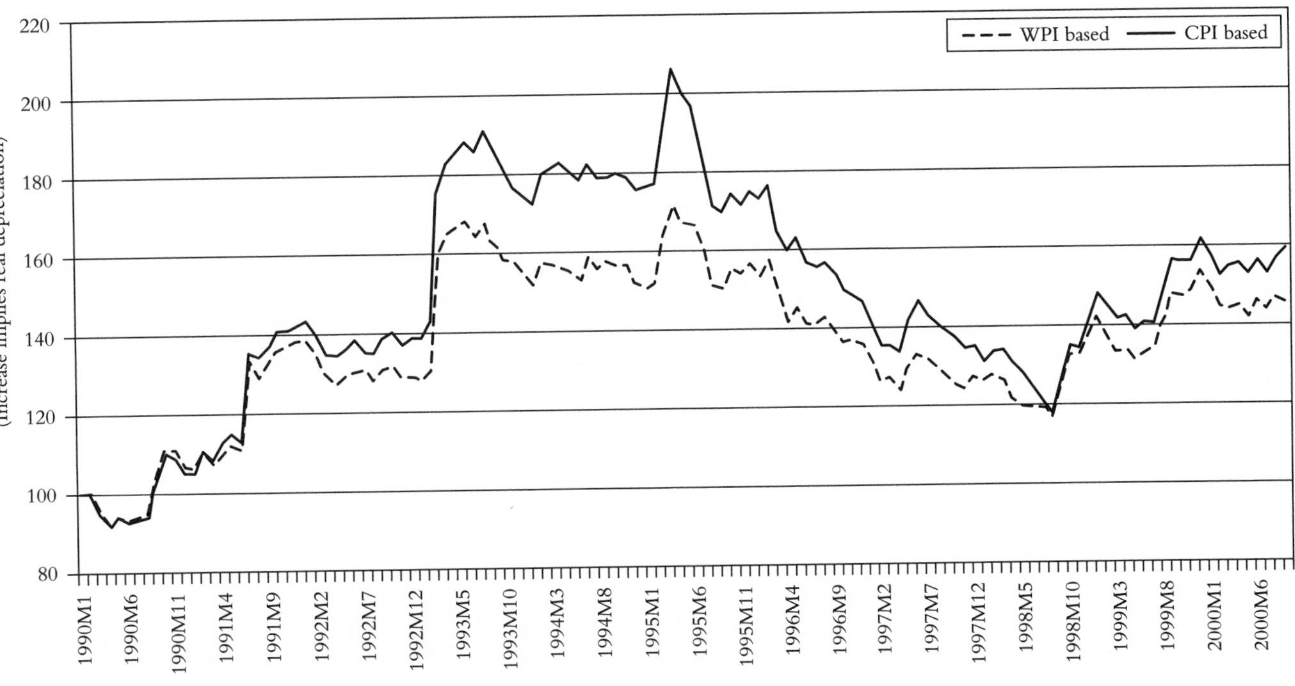

Figure 2.5. India's Real Exchange Rate vis-à-vis Japan, January 1990 to September 2000

SOURCE: International Monetary Fund (2002a).

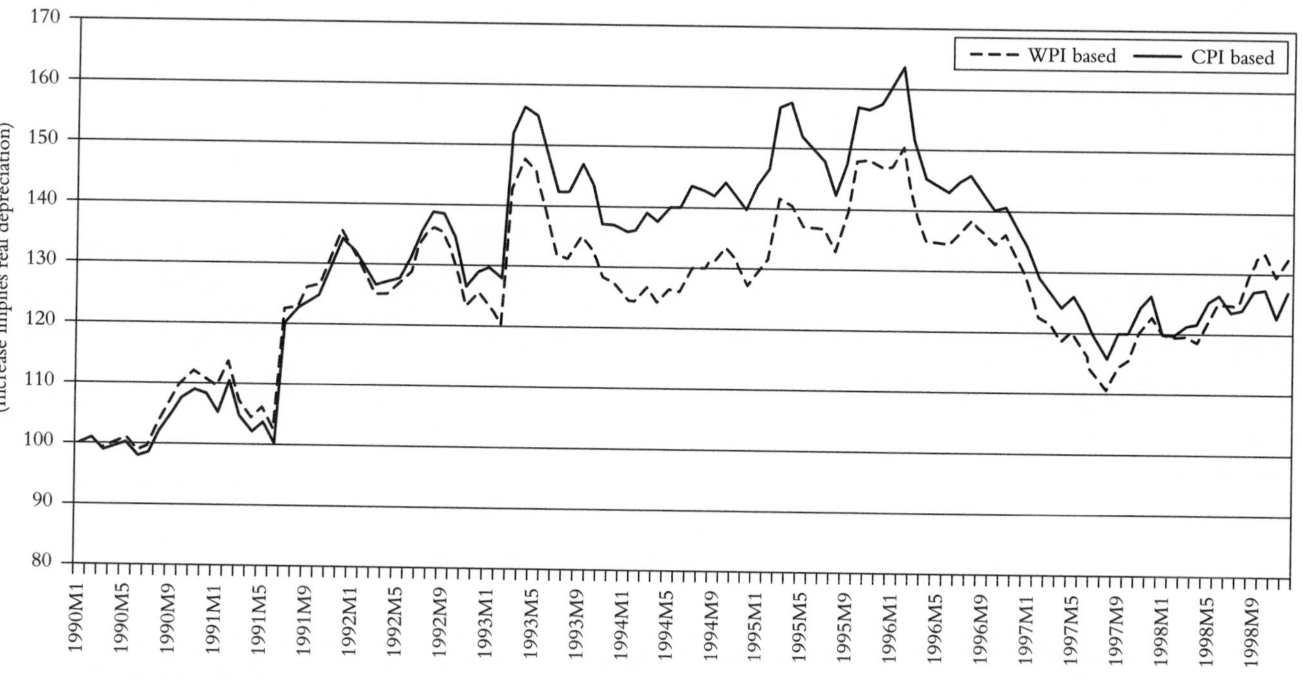

Figure 2.6. India's Real Exchange Rate vis-à-vis Germany, January 1990 to December 1998

SOURCE: International Monetary Fund (2002a).

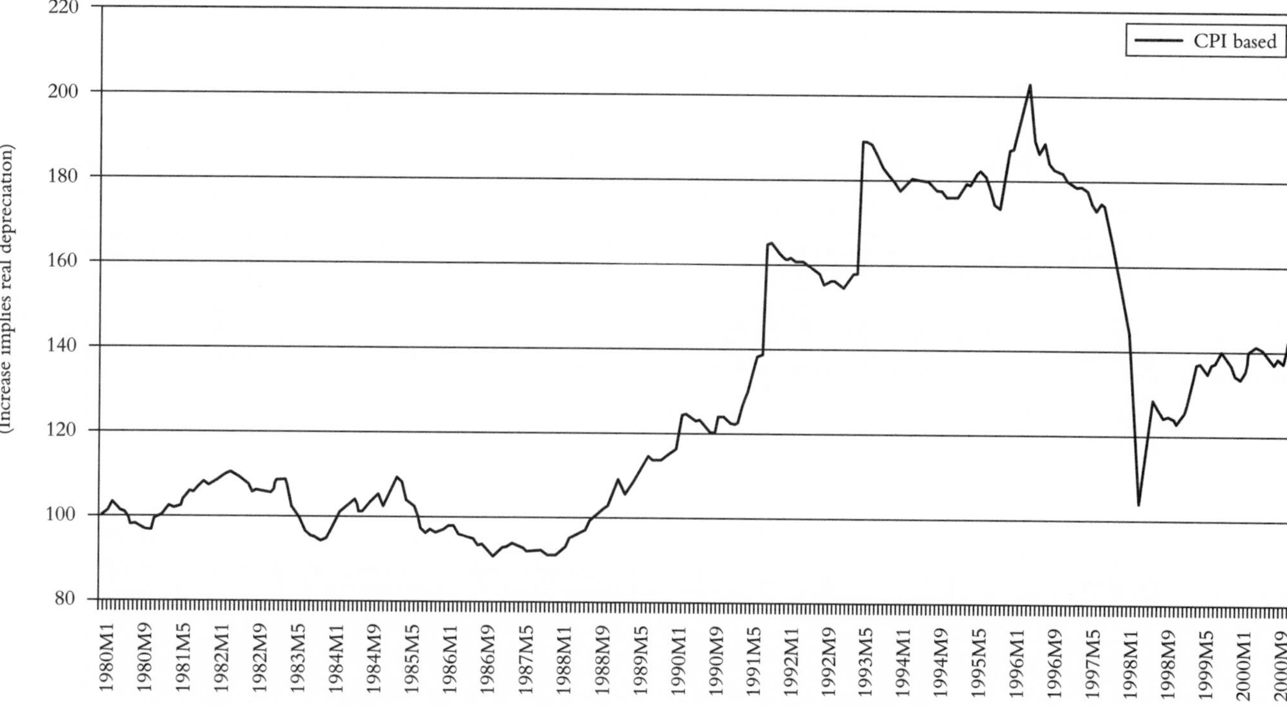

Figure 2.7. Trade-Weighted Average of India's Real Exchange Rate vis-à-vis Six East Asian Competitors, January 1980 to September 2000

Countries (weights): Indonesia (.15), South Korea (.35), Malaysia (.12), Philippines (.06), Singapore (.16), Thailand (.16).

SOURCE: International Monetary Fund (2002a).

75 percent in real terms over its 1980 value vis-à-vis these countries. However, with the onset of the Asian financial crisis, most of the Asian six let their exchange rates depreciate significantly, and India's real exchange rate appreciated sharply vis-à-vis these currencies—as is illustrated in Figure 2.7. Although some of this real appreciation was subsequently reversed (as the East Asian currencies subsequently began to rebound), as of September 2000 India's real exchange rate had still appreciated almost 20 percent in real terms relative to its value just before the Asian crisis.

Figure 2.8 excludes South Korea from the analysis and presents estimates vis-à-vis the other five East Asian countries—in part because South Korea may be judged to have attained too high a wage level to be deemed competing with India in goods intensive in the use of unskilled labor.[23] In this case, India's real appreciation post-1997 is even greater (close to 25 percent) vis-à-vis the other five East Asian countries. Finally, Figure 2.9 presents estimates on India's multilateral real exchange rate from January 1990 to September 2000 vis-à-vis a group of eight countries: the Asian six, China, and Hong Kong.[24] Qualitatively, Figure 2.9 conveys the same story as the earlier figures: real depreciation till the mid-1990s followed by real appreciation for the rest of the decade. Quantitatively, India's post-Asian-crisis real appreciation is more muted—though still significant at about 13 percent—with the inclusion of China and Hong Kong.

As the various figures illustrate, much of India's real depreciation in the early 1990s vis-à-vis its competitors has been undone in the wake of the currency depreciations in East Asia in 1997 and 1998, and, relative to the mid-1990s, Indian goods (at constant rupee prices) appear to be significantly more expensive relative to the goods of the Asian six.

As stressed above, the real exchange rate is important for providing incentives to pull resources into exportable production. One can analyze the appropriateness of the exchange-rate regime by examining the behavior of exports, and export growth, in the postliberalization period. And, when there are traditional exports that cannot expand at rapid rates due to bottlenecks of various kinds, the appropriate criterion shifts to exports of nontraditional goods.

Table 2.1 presents time-series data on Indian exports from 1980 to 1999. As can be seen, India's exports grew hardly at all in volume terms from 1980 until 1985 before growing much more rapidly during the remainder of the decade. These patterns corresponded directly to the strength of the real exchange rate for the first part of the decade and the real depreciation that marked the latter half of the decade. As Siggel (2001) notes: "The sluggish growth of exports in the first half of the 1980s, and subsequent revival, coincided with changes in the real effective exchange rate of the Indian rupee. By 1984, the rupee had appreciated considerably with respect to several country export-weighted indices since the late 1970s. This led to a degree of overvaluation which reduced India's

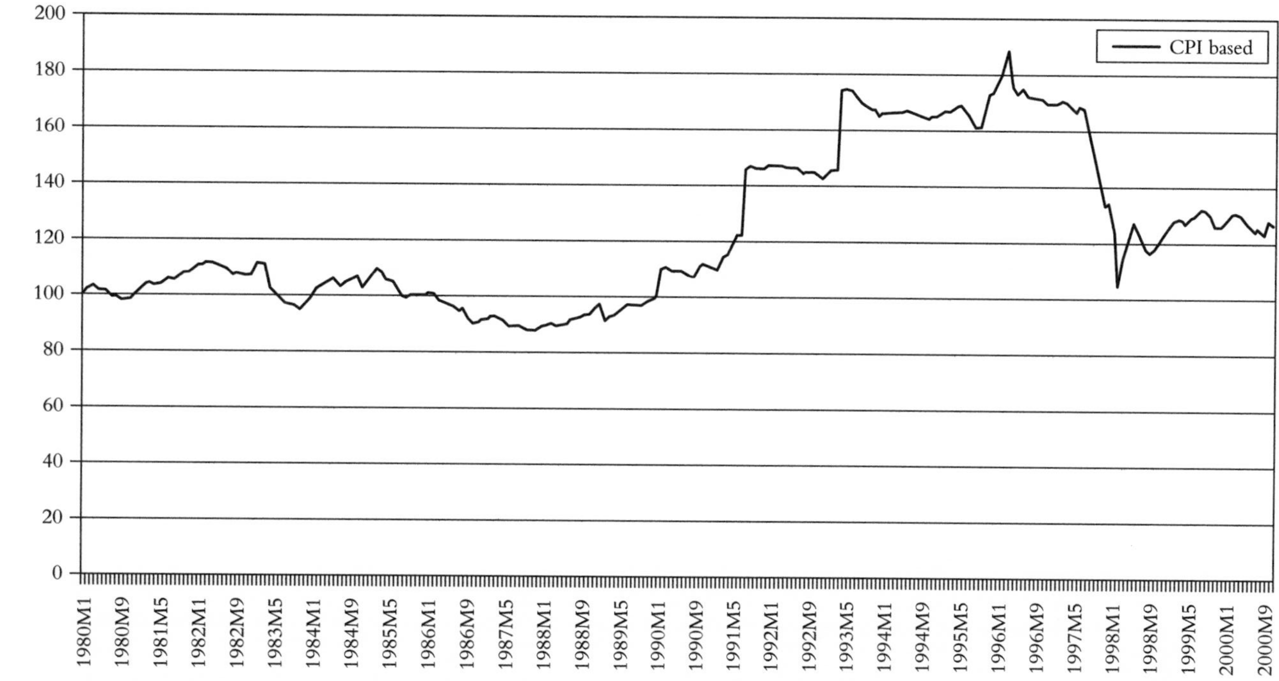

Figure 2.8. Trade-Weighted Average of India's Real Exchange Rate vis-à-vis Five East Asian Competitors (Excluding South Korea), January 1980 to September 2000

Countries (weights): Indonesia (.24), Malaysia (.18), Philippines (.08), Singapore (.27), Thailand (.23).

SOURCE: International Monetary Fund (2002a).

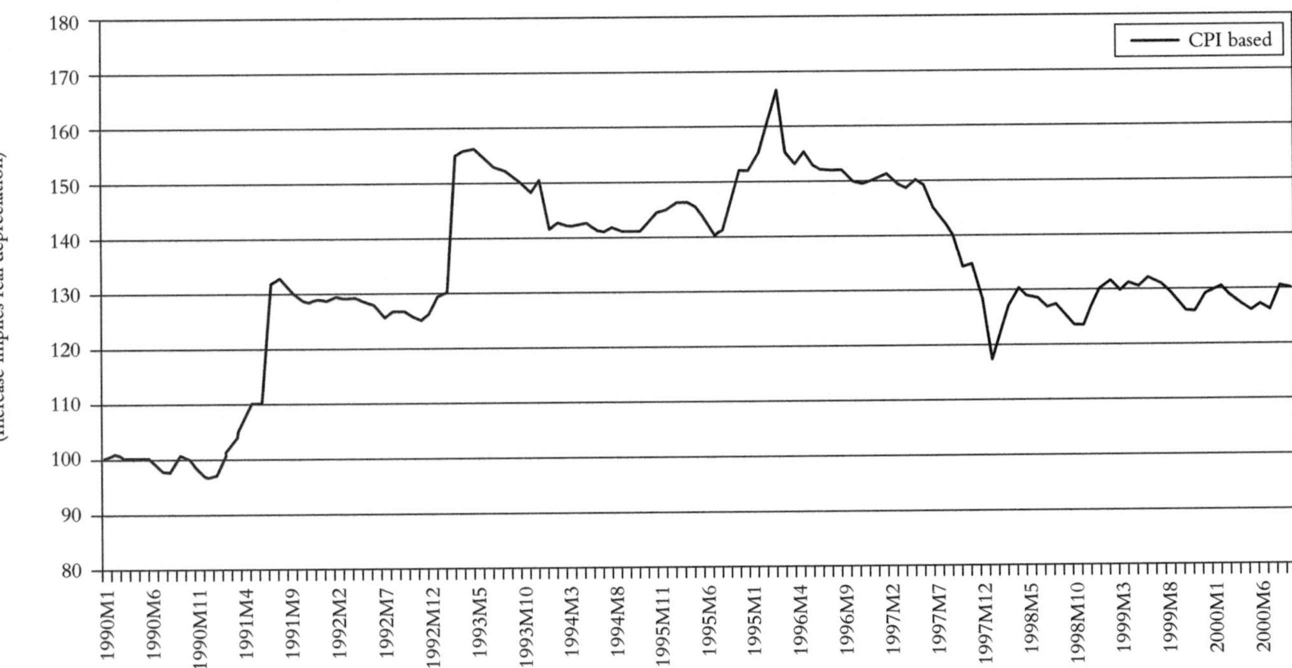

Figure 2.9. Trade-Weighted Average of India's Real Exchange Rate vis-à-vis Eight Asian Competitors (Including China and Hong Kong), January 1990 to September 2000

Countries (weights): China (.23), Hong Kong (.22), Indonesia (.10), South Korea (.16), Malaysia (.07), Philippines (.03), Singapore (.09), Thailand (.10).

SOURCE: International Monetary Fund (2002a).

TABLE 2.1
Time Series of Indian Exports, 1980–1999

	Growth Rate of Volume Index of Exports (%)	Growth Rate of Dollar Value of Exports (%)		Exports of Goods and Services (% of GDP)
		G	G + S	
1980–81	1.8	6.8		6.6
1981–82	1.9	2.6		6.4
1982–83	6.0	4.6		6.5
1983–84	−3.2	3.8		6.3
1984–85	6.9	4.5		6.8
1985–86	−7.9	−9.9		5.7
1986–87	9.0	9.4		5.6
1987–88	15.4	24.1		6.1
1988–89	8.6	15.6		6.1
1989–90	15.0	18.9	16.4	7.1
1990–91	11.0	9.2	8.6	7.1
1991–92	7.5	−1.5	1.1	8.6
1992–93	6.9	3.8	1.3	9.0
1993–94	15.5	20.0	18.5	10.0
1994–95	13.7	18.4	18.0	10.1
1995–96	31.3	20.8	20.2	11.1
1996–97	7.2	5.3	4.9	10.6
1997–98	−6.3	4.6	8.4	10.9
1998–99	3.4	−5.1	5.3	11.2
1999–2000		13.2		

SOURCES: Government of India, *Economic Survey of India* (various issues); International Monetary Fund (2002a).
NOTE: G = Goods; G + S = Goods + Services.

competitiveness across the board. However, by the end of the 1980s the real exchange value experienced a reversal and, with this depreciation, exports became more competitive" (162–63). Srinivasan (1998) estimated export supply elasticities for the period 1963 to 1996 and found that the export response to a depreciation in the real exchange rate was positive and significant, outweighing even the effects of changes in domestic income, and other variables.[25]

The continual depreciation of the real exchange rate in the early 1990s facilitated a rapid growth of export volume for the first part of the decade. However, these impressive gains seemed to stop rather abruptly in 1996–97—around the same time that India's real exchange rate began to appreciate relative to both its export markets and its competitors—as illustrated in Figures 2.2 and 2.7. The slowed export growth during the latter half of the decade meant that by 1999 export volume had hardly doubled over its level at the beginning of 1990—not a sufficient rate of growth to provide a basis for the structural change that should accompany the shift to an outward-oriented trade strategy.

This situation is also reflected in the behavior of exports of goods and ser-

TABLE 2.2

India's Exports as a Percentage of Asian Exports

Importing Country	1993	1994	1995	1996	1997	1998	1999	2000
U.S.A.	3.41	3.45	3.20	3.27	3.48	3.65	3.65	3.73
E.U.	6.95	7.24	7.33	7.09	6.56	6.05	5.79	5.74
Japan	2.73	2.70	2.35	2.16	2.11	2.07	1.81	1.67
Hong Kong	1.46	1.47	1.59	1.60	1.65	1.59	1.85	2.05
U.A.E.	20.25	17.82	18.39	18.52	16.74	17.48	12.33	12.43

SOURCE: International Monetary Fund (2002b).

NOTE: Asian exports = Sum of exports from India, China, Hong Kong, Thailand, South Korea, Indonesia, Philippines, Malaysia, Singapore.

TABLE 2.3

India and China, Percentage of Asian Exports

Importer	Exporter	1993	1994	1995	1996	1997	1998	1999	2000
U.S.A.	India	3.41	3.45	3.20	3.27	3.48	3.65	3.65	3.73
	China	23.85	25.19	25.51	27.24	29.71	31.68	32.86	33.68
E.U.	India	6.95	7.24	7.33	7.09	6.56	6.05	5.79	5.74
	China	22.45	23.20	22.73	22.60	23.72	24.13	26.34	27.59
Japan	India	2.73	2.70	2.35	2.16	2.11	2.07	1.81	1.67
	China	24.65	28.10	28.94	30.66	33.17	35.31	34.78	34.03
Hong Kong	India	1.46	1.47	1.59	1.60	1.65	1.59	1.85	2.05
	China	61.99	61.14	59.05	59.87	60.84	63.23	64.91	63.65
U.A.E.	India	20.25	17.82	18.39	18.52	16.74	17.48	12.33	12.43
	China	23.50	21.88	23.47	24.50	24.85	22.43	15.03	16.16

SOURCE: International Monetary Fund (2002b).

NOTE: Asian exports = Sum of exports from India, China, Hong Kong, Thailand, South Korea, Indonesia, Philippines, Malaysia, Singapore.

vices as a percentage of GDP over the 1990s. While exports were only 7.1 percent of GDP in 1990, they rose to about 10 percent by 1994–95. After that, however, their growth has been very similar to the rate of growth of GDP, and in 1999, the last figure available, they constituted only 11.2 percent of GDP.

The percentage increase in the dollar value of exports reveals much the same trend, an impressive increase in the late 1980s and early 1990s (barring the crisis years at the very beginning of the decade) before an abrupt slowdown beginning 1996–97.[26] As a result, between 1993 and 2000, India's exports—as a share of all Asian exports—had fallen in three of its five largest export markets, as illustrated in Table 2.2. India's relative export stagnation is captured most starkly when compared to the export growth of China over the same years. As Table 2.3 indicates, the relative share of India's exports (as a fraction of all Asian exports) compared to that of China lags behind by an order of magnitude. Furthermore, while India's share declined in three of its largest export markets between 1993 and 2000, China's share actually increased—from an already high base—in four of these same markets.

Quantitatively, India's annual growth rate in the dollar value of exports also pales in comparison with that of some other developing countries during their transition to an outward-oriented strategy. South Korea, for instance, averaged almost 40 percent average annual growth in the dollar value of exports from 1963 to 1973, while Chile's dollar value of exports grew at an average of 17 percent from 1986 to 1991. In sum, if one judges the real exchange rate by the degree to which it has encouraged export growth, the judgment must be that there has been an insufficient stimulus.[27]

The estimates provided thus far suggest that there was a significant real depreciation of the rupee in the early 1990s with the reforms, but that much of that real depreciation has since been eroded. Moreover, in the period since the early 1990s, there has been considerable trade liberalization. Export growth, while much improved over earlier periods, has fallen short of the rate at which one could judge the opening of the Indian economy as having been successfully achieved. On that ground alone, there is a basis for concern about the appropriateness of exchange-rate policy.

However, as seen in the first section, trade liberalization on any significant scale requires an adjustment of the nominal, and hence real, exchange rate. To a first approximation, one might argue that for a given reduction in the average tariff, the offsetting real depreciation should be approximately one half that amount.[28] Since quantitative restrictions on imports were partially removed, and restrictions on consumer goods imports are currently being removed, there are yet further grounds for considering that the real exchange rate may be inappropriate at its present level.

As Table 2.4 illustrates, India's import-weighted, average economy-wide tariff has fallen from 87 percent in 1990–91 to about 30.2 percent in 1999–2000.[29] These significant reductions have spanned almost all sectors: the average import-weighted tariff falling from 70 to 17.7 percent in the case of agricultural products, from 164 percent to 32.4 percent in the case of consumer goods, from 117 percent to 31.9 percent in the case of intermediate goods, and from 97 percent to 32.2 percent in the case of capital goods for the relevant time horizon.

Alongside the drop in tariff rates has been a significant reduction in the non-tariff barriers that governed potential Indian imports at the end of the 1980s. As Table 2.5 illustrates, the weighted-average coverage ratio for economy-wide non-tariff barriers on Indian imports has fallen from over 95 percent in 1988–89 to less than 25 percent in 1999–2000. This significant reduction has occurred in all sectors classified either by activity (primary, secondary), industry, or use (consumer durables, consumer nondurables, intermediate, basic and capital goods). Furthermore, quantitative restrictions (QRs) on most imports have

TABLE 2.4

India's Import-Weighted Tariff Structure, 1990–1999

Sector	1990–91	1992–93	1993–94	1994–95	1995–96	1996–97	1997–98	1998–99	1999–2000
Whole economy	87	64	47	33	27.2	24.6	25.4	29.7	30.2
Agricultural products	70	30	25	17	14.9	14.7	14.0	16.1	17.7
Mining	NA	NA	33	31	27.6	22	21.9	19.5	17.7
Consumer goods	164	144	33	48	43.1	39.0	33.8	39.3	32.4
Intermediate goods	117	55	40	31	25.0	21.9	26.1	31.5	31.9
Capital goods	97	76	50	38	28.7	28.8	24.7	30.1	32.2

SOURCE: World Bank (2000).
NOTE: Numbers are percentages.

TABLE 2.5

Coverage Ratio for Non-Tariff Barriers on Indian Imports, Weighted Average

Sector	1988–89	1995–96	1997–98	1998–99	1999–2000
Average: all sectors	95.2	65.5	64.0	62.2	24.2
Activity based					
Primary	99.9	74.8	76.2	74.9	57.4
Secondary	87.4	46.1	39.4	36.3	27.7
Usebased					
Consumer nondurables	100.0	74.7	75.6	74.0	56.1
Consumer durables	84.3	58.2	46.7	41.5	32.8
Intermediate goods	98.4	47.2	42.0	39.7	33.5
Basic goods	70.3	28.7	22.7	23.2	16.1
Capital goods	74.1	24.0	20.3	18.2	13.8

SOURCE: World Bank (2000).
NOTE: All non-tariff barriers have been assigned equal weights of 100%.

been abolished as of April 1, 2001—though many of these imports now attract tariff rates of 25 or 35 percent.

Given the height of protection earlier, one must judge that a fairly substantial depreciation would have been called for to offset the impact of liberalization over the last decade. In particular, given the significant import liberalization over the last few years and the appreciation of India's real exchange rate relative to its Asian competitors since the Asian crisis, one can wonder whether the current policy may be erring on the side of an overly appreciated real exchange rate.

Finally, it should also be recognized that Indian interest rates are very high, and capital controls evidently are still constraints.[30] As the Indian economy opens up further, liberalization of the capital account will make the maintenance of an appropriate real exchange rate all that much more essential.

Tentative Conclusions

The Indian economy, and foreign trade regime, of 2001 is vastly different from that of the 1970s and early 1980s. The height of protection has been greatly reduced; quantitative restrictions on most imports have been abolished as of April 1, 2001; the exchange rate plays a much larger role in equating the demand and supply for foreign exchange; and export earnings have grown in response to the various policy reforms undertaken.

One can ask, however, whether the situation, and economic growth prospects, could not further improve. The real exchange rate, while significantly depreciated relative to the levels of earlier years, is still not inducing rapid growth of export earnings, and exports are by no means a leading growth sector (with the exception of software industries). Asian competitors have let their currencies depreciate significantly in real terms, and have thus improved their competitive position. Cries from import-competing producers within India suggest that they may be hurting because of the current exchange-rate policy. And prospects for further liberalization of consumer goods imports and of the trade regime more generally also indicate that the current policy may be erring on the side of an appreciated real exchange rate.

To be sure, removal of fiscal pressures on the financial system would provide an important stimulus to the traded-goods sector. Improvement of infrastructure would also significantly enhance prospects for many exportables and import-competing industries. Labor-market reforms, removal of small-scale reservation, and a number of other measures could further improve competitiveness. But, even with all these measures, a strong case can be made that the payoff would be significantly enhanced were the real exchange rate permitted to adjust to a level providing more stimulus for tradable goods in the Indian economy.

Notes

1. There is one other candidate for "most important lesson": the importance of a stable macroeconomic environment. In the 1950s and 1960s, there were even arguments that "inflation is good for growth." Those arguments have been discredited, and many analysts would regard the maintenance of a healthy macroeconomic framework as being as important as policies for keeping an open economy. There would be virtually no disagreement about the paramount significance of these two policies.

2. The desirability of an open economy for economic growth is, to a first approximation, independent of whether the capital account is controlled, or partially or fully liberalized. However, it is questionable whether very stringent capital controls can be effectively maintained in the context of an open economy; the opportunities for arbitrage

between goods and assets is simply too great. For present purposes, focus is on current account transactions, and the question of exchange-rate policy is examined only in that light. Were the capital account as well to be opened, the demands for realistic exchange-rate policy (and a flexible, well-functioning financial system) would be even greater.

3. In the case of a completely market-determined exchange rate (a pure float), the supply and demand for foreign exchange are equated by definition. The exchange rate at each point in time is the price that equates the demand and supply of foreign exchange. However, as Calvo and Reinhart (2000) document, there are very few emerging markets, if any, that allow their currencies to genuinely float. In an environment of "managed" exchange rates, therefore, choosing an exchange rate level that roughly balances the demand and supply of foreign exchange is a very real issue.

4. As the prices of nontradables rise, consumers will shift their consumption toward more tradables (which are relatively cheaper), while producers will shift their resources to nontradables.

5. To simplify the discussion, we are assuming for now a stable foreign price level. Later, it will be shown that the entire discussion still holds when the foreign price level also changes, but language would be far more complex: every time we say that the domestic price level rises more than the nominal exchange rate, we would instead have to say "the domestic price level rises more than the nominal exchange rate relative to the rate of inflation in the rest of the world."

6. These statements assume that there are no significant quantitative restrictions on imports. When there are QRs, the linkage between domestic and foreign prices is broken for import-competing producers, although producers of exportables find themselves doubly disadvantaged: not only do they find their domestic costs rising for goods produced in the domestic market, but they are required to obtain at least some of their inputs from domestic producers of import-competing goods. When those goods are protected by QRs, the prices tend to rise with the domestic price level, and hence raise exporters' costs still further.

7. The opposite occurs with respect to consumption: a real exchange rate depreciation makes the consumption of domestically produced goods relatively more attractive and the consumption of traded goods, both exportable and import-competing, less attractive. These effects are very important in leading to changes in the current account balance after changes (that are expected to continue) in the real exchange rate take place; they are less important in affecting the composition of domestic production between exportables, import-competing, and home goods. It is the latter allocation that has greatest impact on the rate of economic growth and that is therefore the subject of primary concern here.

8. If domestic producers anticipate a nominal exchange-rate change (which in the very short run is a real exchange-rate change), they are likely to accelerate their orders of goods and accumulate inventory, while withholding their exportables from sale in anticipation of greater profitability once the exchange rate is altered. Once the exchange rate is altered, exports accelerate and imports decline, thus leading to a rapid change in the current account balance. This fact makes open discussion of exchange-rate policy exceptionally difficult.

9. Even with devaluations that "fail" in the sense that production of exportables does not respond, there can be short-run effects. Normally, exporters stockpile goods when they anticipate a devaluation, and importers often build up inventory in anticipa-

tion of devaluation. When the exchange rate is altered, exports increase and imports decrease as inventories are reduced.

10. This has often been ignored in trade liberalization programs. The result has been that there has been insufficient inducement to expand capacity and production of exportables, while import-competing industries have languished too much. An exchange-rate adjustment as part of a trade liberalization program is almost always needed. As a first approximation, the adjustment should be approximately half the amount of the average reduction in tariffs (and the tariff equivalent of NTBs).

11. A successful outward-oriented growth strategy must, in its early phases, result in a rate of growth of exports above the rate of growth of GDP (because, almost by definition, an outward-oriented trade regime will entail a higher fraction of exportables in GDP than an inward-oriented regime). This above-average growth rate must result from the allocation of additional resources to exportables, which will come about only when it is profitable to do so. The real exchange rate is virtually the only policy tool that can achieve this. Efforts to achieve rapid growth through an outward-oriented trade strategy have failed when governments have attempted to use commodity-specific incentives. This appears to be both because governments are not effective at "picking winners" and because differential incentives for different industries result in producers' efforts to lobby for larger specific incentives rather than to compete effectively in the international market.

12. It is often forgotten that Brazil had a major liberalization episode in the late 1960s, which lasted for eight years until 1974. During that time, exports grew at an average annual rate of over 20 percent (despite heavy initial dependence on coffee and a few other primary commodities) while real GDP growth averaged almost 10 percent between 1968 and 1974.

13. Chile is an interesting exception, in that Chilean production and exports of fresh fruits and vegetables expanded very rapidly: Chile's trade liberalization encouraged the production of new primary commodities as well as of diverse manufactures.

14. There is actually one method not listed here. That is, the authorities can control imports quantitatively and restrict import licenses to the amount of foreign exchange available. Such a method was used by many countries (including India) for a considerable period after World War II. It is entirely incompatible with an outward-oriented trade strategy. In addition, experience indicated that over time pressures on the exchange rate increased until such time as the authorities were forced to alter the exchange rate. While there is today some argument as to whether fixed or floating exchange rates are to be preferred, there is little disagreement that quantitative restrictions are an entirely unsatisfactory means of adjustment.

15. Even the United Kingdom was following an adjustable peg exchange-rate policy until 1970. By that time, however, the authorities became convinced that they were unable to affect the exchange rate sufficiently to warrant their intervention (and large losses) and moved to a floating rate.

16. This exchange-rate regime has come about because of what Calvo and Reinhart (2000) have termed "the fear of floating." They argue that most countries' authorities do not have sufficient confidence in the market (or willingness to adapt monetary and fiscal policy appropriately) to permit a genuine float. It should be noted, however, that the Mexican authorities shifted from a "managed float" to a "pure float' in 1996, and that Mexican economic performance has improved considerably since that time.

17. A case in point is August 20, 1998, when the Reserve Bank of India (RBI) raised

the cash reserve ratio required of banks by one percentage point and also its repurchase rate to 8 percent (from 5 percent) "to halt the slide in the value of the rupee" (*Financial Times*, August 21, 1998.) In the same article the governor of the RBI was quoted as saying that the RBI "will take appropriate measures as and when necessary" to determine the exchange rate.

18. Patel and Srivastava (1998) believe that Indian exchange-rate policy during the 1990s essentially targeted a given value of the real exchange rate. Even if that were correct, it would imply that the authorities failed to take into account the need for real exchange rate depreciation because of the liberalization of the import regime and, in 2001, the increased price of oil. As will be seen, however, our data suggest that since 1993 there has been a significant real appreciation of the rupee against most of India's trading partners and competitors.

19. The weights used here are the average export weights from 1990 to 1998 for these countries. The weights assigned to each country are United States, .43; Japan, .16; Germany, .15; United Kingdom, .14; and Hong Kong, .12.

20. It is inevitable that there would be some real appreciation after the nominal devaluation of 1993 to account for the pass-through effect of the devalued nominal exchange rate onto domestic prices of tradable goods.

21. The export weights used here are United States, .39; Euro area, .33; United Kingdom, .10; Japan, .09; and Hong Kong, .09.

22. The weights for each "competitor" are assigned by computing the average export weight of each Asian country (relative to the sum of exports for all six countries) for each one-digit SITC code over 1980–96, and in turn, multiplying this by the average share of each 1-digit SITC code in India's export basket over 1980–96. The weights thus computed are Indonesia, .15; South Korea, .35; Malaysia, .12; Philippines, .06; Singapore, .16; Thailand, .16.

23. The corresponding country weights without South Korea are Indonesia, .24; Malaysia, .18; Philippines, .08; Singapore, .27; Thailand, .23.

24. Data unavailability for Hong Kong and China for part of the 1980s constrains the analysis to start from 1990. The country weights with the inclusion of China and Hong Kong are China, .23; Hong Kong, .22; Indonesia, .10; South Korea, .16; Malaysia, .07; Philippines, .03; Singapore, .09; and Thailand, .10.

25. Joshi and Little (1994) also find a positive price elasticity for India's exports. Specifically, they estimate that the elasticity of the supply of Indian exports with respect to the real exchange rate is 0.7 in the short run and 1.1 in the long run. The price elasticity for the demand for exports was found to be 1.1 in the short run and about 3.0 in the long run.

26. The provisional estimates for 1999–2000 indicate an increase in the dollar value of exports of 13.2 percent—giving rise to the hope that the import liberalization of recent years may have provided a further spur to export growth.

27. It should also be noted that, if the real exchange rate had been further depreciated, producers of import-competing goods would have felt some relief contrasted with the situation they were in fact confronted with.

28. This assumes that export and import supply-and-demand elasticities are symmetric, which need not be the case. However, an intuitive way of explaining this result is to note that if import duties are lowered by x percentage points and accompanied by a devaluation of $0.5x$, domestic import-competing prices will fall by only half the amount by which tariffs are reduced, while export prices will increase in comparable measure.

The reduced incentive to import-competing production will be offset, therefore, by an increased incentive to production of exportables.

29. The import-weighted tariffs actually increased since 1996–97, in part because of a 10 percent surcharge imposed in 1997–98. This surcharge was abolished in the budget for 2001–2002.

30. Of course, some part of the high interest rates must be attributed to the need of the banks to finance large fiscal deficits. Even so, high interest rates must surely have helped induce rupee holders to remain in domestic currency rather than to try to shift into holdings of foreign exchange.

References

Calvo, G., and C. Reinhart. 2000. *Fear of Floating*. Working Paper 7993. Cambridge, Mass.: National Bureau of Economic Research.

Government of India. 2001. *Economic Survey of India* (various issues). New Delhi: Ministry of Finance.

International Monetary Fund. 2002a. *International Financial Statistics*. Washington, D.C.: IMF.

———. 2002b. *Direction of Trade Statistics*. Washington, D.C.: IMF.

Joshi, V., and I. M. D. Little. 1994. *India: Macroeconomics and Political Economy 1964–1991*. Washington, D.C.: World Bank.

Patel, U., and Srivastava, P. 1998. Some implications of real exchange rate targeting in India. Working paper. www.icrier.res.in/pdf/Srivastava.PDF.

Siggel, E. 2001. India's Trade Policy Reforms and Industry Competitiveness in the 1980s. *World Economy* 24 (2): 159–83.

Srinivasan, T. N. 1998. India's Export Performance: A Comparative Analysis. Ch. 9 in *India's Economic Reforms and Development: Essays for Manmohan Singh*, edited by I. J. Ahluwalia and I. M. D. Little. Delhi: Oxford University Press.

World Bank. 2000. *India: Policies to Reduce Poverty and Accelerate Sustainable Development*. Report No. 19471-IN. Washington, D.C.: World Bank.

Comment
Indian Exports and Exchange Rate Policy

Naushad Forbes

Anne Krueger and Sajjid Chinoy's chapter makes a most persuasive case (as does T. N. Srinivasan's chapter in this volume) for both the importance of exchange rates and their current impact on the Indian economy. They argue that exchange rates are important both to balance out foreign exchange receipts and expenditures and as a competitive measure to provide a sufficient incentive to exporters. In these comments, I will focus on the importance of exchange rates to exports, as these will in themselves contribute to foreign exchange receipts.

I will address three issues: first, how important exports are to the Indian economy, and what potential they have; second, that exchange rates need to be seen as a political issue and not only an economic issue; and third, as a way of thinking through the implications of Krueger and Chinoy's analysis, some speculation on what would happen if the real effective rate of return depreciated by 25 percent.

Importance of Exports

Exporting has several benefits. At the most obvious, exporting firms access larger markets for their products. Serving larger markets allows firms to operate at international scales of production. People get put to work in higher-value-added manufacturing activities, and exports can become an engine of growth for the entire economy as it develops.

India's software industry is properly seen as a great success story, indeed a great *export* success story. In 2001, it employed 400,000 people, and the optimistic projections of NASSCOM, the software industry association, are that software export will continue to grow at 40 percent plus through 2008, by which time the industry will employ 2 million people. These projections have led some, such as the Indian prime minister, to claim that while India may have missed the industrial revolution, it will get rich by being at the forefront of the knowledge revolution. This argument misses a crucial point: no major country has developed without industry. The employment potential of much less seductive low-technology industry can be far greater. Compare NASSCOM's projection of 2 million software employees in India by 2008 with the fact that China's export manufacturers in 2000 employ over 50 million people. Similarly, in 2000 about 3800 maquiladora export-assembly plants in Mexico employed 1.4 million people, accounting for fully 40 percent of total Mexican manufacturing employment.

If China is a more recent example of export success, Krueger and Chinoy properly point to the South Korean example as the archetypal story of export-driven growth, with exports growing at 40 percent annually over a 20-year period, turning the country into a key industrial nation.

However, I would argue that the key benefit for South Korean firms, and indeed East Asian firms in general, was not export employment or export markets, but the learning that was forced within firms as a result of exporting. Competing with international best practice forces firms to provide value for money. Selling in export markets was an essential disciplining tool that focused South Korean technological effort on making firms internationally efficient and pushing them up the product-value chain as local wages rose. Howard Pack and Michael Hobday discuss these learning benefits:

> [P]urchasers, having discovered a reliable source of low-cost, high quality products, were anxious to enhance the quality of local production. Thus, the very act of exporting be-

came a source of improved technical knowledge substituting for expensive domestic research institutes.

(Pack 2000, 80)

[Exporting became] a training school for technological learning. (134)
Transnationals and other buyers sought to ensure that production was of the highest quality at the lowest possible price. (138)
[U]tilise exports to force the pace of learning, innovation and industrial development. (162)

(Hobday 2000)

These learning benefits are a considerable missed opportunity for an inward-oriented economy like India's.[1]

Do Exports Necessarily Involve Openness and Free Markets?

Krueger and Chinoy imply in their arguments that export orientation goes with an open-trade regime and, indeed, free markets in general. While this may be true in the aggregate, other observers of their South Korean export example have concluded differently. Kim (1993), Lall (1990), and Wade (1990) have argued that export orientation in South Korea (and Taiwan) went together with import substitution and were the focus of a very activist and interventionist state. There are reports of President Park holding weekly meetings with the heads of the leading *chaebol* to specifically review their performance in meeting export targets. Wade talks of a reciprocity principle in East Asia, where the state "traded" subsidies for firms (such as subsidized credit and protection) with the requirement that they meet explicit export targets. These descriptions provide a different impression from one of exports going with an open- and free-market regime. The impact on firms, though, was the same, whether the perspective used is one of intervention and protection or free markets and openness: rapid export growth fostered learning by firms, which in turn fostered a move to higher value-added activities as wages rose.

That, though, is merely a qualification: exports are vital to industrial growth, both for the quantitative market benefits and the qualitative learning and disciplining effects. The relative mix of market and state action in growing exports is secondary.

Exports as a Political Issue

My second point is that exports need to be seen as a political issue in India, and not just an economic one. A fall in the rupee against the dollar by even a fraction of a percent leads to headlines in the popular press. Every fall is seen as weakness, even as failure. Indeed, devoid of Krueger and Chinoy's analysis of real exchange rates, the well-educated Indian would today think the rupee weaker than it was in 1993.

This perspective on exchange rates is neither new nor limited to India. One is reminded of Oscar Wilde's *The Importance of Being Earnest*, where Miss Prism assigns Cecily her political economy reading: "The chapter on the Fall of the Rupee you may omit. It is somewhat too sensational. Even these metallic problems have their melodramatic side." That was in 1895. Things haven't changed.

What is unique to India is that this perspective is shared by industrialists, who also see a fall in exchange rates as a negative development. In all the analysis of Indian competitiveness and arguments by the Bombay Club for a level playing field for Indian industry, I have never seen exchange rates included. Why? A significantly cheaper rupee would at a stroke neutralize all the arguments about India's lack of competitiveness coming from electricity tariffs, poor infrastructure, and high interest rates and provide the level playing field so sought by these groups of Indian industrialists. Why are exchange rates not included in this analysis? No industry body, not the Confederation of Indian Industry, not the Federation of Indian Chambers of Commerce and Industry, has placed exchange rates on the agenda, and their staff includes skilled economists. I would suggest three reasons:

First, forty years of inward-looking policies have left a legacy behind in the mindset of industrialists. In an inward-looking environment, the industrialist benefits from a strong rupee—imports (the TV sets or computers they trade, the components they buy, or the new machine they invest in) are cheaper. And competing with the cheaper imports for their own products can come from protective tariffs. So a combination of a strong rupee and high protection is best.

Second, it is an obvious statement that Indian industry is not export oriented. Exports are not of low concern to the average Indian industrialist—they are of *no* concern. As such, most Indian firms simply do not have a mindset to search for opportunities overseas.

Third, as I said earlier, Indian industrialists simply would not know the rupee was in 2001 stronger against several major competitors than in 1997. Krueger and Chinoy's analysis of real exchange rates is hardly within the mainstream of economic thought in India today.

What If the Rupee Dropped 25 Percent Against the Dollar?

There is no question that a fall of 25 percent would give Indian industry relief from imports, as Krueger and Chinoy say. But will it lead to an export boom? What Indian industry and the economy generally need, as Krueger and Chinoy argue, is export growth of 40 percent a year for a decade as South Korea had in the 1960s and 1970s and China had in the 1990s. (As Srinivasan points out, the ninth Five-Year Plan targets just 12 percent.) Answering this question is, of course, speculation, and I will approach it at two levels: at the macrolevel of India's main export industries, and at the microlevel of three Indian firms.

India's three largest export industries are textiles, software, and gems and jewelry. Textiles would probably grow, as India is present in many international markets and competes directly with China, Sri Lanka, and Southeast Asia. Software, which has grown at 50 percent annually in the 1990s, would probably not be significantly affected. Indian firms do not seriously compete with foreign firms, with the main "competition" being continuing to do the job in-house; a cheaper rupee would just make the industry still more profitable. Gems and jewelry, and in particular cut diamonds, could grow, but my understanding is that this is a fairly small industry internationally, and India already has a high market share.[2]

Next, consider three engineering firms. Hero Cycles is the world's largest bicycle manufacturer (at 5 million bicycles), and has a dominant 52 percent share of the Indian market. Hero has seen its exports to the United States replaced by Chinese imports (which sent 10 million bicycles to the United States in 2000). A 25 percent fall in the rupee would make it competitive and attractive for Hero to invest in capacity for the speciality bicycles (sports bikes, mountain bikes, children's bikes) that the U.S. imports.

Bajaj Auto is India's largest scooter manufacturer, and the world's fourth largest two-wheeler manufacturer. A 25 percent fall in the rupee would not significantly impact BAL in the short term, as it does not seriously export today. But in the longer term, it could make export markets much more attractive, especially since the Indian market has become so difficult for it with Hero Honda motorcycles and Honda scooters.

Speaking more personally, Forbes Marshall is India's leading steam engineering and control instrumentation firm. FM exports one product globally, a vortex meter that primarily finds use in measuring process utilities such as steam and compressed air. A 25 percent fall in the rupee would immediately make that product more competitive globally, and would lead to an estimated doubling of sales. In the longer term, a 25 percent cheaper rupee would make it a much higher priority for FM to export other products too.

I would speculate, then, that the overall impact of a 25 percent depreciation in the rupee would be mixed in the short term: a few firms and sectors that are present in competitive international markets would benefit. But most Indian firms would not export more as they do not have the presence in international markets needed to take advantage of depreciation. With such depreciation being credible for the longer term, the impact on Indian industry should be much more widespread and fundamental.

This suggests a useful microanalysis that looks at particular industrial sectors for the impact of real effective exchange rate changes. What happened to existing sectors from the 1991–93 depreciation? What new sectors (the software industry being the most striking example) emerged as exporters? And how sensitive were they to the real effective exchange rate?

The India-China comparison is also striking, but the real effective exchange rate has not changed against China in the last four years, and China, one would argue, is India's number one international competitor. This says that while real effective exchange rates are important, they need to be situated within an overall analysis of industrial competitiveness to determine their impact on industrial exports. Do Indian firms have the necessary products to compete internationally, whatever their price? Do Indian industrialists have the ambition and entrepreneurship to become export powerhouses? Most would agree that Indian industry ten years after liberalization is still largely inward-looking and not oriented to exports. Krueger and Chinoy's paper should lead to a more informed debate about what it would take to increase the exports of Indian industry. Ultimately the success of liberalization will hinge on the ability of Indian firms to compete internationally. This essay on so crucial a topic requires the widest possible readership and is to be greatly welcomed.

Notes

1. We have dealt with these learning benefits from exports at length elsewhere. See Forbes and Wield 2002.

2. The importance of cut diamonds in India's international trade is best illustrated by the dominance of a tiny country, Belgium, in India's total imports. In 1999, India imported more from Belgium than any other country. In 2000, Belgium was still number three, ahead of the United Kingdom and Germany.

References

Forbes, N., and D. Wield. 2002. *From followers to leaders: Managing innovation in newly industrialising countries*. London: Routledge.

Hobday, M. 2000. East versus Southeast Asian innovation systems: Comparing OME- and TNC-led growth in electronics. In *Technology, learning, and innovation: Experiences of newly industrializing economies*, edited by L. Kim and R. R. Nelson. Cambridge: Cambridge University Press.

Kim, L. 1993. National system of industrial innovation: Dynamics of capability building in Korea. In *National innovation systems: A comparative analysis*, edited by R. R. Nelson. New York: Oxford University Press.

Kim, L. 1997. *Imitation to innovation*. Boston: Harvard Business School Press.

Lall, S. 1990. *Building industrial competitiveness in developing countries*. Paris: Development Center, Organization for Economic Co-operation and Development.

Nelson, R.R., and H. Pack. 1999. *Firm competencies, technological catch-up, and the Asian miracle*. In *Development, duality, and the international economic regime: Essays in honor of Gustav Ranis*, edited by G. R. Saxonhouse and T. N. Srinivasan. Ann Arbor: University of Michigan Press.

Pack, H. 2000. Research and development in the industrial development process. In *Technology, learning, and innovation: Experiences of newly industrializing economies*, edited by L. Kim and R. R. Nelson. Cambridge: Cambridge University Press.

Wade, R. 1990. *Governing the market*. Princeton, N.J.: Princeton University Press.

Part II

THE FINANCIAL SECTOR

3

INDIAN BANKING

Market Liberalization and the Pressures for Institutional and Market Framework Reform

James A. Hanson

Overview

In the early 1990s, India began to reverse the financial repression and heavy intervention that had characterized its banking sector for many years. The government liberalized interest rates, directed credit, and increased competition. Regulation and supervision were also strengthened substantially. These policies yielded some substantial benefits. However, the gains were limited by three factors. First, government debt arising from high fiscal deficits continues to crowd out credit to the private sector, albeit through markets rather than forced investments rules. Second, the banks' non-government loan portfolios, though improved, still suffer from high rates of non-performance, reflecting the limited changes in the legal and informational framework. In addition, the dominant public sector banks are still characterized by low lending quality and collection, reflecting the inadequate incentives that characterize public sector banks worldwide. Third, some public sector banks are recognized as weak, and many others are unable to generate enough capital internally to keep up with deposit growth, reflecting their inability to cross-subsidize their weak lending and high costs under the increased competition. It is gradually being recognized that the legal, informational, and incentive frameworks need reforms. Such reforms will involve a much greater private sector role in the banking sector and, correspondingly, will require much stronger regulation and supervision to limit moral hazard.

The first section of this chapter describes the situation in Indian banking prior to the reforms. Section 2 discusses briefly the wave of liberalization of markets and the strengthening of regulation that began in the early 1990s and was largely completed by 1997–98. Section 3 discusses some of the main impacts of the liberalization: the resumption of deposit mobilization, the increase in credit to the private sector, and the reduction in spreads because of increased competition. Section 4 focuses on the problems created by issues related to the macroeconomic, institutional, informational, and incentive framework. In particular, it discusses (a) the continuation of large government deficits, which means that the government continues to crowd out private borrowing from the banks; (b) the continued large fraction of credit to the private sector that is nonperforming, reflecting the poor judicial framework, the poor quality of credit information, and the lack of incentives for sound lending in the still-dominant public sector banks; and (c) the public sector banks' difficulties in generating sufficient capital internally to keep up with the regulatory needs associated with credit growth, reflecting in turn the public sector banks' relatively high nonperforming loans and costs. Section 5 discusses the government's recent attempts to deal with these framework issues. The last section briefly argues that not only is there a need to reduce the deficit and improve the judicial and informational framework, but also that incentives for sound lending will need to be improved. Improving incentives probably entails a much greater private sector role in bank management. However, to limit the well-known moral hazard associated with private sector banking and high deposit insurance, India's regulation and supervision will also need substantial improvement.

1. The Indian Banking System Before Market Liberalization

At the end of the 1980s, Indian commercial banking and the financial sector were dominated by public sector banks.[1] They mainly financed the government deficit and supported priority sectors, both at controlled interest rates. The 1969 nationalization of the 14 largest private banks had raised the public sector banks' share of deposits to 86 percent, from the 31 percent share represented by the State Bank of India. In 1980, the nationalization of 6 more banks raised the public sector banks' share to 92 percent.

The 1969 nationalization reflected the "statist" approach to development prevalent at that time, both inside and outside India. However, there were also some important financial issues, involving insider lending and the frequent bankruptcies of the private banks—issues that remain today in private sector-dominated banking systems in developing countries. Making India's banks part of the public sector made it easier to ensure that they would support government policies, such as the "need to control the commanding heights of the economy and to meet progressively the needs of development of the economy in conformity with national policy objectives" (Preamble of the Banking Companies [Acquisition and Transfer of Undertakings] Act of 1969). Financing agriculture was also an important goal, particularly with the green revolution starting and requiring more commercial inputs. Also, political pressures existed against conglomerates, and in favor of more loans to small farmers and businessmen, who were considered to be neglected by the formal credit system and who were thought to be able to use credit more productively than the traditional clients of banks. These issues became even more important with the 1971 Abolish Poverty (*Garibi Hatao*) campaign of Indira Gandhi. Priority sector lending and extension of a massive network of branches were used to reach the poor.[2]

By the end of the 1980s, as pressures to fund the rising public sector deficit grew, the cash-reserve requirement (CRR) had been raised to 15 percent of deposits and the statutory liquidity requirement (SLR) to 38.5 percent (see Table 3.1)—both requirements being the maximum permitted by law. Eligibility for the statutory liquidity requirement had been expanded to include some non-government borrowers, a political economy development that tends to occur when credit becomes scarce and underpriced (see Caprio, Hanson, and Honohan 2001).

In the 1980s, the priority sector lending requirement also was raised to 40 percent of net loans[3] (effective as of 1985) from the 33 percent that came into effect in 1979. Of the priority sector lending, 18 percentage points had to be for agriculture and 10 percentage points to the weaker sectors. In addition to this priority sector requirement, other requirements also were imposed, including credit for public food-procurement schemes (10 percent of credit) and targets for export and housing credit. The rates on the various types of priority credits and the volumes of credit on individual loans were set in minute detail and supervised by the Reserve Bank of India (RBI). Lending to the largest corporations required prior approval by the RBI.

The main beneficiaries of this financial repression were the government and other borrowers eligible for the statutory liquidity requirement. Rising public sector deficits were funded with increases in both the cash reserve requirement, which provided low-cost resources for the RBI[4] to absorb government debt without raising money growth, and the statutory liquidity requirement, which increased the demand for eligible paper even if it paid low interest rates. In 1986, for example, the average interest rate earned on banks' investment in government debt was 8.7 percent, compared to an average deposit cost of 6.2 percent plus an operating cost of about 3 percent of assets—that is, the average return on government debt was less than the average costs of the banks. Other large beneficiaries of financial repression were agriculture and the miscellaneous category of "other borrowers," a group that included bank employees, part of whose compensation came in low-cost loans. Including the high rate of non-performing loans, the average cross subsidy on lending to the priority sector was probably equivalent to about five percentage points per year (Hanson 2001).

The public sector nature of banking weakened the incentives for lending based on commercial considerations and the concern and accountability for

TABLE 3.1

Indicators of Indian Banking Policy, 1968–2000: Deposit, Lending Rates, and Reserve and Liquidity Requirements in Selected Years

Year	Deposit Rate (1 year) (% per annum)	Ceiling or *Minimum* Loan Rate (% per annum)[a]	Cash Reserve Requirement (% of deposits)	Statutory Liquidity Requirement (% of deposits)
1968		NA		25.0[b]
1974 (Dec.)	8	16.5, Mar. '76[c]	4.0	32.0
1978 (Dec.)	6	15.0, Mar.[d] 18.0, Sept. '79	5.0	34.0
1981 (Dec.)	7.5	19.5, Mar.[c]	7.5	35.0
1983 (Nov.)	8	18.0, Apr.	8.5[e]	35.0
1984 (Sept.)	8	18.0	9.0[e]	36.0
1987 (Oct.)	9	16.5, Apr.	10.0	37.5
1989 (July)	9	*16.0, Oct. '88*	15.0[f]	38.0
1990	9	*16.0*	15.0[f]	38.5,[g] Sept.
1991	10, July; 12, Oct.	*19.0, Apr.*	15.0[f]	38.5[g]
1992	<13, Apr.; <12, Oct.	*19.0*	15.0[f]	30.0,[h] Apr.
1993	<11, Mar.; <10, Sept.	*17.0, Mar.*	14.0, May	25.0,[h] Sept.
1994	<10	*14.0, Mar.,* *Free, Oct.*	15.0,[f] Aug.	25.0[h]
1995	<11, Feb.; <12, Apr.	*Free*	14.0, Dec.	25.0[h]
1996	Free, July	*Free*	13.0, May; 11.0, Nov.	25.0[h]
1997	Free	*Free*	10.0, Jan.	25.0[b]
1998	Free	*Free*	11.0, Aug.[i]	25.0[b]
1999	Free	*Free*	10.5, Mar.; 10.0, May; 9.0, Nov.	25.0[b]
2000	Free	*Free*	8.0, Apr.; 8.5, July	25.0[b]

NOTE: Months refer to dates after which policies took effect. $<x$ means that the rate is less than x%.

[a]Effective October 1988, the ceiling interest rate on loans was abolished and minimum interest rate imposed. Minimum loan rates are in italics.

[b]Legal minimum.

[c]Includes 7% tax.

[d]Excludes 7% tax.

[e]Marginal requirement on deposit increases after November 1983 was 10%.

[f]Marginal requirements and special requirements on non-resident accounts removed.

[g]Legal maximum.

[h]Applied to increase over deposits on a base date; base date moved forward and SLR rate on base reduced at various times.

[i]Impounded cash balances from period of high rates were released in 12 installments from May 1998 to March 1999.

performance in areas such as credit risks, exposures, maturity mismatches, collections, and profits. Instead, the main way in which public sector banks were judged was the fulfillment of lending targets set by the government (Ahluwalia 1997). The incentives for sound lending and collection were also weakened by the high percentage of directed credit and by political interference, which began with individual loans and culminated in the late 1980s in loan "fairs," where loans were given to masses of individuals at the behest of local politicians. An example of how the lack of appropriate incentives affected the institutions' behavior was the quality of loan documentation by the public sector banks. Generally, borrowers consider its quality to be lower than that of foreign banks', and in many cases it was insufficient to meet court challenges when the public sector banks were ordered to improve collections by taking defaulters to court in the 1990s.

As also often occurs with public enterprises, the interests of the employees also became important. The bank employees formed a strong union and began to play a role in decision making—for example, delaying the introduction of modern technology. Finally, regulation and supervision of banking also reflected the government's use of the financial sector as an arm of fiscal policy; it did not focus on prudential issues but on whether loan allocation and interest rate regulations had been met. The combined effect of this approach left India with public banks, civil service bankers, a large stock of non-performing loans (NPLs), and a weak regulatory and supervisory framework—problems that the government has been trying to correct since the early 1990s.

2. *Liberalizing Banking: Freeing Interest Rates and Credit Allocations, Increasing Competition, but Maintaining Public Sector Dominance*

A substantial liberalization of India's banking and financial sector began in 1992, as part of the liberalization of the economy that was stimulated by the 1991 balance of payments crisis.[5] The intent of the general liberalization was to speed up growth and thereby reduce poverty. The general approach of the economy-wide liberalization was to open up the economy, give the market a greater role in price setting, and increase the private sector's role in development.[6] In the financial sector, the 1991 Narasimham Committee recommendations provided a blueprint for the reforms (Narasimham Committee 1991). The government gradually freed interest rates. It also reduced the volume and burden of directed credits, in order to increase credit to the private sector. Table 3.1, Box 3.1, and appendix Table A.3.1 provide some indicators of the policies.[7] By 1997–98, most of the financial market liberalization was complete.

Unlike financial liberalization in many countries, India's reforms also strengthened regulation and supervision significantly. In addition to recapitalizing the public sector banks, the government set the minimum capital adequacy

Box 3.1
Summary of Principal Market Liberalization Policies

Freeing Interest Rates

- A single-term deposit-rate ceiling replaced the multiple ceilings in 1992; it was varied according to credit conditions, and, beginning in 1995, different maturities were gradually freed starting with the longest maturities and reaching all maturities by 1997. As of March 1998, banks were allowed to set different rates for the same maturity deposits and set their own penalties for early withdrawal.
- Loan rates actually began to be liberalized in 1988, when the maximum rate on nondirected credit was turned into a minimum; after 1992, the number of rate categories for different types of loans was reduced sharply, and most directed credit (priority sector credit) was gradually shifted to free rates (see below).
- Interest rates on more and more of government debt are determined in auction (although the statutory liquidity requirement, the low risk weight of government debt, and the threat of investigation of lending to nonpublic sector corporations still make government debt attractive to banks). Low rates still prevail on the reduced volume of the RBI's automatic Ways and Means advances and "private placements" with RBI. One of RBI's monetary policy instruments is to absorb government debt when it considers the auction rate above its monetary policy target.

Reducing Directed Credit and Its Burden

- The cash reserve requirement has been reduced from 15 percent to the 8–10 percent range and remuneration simplified.
- The statutory liquidity requirement has been reduced to 25 percent and limited to government debt (1993).
- Priority sector credit continues to be targeted at 40 percent of net bank credit, but its burden was reduced by freeing rates (1997), except on credits under Rs 200,000 where the ceiling was raised to the prime rate in 1998. The definition of priority sector lending has been expanded, beginning with foreign bank export credits (1993); it now includes lending for information technology. Shortfalls in meeting the target by direct lending can now be made up through loans to government banks (transferring the burden of non-performing priority sector loans to them).

- The new private banks were allowed to make up shortfalls by deposits with the National Bank for Agricultural and Rural Development or the Small Industries Development Bank of India, a policy that has been extended to other banks.
- "Investments" have been allowed that are not eligible for the statutory liquidity requirement. These investments are not subject to the priority lending requirement (they are not part of net credit) and have grown sharply in recent years.

requirements of 8 percent of risk-weighted assets by 1995 for Indian banks with foreign branches or 1996 for other Indian banks—that is, over two (three) years. In 1998 the standard was raised to 9 percent (effective as of March 2000), with government securities given a 2.5 percent risk weight to begin reflecting interest-rate risk. Recognition of NPLs was gradually tightened, so that by March 1995 assets with unpaid interest of more than two quarters were considered non-performing (with some exceptions). On-site supervision of banks was introduced in 1995, a CAMELS system of annual supervision was introduced in 1997,[8] and, in 1998, the RBI judged that it fully met 14 of the 25 Basel Core Principles of Supervision and was implementing compliance with the other 11 (Reddy 1999)

Competition with banks and within the banking industry was encouraged in various ways. Non-bank financial corporations were allowed to grow rapidly under a regime of freer interest rates, less directed credit, and easier regulation and supervision than banks. They provided additional funding for industry and new firms, and for hire-purchase, housing, leasing, and so on. The capital market became a major source of equity finance with the easing of requirements for new issues and improvements in market infrastructure (tightening of regulation and supervision, the creation of depositories, and the shift toward rolling settlements). The partial opening of the capital account brought foreign institutional investors into the domestic capital market (1992) and allowed firms to issue bonds and global depository rights (GDRs) offshore, albeit under tight control, thereby providing a new, market-based source of finance for the larger companies and a stimulus to the stock market.

Within banking, competition was encouraged by granting licenses to new private banks (9 in 1994) and new foreign banks (21 between 1994 and 1999) and easing of restrictions on foreign banks' operations. Consortium project lending led only by development finance institutions was phased out and bank-led syndications were allowed. The restrictions on borrowers switching banks and the requirement that the RBI approve lending to large companies were also gradually phased out.

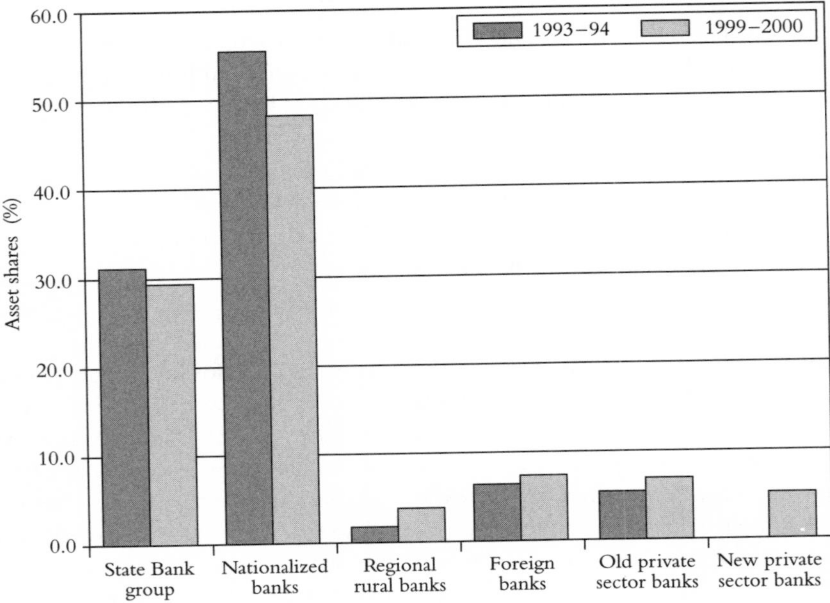

Figure 3.1. Asset Shares of Commercial Banks by Type

Although competition has reduced the public sector banks' importance, as a group they still control a dominant 80 percent of commercial bank assets (Figure 3.1). The Ministry of Finance continues to run the public sector banks. No public sector banks were sold to private owners, although nine banks have sold some equity in the capital market. Sale of over 51 percent of a public sector bank's equity would have required amendment of the Bank Nationalization Act and still faces substantial political opposition.

As discussed below, although gains from India's financial sector liberalization were substantial, the public sector's continued large role in banking limited the gains. Recent cross-country evidence is consistent with this result; it suggests that greater public presence in banking tends to be associated with lower growth, lower aggregate productivity growth, higher spreads, and less private credit (La Porta, Lopez Silanes, and Schleifer 2000; Barth, Caprio, and Levine 2000). This result reflects the difficulties inherent in making public sector financial institutions respond to market incentives for loan quality and collection of debt service, given the other objectives that the government imposes on them and the weak links between standard measures of efficiency and public sector bank officers' pay and advancement.

3. *Outcomes of the Market Liberalization*

One positive outcome of the financial market liberalization was a substantial increase in the availability of finance for the private sector. One factor in that increase was the rise in banks' funds from resumption of real bank deposit (M3) growth. Real deposit growth had stagnated from 1987 until the crisis was resolved. The market liberalization described above, along with the stabilization program of the early 1990s, seems to have contributed to the resumption of real M3 growth. Until 1997, deposits also grew rapidly in non-bank financial corporations (NBFCs). The NBFCs took advantage of the easy regulations they faced and the liberalized interest rates to mobilize a substantial volume of deposits, equal to about 6 percent of M3 in 1996. The NBFCs used much of these funds to finance nontraditional clients and consumer credit. However, in 1997, NBFCs' deposits declined by almost 50 percent, after the collapse of a major corporation led to system-wide withdrawals, wind-downs of numerous corporations, and the RBI's imposition of substantially tighter regulation under new legal authority. It seems likely that some of these deposits shifted to banks, which is one explanation for the rapid growth of M3 from 1996 to 1999.

Liberalization also opened up other sources of funding for the private sector. Capital market finance for the private sector increased sharply in the 1990s, first through equity, then bonds and "private placements" (RBI 1999c). The liberalization of GDR issues and commercial borrowing offshore by top corporations, albeit under tight control by RBI, was another source of additional funds for the private sector, particularly in the mid-1990s.

Another important outcome of liberalization was a decline in the average interest margin (total interest earned less total interest paid, as a percentage of assets). Interest margins have declined after 1996–97 in all groups of banks (Figure 3.2). This decline followed a rise immediately after liberalization. The post-1997 decline probably reflects increased competition in various forms, even though the different groups of banks operate with different clients (as discussed below) and may respond differently to competition.[9]

One way in which competition manifested itself after liberalization was the competition between all banks for prime borrowers. This competition probably drove down the spreads on lending to these borrowers to minimum levels. To some extent, competition from the growth of non-bank financial companies from 1993 to 1997 may also have put pressure on banks' spreads, although much of their lending was to previously unserved borrowers, such as credit for consumers.

Competition with and through the capital markets for bank borrowers was perhaps even more important in reducing banks' interest margin, a process that is going on worldwide. The largest Indian borrowers (the largest 1800 firms,

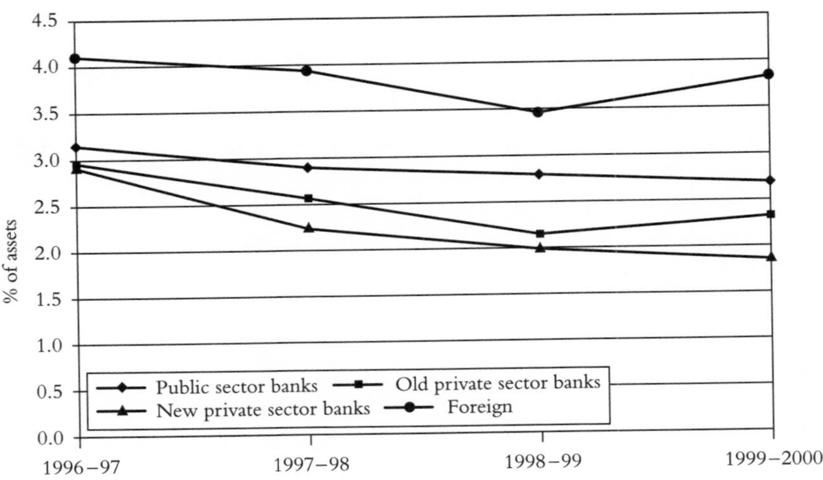

Figure 3.2. Average Interest Margins by Bank Group

which are tracked by the RBI in its sources and uses of funds) have increasingly turned from banks to capital markets for their funding during the 1990s. In the mid-1990s, they used the equity markets. In the latter part of the 1990s, they used "private placements" of commercial paper and debentures (RBI 1999c). To make a "private placement," these firms called various banks and sold their debt instrument to the bank offering the lowest rate (rather than going through the market with its listing requirements). Banks would make offers because of competition and because investments in "private placements" offer some advantages compared to loans.[10] In addition to banks and other financial intermediaries, firms with temporary excess liquidity might also be tapped. Through this mechanism, the average interest rate earned on banks' funding of these firms has been driven down, compared to the banks' average cost of funds. Obviously an important element in the growth of these types of funding has been the development of a rating industry. However, rating agencies deal only with the largest firms. Small and medium firms cannot access these funding sources because they lack ratings, or histories of debt repayment.

Offshore funding was another source of competition for banks, particularly for the top borrowers. However, this type of funding declined toward the end of the 1990s. After 1998, some firms even let their permits to raise funds offshore expire.

Market liberalization thus was an important factor in the increase in competition and the decline in spreads.[11] Increased competition between banks was, of course, dependent on the growing ability of borrowers to switch banks. It was also dependent on the relaxation of restrictions on "investments" by banks in assets that are not eligible for the statutory liquidity requirement. This category of assets had grown to 9 percent of assets in March 2000. Competition between banks and the equity market was dependent on the easing of requirements on new capital market issues and the fall in costs of capital market transactions related to increased competition (Shah and Thomas 1999). Competition from the international capital market was, of course, dependent on the partial liberalization of the capital account. Increased competition was also dependent on the availability of ratings on firms and information on their past performance in servicing debts.

4. Continuing Problems and Their Relation to the Macroeconomic, Institutional, Informational, and Incentive Frameworks

Although the financial market liberalization yielded important benefits, a number of problems remain. First, as discussed below, the large volume of government debt has continued to limit the volume of credit to the private sector, albeit through market sales rather than through forced investments. This crowding out reflects the macroeconomic framework, in particular the continued large government deficit. Second, NPLs, though reduced, remain a large fraction of the loan portfolio by international standards. The poor quality of lending across all banks reflects the lack of changes in the legal and informational framework. It also reflects the poor performance of the dominant public sector banks, which have fewer incentives for sound lending than the private sector banks. Third, the problems with poor loan performance and high costs in the public sector banks have been exposed by competition, which has made it increasingly difficult to cross-subsidize weak loans with high provisions and cover high costs.

Crowding Out of Private Debt in the Bank's Portfolio

Total government debt held by the banks (including the cash reserve requirement) actually absorbed a higher percentage of deposits in the 1990s than in the last half of the 1980s—an average of 40 percent compared to 36 percent (Figure 3.3). This rise in government debt holdings has occurred despite the large reductions in the cash reserve requirement and the statutory liquidity requirement that occurred with liberalization (Table 3.1). The reduction in the statutory liquidity requirement mainly affected new issues by "other eligible borrowers," the non-government borrowers—public enterprises, quasi-public borrowers, and private enterprises—that were excluded from the statutory liquidity requirement in 1993.[12] These "other eligible borrowers" lost their implicit interest-rate subsidy on new issues and now have to compete with private sector borrowers for

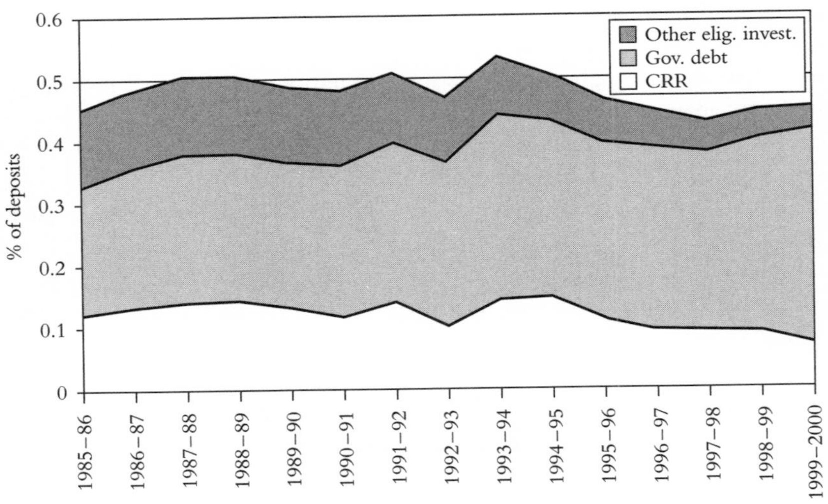

Figure 3.3. Banks' Cash Reserves and Investments Eligible for the Statutory Liquidity Requirement

funds, an important outcome of the liberalization. Meanwhile bank holdings of government debt have trended upward.

The large holdings of government debt by the banks reflect the large general government deficit during the 1990s, which averaged 8 percent of GDP.[13] The deficit generated new debt that had to be held by someone, a macroeconomic constraint. In fact, banks actually have held more government debt than required by the statutory liquidity requirement in recent years, while they just met the statutory liquidity requirement in the 1980s. And banks have increased their holdings of government debt substantially in the last two years, as the deficit rose to an average of 9.4 percent of GDP.

Public debt is less of a burden for the banks today than in the 1980s. In the 1980s, the interest rate on government debt was kept only slightly above the average interest cost of funds by fiat, and demand for it was generated by the statutory liquidity requirement. Currently the government pays an interest rate that is much higher than the average interest cost of funds and which is largely determined in auctions.[14] Moreover, public sector debt carries a low risk weight for purposes of capital adequacy (2 percent), and it has no priority sector lending requirement and no risk of default. All these factors make public debt more attractive than in the 1980s.[15]

It is important to note, however, that all these factors mainly affect the rates offered by buyers in the government debt auctions. To repeat, the macroeconomic constraint remains that all the government debt that is offered has to be held, one way or another. If it is not bought by the banks, then it will have had to be taken up by individuals and non-bank institutions.[16] Thus, one way or another, the large and growing government debt would reduce the availability of credit to the private sector.

The Continuation of High NPLs

Indian banks' non-government lending tends to have high rates of non-performance by international standards (Table 3.2). Although the NPL rates appear to have been reduced since liberalization began,[17] NPLs remain high compared to international best practices. The systemic risk of these NPL rates is limited by the banks' provisions and the large share of government debt in banks' portfolios, which together reduce reported net NPLs to only about 3 percent of banks' *assets* and about 1.5 percent of GDP.[18] Of course, reported NPLs are only an indicator of potential systemic problems in all countries.[19]

The interest here is not, however, the systemic risk posed by India's NPLs, but what they indicate about the quality of lending and collection by Indian banks. The continued problems in the quality of lending and collection in India are indicated by the high ratio of non-performing loans to non-government loans, before provisioning. The following discussion focuses on three main factors affecting the quality of lending: the poor legal framework for executing collateral, the poor information on borrowers, and the still-dominant role of public sector banks, which have higher rates of non-performing loans than the other banks.

The poor quality of lending by Indian banks, particularly by the public banks, is important because it means that banks are not contributing to development as well as they might. Either the banks are (a) not allocating scarce resources to sound projects, or (b) hidden "subsidies" are being provided to delinquent borrowers that must be covered by depositors, or by other borrowers or the banks' owners, through provisionings and recapitalizations. Of course, the ability to transfer the costs of non-performing loans to depositors is limited by competition for deposits, which is reasonably high in India. The ability to transfer the costs to borrowers in general is limited by individual borrowers' ability

TABLE 3.2

Non-Performing Loans of Commercial Banks

Non-Performing Loans	End of March 1997	End of March 1998	End of March 1999	End of March 2000
Gross NPLs (% of loans)	15.7	14.4	14.7	12.8
NPLs net of provisions (% loans)	8.1	7.3	7.6	6.8
Net NPLs (% of assets)	3.3	2.7	2.9	3.0

SOURCE: RBI, *Report on Trend and Progress in Banking 1998–99; 1999–2000.*

to signal their creditworthiness and by competition. The three factors contributing to the high rate of NPLs mentioned above probably also contribute to the transfer of the costs of non-performing loans to borrowers in general, by raising interest rates to cover high provisions, as discussed below.

One major factor in India's high NPLs is the weak legal framework. The weak legal framework limits creditors' ability to execute collateral and thereby provides weak incentives for borrowers to service debts promptly, especially if unforeseen problems develop.[20] Although the law on debt recovery is fairly clear, the judicial system makes it difficult to execute collateral. An RBI study of 10,000 large NPLs (over Rs 10 million) in 15 public sector banks found that obtaining a judgment to execute collateral usually takes 10 years and then may be difficult to execute—only one case of the 10,000 studied had actually obtained a judgment and executed the collateral (RBI 1999b). Indian courts work slowly (World Bank 2000), and in 1998 an estimated 1.4 million debt recovery cases were pending, representing about 47 percent of the accounts in arrears (RBI 1999b). Moreover, suits for debt recovery are prohibited once a company is declared "sick" and are transferred to the Board for Industrial and Financial Reconstruction (BIFR), which is supposed to act like a U.S. Chapter 11 rapid bankruptcy proceeding. According to newspaper reports, about one third of banks' non-performing corporate loans are debts of companies in BIFR. The BIFR also is slow acting. Of the roughly 4000 firms that have entered the BIFR since 1987, 80 percent are still under consideration.[21] Moreover, once BIFR reaches a judgment, it can be appealed through the court system.

In an attempt to speed debt recovery, special debt tribunals were set up in 1993 following the recommendations of the first Narasimham Committee on financial reform. However, by 1997 only about 1 percent of the pending cases had been transferred to them and only 10 percent of them had been resolved (RBI 1999b). The poor performance of the debt tribunals reflects the slow implementation of the legal authorization, legal challenges, and lack of resources, relative to the massive number of potential cases.

A second major factor in India's high NPLs is the lack of information on borrowers' repayment records. Prior to liberalization, borrowers were effectively limited to one bank or group of banks, who maintained their credit records. Liberalization allowed borrowers to switch banks. While banks obviously could ask new clients to provide a credit history, individual banks are naturally loath to share credit records with another bank to which they might lose a client. Credit ratings have been established for the larger firms, but credit ratings of small and medium firms and consumers are nonexistent. The government is considering setting up a credit bureau to supply credit information. Currently, however, the absence of shared data not only makes lending difficult but naturally means less incentive for borrowers to maintain a good credit rating.

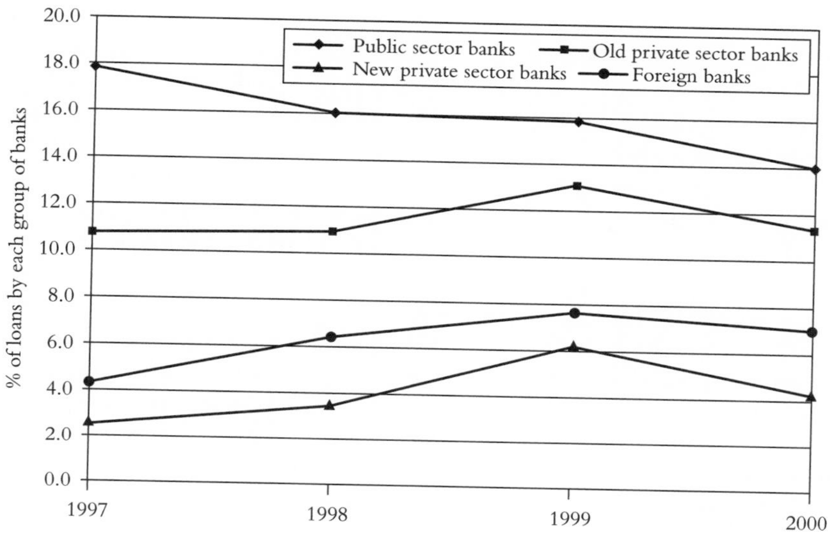

Figure 3.4. Non-Performing Loans by Bank Groups

A third major factor in the high rate of non-performing loans is the high rate of non-performing loans by the still-dominant public sector banks. In 2000, the public sector banks' NPLs were 14 percent of loans on average (Figure 3.4), a substantial reduction from the more than 20 percent rate around the time of liberalization but still high compared to the 7.9 percent average for all other types of banks in India. The public sector banks have reduced their NPLs substantially since the early 1990s, with most of the reduction coming between 1994 and 1997. The reduction in NPL rates over time was almost wholly due to loan growth in excess of NPL growth and some write-offs associated with the recapitalization of the public banks in 1995. Various governments have continually pressured the public sector banks to reduce NPL rates and some reduction has occurred, although largely because of loan growth. To the public sector banks' credit, their post-1997 improvement, although slow, has taken place while NPL rates were rising in private and foreign banks.

The NPL rates of other types of banks are much lower than those of the public sector banks, though generally higher than international best practices (Figure 3.4). In 1997, the first publicly available data on NPLs for non-public sector banks showed that NPLs averaged about 6 percent of advances for the non-public sector banks as a group. This figure had worsened to 7.8 percent by March 2000.

The old private sector banks have higher-average NPL rates than the new foreign banks and than the new private banks licensed in 1994, which have the lowest NPL rates of all. Some of the new foreign banks have suffered high NPLs. As noted, the average NPL rates in all these banks exceed best international practices.

Differences in NPL rates across bank groups partly reflect differences in borrowers, particularly differences between bank groups in priority sector lending.[22] Priority sector borrowers, particularly in public sector banks, have higher NPL rates than non-priority sector borrowers, although the non-priority sector borrowers' NPL rates are also high compared to the best international standards.[23]

The foreign banks have a lower (32 percent) priority sector lending requirement—of which at least 10 percentage points must be for small and medium industry and at least 12 percentage points must be export credit. Export credit is, of course, low risk, and the foreign banks far overfulfill their requirement, which contributes to their low NPLs. The private and public sector banks have a 40 percent priority sector lending requirement, which involves agriculture (18 percentage points), small and medium industry (40 percent of which is supposed to be for small and tiny), other small firms, and the self-employed, with the "weaker sectors" accounting for 10 percentage points. Until recently, the public sector banks and the old private sector banks had to fulfill this requirement largely by direct lending, while the new private banks (and the foreign banks) were allowed to fulfill all (some) of their requirement by lending to government second-tier institutions (the National Bank for Agriculture and Rural Development and the Small Industries Development Bank of India), thereby shifting the burden of NPLs on direct lending to them.

The burden of the priority sector requirement on the public sector banks has been eased recently, and this may partly explain their reduced NPLs. Since 1994–95, the banks have increasingly been allowed to fulfill more of their priority sector obligation by extending credit to government second-tier institutions.[24] Moreover, the definition of priority sector loans has been expanded to other sectors, including the software sector. Another factor in improving the performance of priority sector loans in the public sector banks is a shift in lending to larger borrowers by the banks themselves: the public sector banks have reduced the number of direct agricultural loans and small-scale loans by 25 percent since 1997, suggesting that they are concentrating more on larger borrowers. Some public sector banks have also tried to use new approaches to improve the performance of priority sector loans, such as Grameen-type social contracts with villages. Finally, RBI directives were issued recently regarding acceptable settlements on old NPLs, which protect public sector bank managers who settle NPLs provided their bank's earnings permit them to do so. All these factors, along with the response to government pressure to reduce NPLs and the lack of new priority sector lending campaigns, probably explain why NPLs have declined in the public sector banks. Of course, to some extent, this reduction in non-performing loans has come by transferring part of the burden to the government second-tier institutions.

The NPL rates of public sector banks nonetheless remain much higher than even those of the old private sector banks, whose clientele most closely resembles that of the public sector banks. The difference in NPLs between these two sets of banks probably reflects the public sector banks' lesser attention to loan quality at entry and to collection, reflecting in turn weaker incentives within the public sector banks for sound lending and collection and the continued, albeit reduced, pressure on them to make loans to noncreditworthy borrowers. These problems even show up in the lesser quality of loan documentation that is exposed when non-performing loans are taken to court, as noted above.

As discussed below, increased competition is making it more difficult to cross-subsidize weak lending in the public banks, increasing the likelihood that the taxpayers will have to pay the costs of poor lending at some point. To some extent this has already begun: from 1992–93 to 1998–99, the government provided an average of about 0.25 percent of GDP p.a. for recapitalization of public sector banks.[25] Most of the recapitalization came in the early 1990s, but some banks have been recapitalized more than once.

The Profit Squeeze on Indian Banks

Indian banks are caught in a profit squeeze between the competitive pressures on their interest margins on the one hand and their high NPLs and wages on the other. The squeeze is worst on the public sector banks, particularly the nationalized banks.[26] Many of the old private sector banks are also feeling the squeeze (Figure 3.5). The other banks operate at reasonable profit rates because the weak status of many of the public sector banks limits their ability to compete.

A major factor in low public sector bank earnings is their high NPL rate. Once actual debt service stops on a loan and the loan is recognized as non-performing, then income accrual is stopped. NPLs also mean a provision is charged against earnings. Indian regulations on income recognition roughly meet international standards but are below best practices. Required provision rates are low.[27] However, even at the low required provisioning rates, the public sector banks' profits are hurt by provisioning. The public sector banks have provisioned about 0.9 percent of assets recently. Non-public sector banks provision at much higher rates, despite lower NPLs. For example, the public sector banks provision about the same percentage of assets as the new private banks and only half of the rate in the foreign banks (Figure 3.5). However, the public sector banks have NPL rates that are roughly twice as high as those of the foreign banks, and three times those of the new private sector banks (Figure 3.4). Even

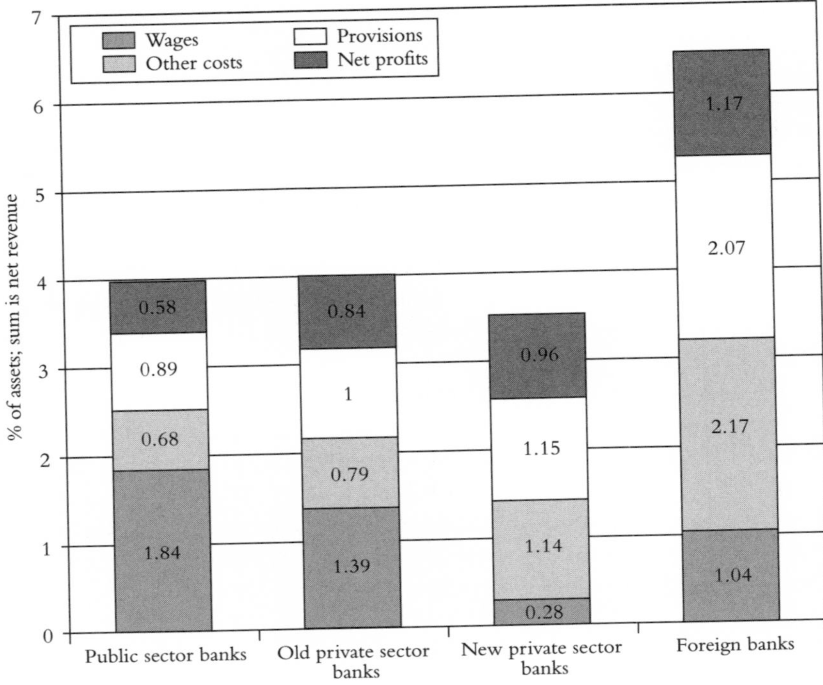

Figure 3.5. Costs, Provisions, and Net Profits

the old private sector banks provision slightly more than the public sector banks, and they have lower NPL rates, as discussed above.

Public sector banks' high wage costs also cut into their profits (Figure 3.5). The public sector banks' wage costs average about 1.84 percent of assets, 35 percent higher than the old private banks and 75 percent higher than the foreign banks.[28] Thus, even the old private sector banks, which have roughly the same net revenue (as a percentage of assets) as the public sector banks, have room to provision more than the public sector banks, pay slightly higher "other costs," and still make higher profits. The comparison between the public sector banks and either the new private banks or the foreign banks is even worse.

The public sector banks' high wage costs mainly reflect overstaffing and are a legacy of their branch expansion in the 1970s and 1980s and their protected position until recently. With about 900,000 employees, public sector banks have about 10 times as many employees per billion Rs of assets as the new private banks (in 1998), 6.5 times compared to the foreign banks, and 30 percent more than the old private banks.[29] Moreover, the comparison understates the overmanning in public sector banks, given the larger amount of "other business" and corresponding larger amount of noninterest income in the other bank groups compared to public sector banks (other than the State Bank group). Wage and salary rates in public sector banks are much lower than the figures for comparable jobs in non-public sector banks, which partially offsets the overmanning.[30]

Both employment and high wage costs reflect the strong position of bank unions in India, particularly in the public sector banks. The costs in the foreign banks and the new private banks are much lower because they have new employees and their unions have allowed different work arrangements. The public sector bank unions have been a major factor in delaying the introduction of technology. In the late 1980s, there was even a strike against the introduction of calculators.

More generally, the high wage costs of public sector banks are another confirmation of the hypothesis that industries protected from competition tend to share their potential excess profits with their employees. The public sector banks also shared their potential profits with preferred borrowers, in terms of lower interest rates and in loans that were not repaid (Hanson 2001). However, now that competition has increased, the public sector banks are squeezed between declining margins, still-high non-performing assets, and high labor costs.[31]

Profit rates in the public sector banks are not only much lower than in the other bank groups (Figure 3.5), but insufficient to keep pace with the normal growth of lending, let alone a higher ratio of lending to the private sector. Thus the problem in the public sector banks goes beyond the standard problem of low returns to government capital in public enterprises to the issue that in banking more capital will have to be injected for banks to continue to grow, because of the capital adequacy requirements on banking. Capital (including reserves and surpluses) in the public sector banks was about 5.2 percent of assets (not risk weighted) at the end of March 2000. A 15 percent annual growth in credit (and other assets) means that profits before taxes must be 0.8 percent of assets annually to maintain the ratio of capital to assets through internal capital generation. Yet, the profits before taxes in the Indian public sector banks averaged only 0.66 percent in 1999–2000, with roughly half of the public sector banks falling below that figure. To increase lending to the private sector, capital would have to grow even faster, because of the high (100 percent) risk weight of loans to the private sector.

Thus, without substantial changes, the Indian public sector banks will increasingly face a constraint on growth from low profits or require further capital injections from the government to maintain their growth. The old private sector banks face a similar, though less pressing problem. Fundamentally, this squeeze reflects the pressure for change, in terms of better lending and lower costs, from the increased competition that arose after market liberalization.

5. Recent Government Efforts at Further Reform in Banking

The government has made various attempts to address the problems of public sector banks in recent years, the most important of which is the voluntary retirement scheme (VRS). Under VRS about 11 percent of the employees in the public sector banks have chosen to voluntarily retire, in exchange for a retirement bonus and payment of their retirement benefit. The average payment of about $13,000, plus another $13,000 in accumulated retirement benefit (paid as a lump sum on retirement under the Indian public sector pension system) was sufficiently attractive for the union members to back it wholeheartedly. In the short run, however, the VRS results in a one-time charge against profits/capital.

Translating lower employment into higher profits and more efficiency will not be automatic, however, unless the early retirees indeed had zero productivity. Typically, employees with the most options are those who leave under voluntary retirement schemes. In the Indian scheme, the bank retained the option to reject any employee's request for early retirement to avoid the loss of key employees. However, it is doubtful that banks exercised this option much. Thus, new ways of doing business will be needed to reap the benefits of lower labor costs. This process has begun, including dropping one intermediate layer of reporting responsibilities. However, much more change in business practices is likely to be needed, including a sharp reduction in unprofitable branches, improved communication, and greater computerization.

Commenting on the lack of computers in Indian (public sector) banking, the second Narasimham Committee report said, "No area of commercial activity has been influenced more by the ongoing revolution in information and communications technology than the banking and financial systems. . . . This phenomenon has largely bypassed India" (Narasimham Committee 1998, 40). In 1999, the beginnings of a strategy for computerization of the public sector banks were laid out by the Vasudevan Committee (Vasudevan 1999). However, computerization and the associated training of staff will require funding, again an up-front cost with uncertain returns only later. Unions are likely to continue their resistance to computerization, and to outsourcing, which would be one way to jump-start the process. But computerization also is a management issue—in the mid-1990s, the government and the public sector bank unions agreed upon a limited program to computerize particular branches, but the actual numbers of branches that were computerized were less than had been agreed.

The government's direct efforts to improve the public sector banks' performance have focused mainly on the weak banks. A few weak public sector banks (and a few old private banks) have been allowed to operate for some time with much less capital than required. The government has injected new capital in banks that had been recapitalized over the early 1990s, in some cases more than once, and insisted on new business plans that include measures like closing foreign branches and not opening new domestic branches. Extensive discussions have taken place regarding the setup of Asset Recovery Corporation(s), for the weak banks and public sector banks in general, but no policy has been established legally, as yet. Concerns remain regarding what is the best approach and whether Asset Recovery Corporation(s) will indeed reduce NPLs or simply take them off banks' books and allow banks to focus on lending without appropriate concern for recovery.[32] Various committees and observers have discussed alternative solutions for the weak banks, such as sale or turning them into narrow banks.[33] Most recently, the 2000 Verma Committee identified nine weak public sector banks and laid out a series of recommendations that, if carried out, would turn them into the most productive public banks. The difficulty, of course, is that the committee's charge to improve the existing weak public sector banks neglected the more fundamental issue of how making the weakest much stronger would affect competition and the sector, in particular the banks that would now fall into the bottom tier.

The efforts to improve the legal framework are just beginning and have not made much of a dent in the overhang of court cases on debt. The attempt to use debt tribunals that began in 1993 got a slow start, as discussed above based on an RBI study (RBI 1999b). The problems included legal challenges, the limited number of tribunals, and their lack of funding. The legal challenges are nearly resolved, recent budgets have set up new courts, and there have been proposals to speed execution of collateral by making it easier for creditors to take over collateral. However, concerns have increasingly been expressed that the tribunals are becoming mired in their own set of extended legal proceedings, with the proceedings becoming subject to delays similar to those in the regular court system, leading to a rise in the number of unresolved cases. The tribunals also appear to remain strapped by lack of funds, facilities, and personnel, problems that have plagued the BIFR. Discussions have begun on replacing the BIFR/Sick Industries Act with new bankruptcy legislation. In addition, the government has considered legislation to ease problems of collateral execution. Arbitration clauses are supposed to be introduced in all loan contracts, but it remains to be seen whether that will help settlements or simply delay the entry of NPLs into the courts, as has occurred in other countries. The government has also discussed setting up a credit registry, but issues remain of confidentiality, which institutions will be included, and how data will be recorded (particularly if the registry is a public sector institution).

The government has also engaged in some partial privatization of public sector banks, but the efforts have been aimed more at raising capital than changing incentives for management and staff. During the 1990s, nine banks sold shares to the public, including the State Bank, with both a GDR and a domestic issue. However, these shareholders are represented only on some of the banks' boards and then by appointees of the government. The second Narasimham Committee recommended reducing the government's equity stake to 33 percent, and the government has proposed a bill to do so. However, immediately after the announcement, the finance minister's office also announced that the public sector character of the banks would be maintained (presumably through either a golden shareholding by the government or cross holdings of shares by the banks). Nonetheless, the bill met strong opposition in Parliament, and a parliamentary vote was needed merely to commit the proposal to committee discussion. In that context, and given the poor performance of bank shares (RBI 1999a, 42–44), it is likely that any share offering would not be well received and that management and incentives would not change much.

6. *The Road Forward: Beyond Market Liberalization to Reforms of Institutions and the Frameworks in Which Markets Operate*

Improving the development contribution of India's banks will require a reduction in the fiscal deficit and a clear focus on improving incentives for sound banking, which means more vigorous efforts in the areas discussed above. For example, improving the legal framework will require more funding of and better processing by the debt tribunals and a better bankruptcy law. But greater speed and penalties for willful delay in the courts are also needed to provide appropriate incentives for reducing the volume of cases that otherwise will be hard to handle even with more and better tribunals. Unless collateral is rapidly executed, and debt service cannot be delayed without suffering large penalties (essentially limiting automatic rollovers at the behest of the borrower), there will be little incentive to service debts when the borrowers experience problems and little incentive to avoid court cases.

Better information would make it possible for banks to avoid borrowers that systematically default on debt service. For example, it should be easy to require public sector banks to avoid such borrowers. Better information on debt-servicing histories would also tend to improve debt service by providing an incentive for the borrower to pay promptly to protect their credit ratings. Moreover, better information would also improve access to credit. Smaller borrowers often suffer from lack of access because they cannot demonstrate their willingness to pay and lack collateral. Thus, to improve credit access, the credit registry should include information on small-sized borrowers from non-bank institutions that service them.

Improving the banks will also depend on providing better incentives for selection of sound borrowers and collection of debt service. These are principal agent tasks—indeed banking is a principal agent business: the depositors turn over their funds to the bank's management on the expectation that it will carry out a task that the depositors cannot monitor directly. Given the number of variables and the amount of judgment involved in individual loans, it is difficult to improve lending in the command and control system that characterizes public sector firms, as discussed earlier. Incentives in salary and advancement are needed for bankers who perform these micro tasks well. Although in theory public sector banks could offer incentives for sound performance of these tasks, in practice there are few cases where this has been done.[34] It is worth noting, again, that Indian banks consider the limits on interest rates charged to small borrowers too low to cover the costs of dealing effectively with these borrowers.

Privatization of bank management and ownership would provide better incentives for improving lending quality, thereby increasing the contribution of the banks to India's development. But, privatization of banks also creates some well-known perverse incentives—the moral hazard that exists in a banking system where capital is only a small fraction of loans/deposits and depositors are protected against loss by deposit insurance (which is a high percentage of per capita income in India compared to other countries). In that context, a bank owner may be encouraged to adopt a high-return/high-risk strategy, and leave the government to pay the depositors if the risks become realities.[35] In this context, it is worth recalling that one of the reasons the banks were nationalized was to limit losses that had been incurred by private banks.

Reducing moral hazard for private bankers involves making them (and depositors) pay more of the cost of their mistakes. That is, private bank owners must maintain relatively high levels of capital, must promptly recognize and provision substantially for bad debts, must be monitored closely to ensure these requirements are fulfilled, and must be replaced quickly (before capital is gone) in the event that they fail to do so. Generally speaking, Indian regulation and supervision is not as strong as in many other developing countries, in terms of income recognition and provisioning. Thus, Indian banking needs not only more private management and ownership to create appropriate incentives for sound banking that will contribute to development, but much better regulation and supervision to limit the moral hazard associated with private owners and high deposit insurance.

Appendix

TABLE A.3.1

Major Events in the Banking Sector

Date	Event
1969	Nationalization of private banks (first round)
1973	Foreign Exchange Regulation Act (FERA)
1979	Priority sector lending requirement of 33% (effective date)
1980	Nationalization of private banks (second round)
1985	Priority sector lending requirement raised to 40% (effective date)
1991	(Narasimham) *Report of the Committee on the Financial System*, outlining reform strategy
1992–93	Financial liberalization begins with gradual liberalization of interest rates, easing of CRR and SLR, beginning of recapitalization of public sector banks, gradual introduction of 8% capital norm (on risk-weighted assets), tightening of income recognition and provisioning norms, and easing of controls on offshore financing by corporations
1993	Recovery of debts due to Banks and Financial Institutions Act creating debt tribunals
1993	Board of Financial Supervision and Department of Supervision set up in Reserve Bank of India
1993	State Bank becomes first public sector bank to issue shares in the capital market (33% of equity)
1994–95	Six new private banks commenced operation, with four more the next fiscal; entry limitations on foreign banks eased, resulting in increase in foreign banks
1997	Priority sector lending eased by allowing free rates on loans except for loans under Rps 200,000 (ceiling raised to the prime rate in 1998)
1997	Crisis in non-bank financial corporation sector, leading to elimination of public deposit-taking for 90% of the institutions
1998	(Narasimham) *Report of the Committee on Banking Sector Reforms*, outlining second-round reform strategy
2000	Foreign Exchange Management Act (replaced FERA) eased capital controls

Notes

1. See Sen and Vaidya (1997) and Hanson (2001) for further discussion of the preliberalization period.

2. Between 1969 and 1979 public sector bank offices nearly tripled, rising from about 7200 to 22,400; in addition, regional rural banks were created in the 1970s and had 2400 offices by the end of the decade. The growth of public sector bank offices continued in the 1980s, albeit at a slower pace. By 1992, there were about 44,000 offices and 14,700 regional rural bank offices. Since 1992, the growth of public sector bank offices has been only about 1 percent per year. Branching by the non-public sector banks was and is restricted by the Reserve Bank of India.

3. Net loans are essentially equal to deposits less the cash reserve and statutory liquidity requirements—that is, 46.5 percent of deposits at the end of the 1980s.

4. The cash-reserve requirement was remunerated beginning in 1962. During the 1980s the remuneration rate was changed at various times both on the basic amount of the reserves and on the marginal increases in reserves, and reached a maximum of 5 percent at the end of the decade.

5. Some liberalization had been begun during the initial years of the prime ministership of Rajiv Gandhi but slowed at the end of the 1980s (Joshi and Little 1994).

6. For example, tariffs were lowered significantly and quantitative restrictions on trade reduced.

7. Reddy 1999 and various issues of the RBI's *Report on Trend and Progress of Banking in India* and *Annual Report* provide more details.

8. CAMEL is a standard acronym that refers to supervision of Capital Adequacy, Asset Quality, Management Quality, Earnings, and Liquidity, to which India added an "S" for Systems Evaluation.

9. An indication of the four bank groups' different clientele is the difference in their average interest earned (as a percentage of assets). The foreign banks' average interest earned is about 1 percentage point higher and the old private sector banks' about 0.6 percentage points higher than the average for the public sector banks. The new private sector banks' average interest rate has actually fallen below that of the public sector banks, apparently reflecting the new private sector banks' concentration on the best clients and their passing on the drop in their funding costs associated with the softening of interest rates on short-term funds that form a major part of their resources. The difference between the average interest earnings of the public sector banks and the other bank groups has declined since 1996–97, suggesting that the composition of borrowers is becoming similar across all bank groups, as the borrowers switch banks.

10. As investments, private placements are not subject to the priority sector lending requirements that apply to loans (Box 3.1), and thus are more profitable for the banks than loans. The RBI has recognized the similarity between private placements and loans and has applied the same provisioning rules to both assets. Another element in the growth of the private placement market has been the peculiar role that the prime rate played in India. The banks are required to use their "prime rate" for lending to the smallest borrowers eligible for priority sector lending (Box 3.1). This requirement meant that setting a prime rate appropriate for the best borrowers would make lending to the smallest borrowers unprofitable, given their higher costs of loan origination and higher rates of nonperformance compared to loans to the best borrowers. A 1997 survey suggested that banks found the interest rate structure too low to lend to small clients—that is, the remaining regulation that small borrowers had to get the prime rate was binding. To get around this requirement, some banks quoted a prime rate that was higher than would have been appropriate for the best borrowers, and then provided the best borrowers funds through "private placements" at subprime rates. Banks also began to quote lending rates to prime borrowers as a spread over their cost of funds. Recently, the RBI has allowed banks to make loans at less than the prime rate.

11. Some institutional and political factors also have tended to drive down average lending rates faster than average deposit rates, particularly in the public banks. On the deposit side, interest rates have probably been kept up by the "stickiness" of the rates on the government's direct mobilization of funds through "small savings," 70 percent of which is on-lent to the states. The government has tended to keep this rate high because

of the need to finance the states' growing deficits (World Bank 2000). Second, banks, particularly public sector banks, tend to have longer maturity deposits, compared to loan maturities, than in most countries. In the context of the falling interest rates in India after the mid-1990s, this meant that deposit costs declined slowly compared to loan rates, particularly in the public sector banks and the old private sector banks, which depend more on longer-term deposits than the new private sector banks and the foreign banks. Third, public sector bank boards have directors representing consumer interests, and they were loath to cut deposit rates. On the lending side, interest rates of the public sector banks have been subject to political pressures for cuts, notably in March 1999, after the budget speech, when the finance minister exhorted the financial sector to do its part in restarting the economy, the RBI cut the bank rate and its repo rate, and the public sector banks reduced the lending rates. Private and foreign banks cut their rates with a lag, and by less. Beginning in March 2000 a similar pattern of rate cuts occurred.

12. Debt issues of these borrowers that were in banks' portfolios in 1993 were granted eligibility to meet the statutory liquidity requirement until they matured. This exemption explains the existence and decline of the other eligible investments shown in Figure 3.3.

13. The general government deficit refers to the combined central and state deficit, netting out intragovernment net borrowing, and includes the oil pool subsidy account and excludes disinvestments revenues. Annual figures are as follows:

India: General Government Deficit as Percentage of GDP

1990–91	1991–92	1992–93	1993–94	1994–95	1995–96	1996–97	1997–98	1998–99	1999–2000
9.4	7.8	7.4	8.2	7.4	6.7	7.1	6.9	8.9	10.0

SOURCE: World Bank 2000 and World Bank estimates.

The central government deficit averaged 6.2 percent of GDP in the 1990s. This includes about 1.5 percent of GDP p.a. of net central government lending to the states, which are limited in their direct borrowing by the central government. The public enterprises reduced their deficit during the 1990s (World Bank 2000), which means that they left more room for private borrowings from banks.

14. The RBI takes up government debt issues if it considers the interest rates offered in the auction to be too high, and occasionally receives "private placements" of government debt. Thus, the interest rates on government debt are not completely based on the auctions.

15. The public sector banks hold only a slightly higher percentage of public sector debt than the other banks, 32 percent of deposits, compared to 31 percent for the other groups of banks in March 2000. This similarity suggests that pressures on public sector banks to hold government debt are not important in determining holdings.

16. The Life Insurance Corporation is required to hold over 50 percent of its assets in government debt and holds an even larger fraction; the pension funds also hold much more government debt than required.

17. No overall figures on NPLs are available for the first half of the 1990s. However, in 1993–95, the NPL rates of the public sector banks averaged 22.5 percent of loans and NPLs accounted for over 80 percent of the system in that period (RBI 1998). These NPL figures probably reflected the recognition of the existing stock of NPLs under the tight-

ened regulatory standards that accompanied liberalization. The public sector banks tend to have much higher NPL rates than the other banks, for reasons discussed in the rest of the section.

18. The large proportion of government sector debt or government guaranteed debt in the portfolio reduces the ratio of non-performing loans to *assets* to 5.5 percent, compared to 12.8 percent for *loans*. This means that systemic risk is related mostly to the sustainability of the fiscal accounts and not so much to the banking system. From the standpoint of comparing portfolio quality in India to other countries, this large difference between NPLs as a percentage of loans and as a percentage of assets must be borne in mind. In addition, provisions must be deducted to get a comparable cross-country measure (net NPLs), because in India NPLs tend to be settled or written off much more slowly than in most other countries. The slowness in public sector banks' write-offs and settlements occurs because of the potential political problems associated with settlements and write-offs of large loans and because the banks may lack sufficient earnings to settle or write off NPLs. The 2000–2001 program to settle public banks' NPLs achieved only limited success.

19. As in most countries, India's reported NPL data must be regarded only as an indicator of loan performance. The degree to which it measures actual NPLs depends on the quality of accounting, auditing, regulation, and supervision. In particular it depends on the amount of "evergreening" of weak loans through restructuring, which is a continual problem in India to judge from the numerous circulars against the practice that the RBI has issued over the last decade. India's easing of regulations on income recognition and provisioning of restructured loans in 2000, taken in the name of allowing adjustment to the general decline in interest rates, is likely to reduce NPL rates and pressures for provisioning temporarily in 2000–2001, but is unlikely to reduce NPL rates much over the medium term.

20. The problems in the legal framework have been raised by the two Narasimham committees, the RBI, the World Bank (2000), and Hanson and Kathuria (1999), among others.

21. Of those released, 6 percent were brought back to health and 13 percent were judged to have been healthy when they were brought into the BIFR.

22. Another factor in the non-public sector banks' lower NPL ratios is their faster settlement and write-off of NPLs , made possible by their higher provision rates and profits and the lack of political constraints on settlements and write-offs.

23. No separate figures are published on NPL rates in priority sector lending by banks as a whole. It is also difficult to estimate non-performing rates on priority lending, because there are two sets of data on priority sector lending, one of which shows rising rates of priority sector lending (RBI 2000, 226 and 227) and the other showing a constant rate of priority sector lending (RBI 2000, 53). Moreover, as discussed above, there have been significant changes in the composition of priority sector lending. By 1997, when lending rates had been liberalized and the stock of NPLs had been cleaned up to some degree, priority sector loans in public sector banks accounted for 47.7 percent of their NPLs, but only 41 percent of their lending. Using the first set of data on total lending, this generates a rate of NPLs on priority lending that is more than 25 percent higher than on non-priority sector lending. However, by 2000, the rate of NPLs on public sector banks' priority sector lending, using the same set of data, was only about

4 percent higher than on non-priority lending, for the reasons discussed in the rest of the paragraph.

24. In addition, the public sector banks can count some of the funds they transfer to associated regional rural banks as priority sector lending, and it is not clear how these funds are treated as NPLs. However, these transfers are generally small; often the net flow is from the regional rural banks to the public sector banks, because the regional rural banks mobilize more deposits than they lend.

25. The recapitalization takes the form of bonds bearing 10 percent interest. Because the recapitalization represents an exchange of assets (more government capital in the banks), it shows up in the capital budget and not the annual deficit, except for the interest payments on the bonds.

26. The State Bank group has resisted the squeeze, because of somewhat better loan performance and its higher noninterest earnings.

27. Indian regulations require nonaccrual of income after debt service has been in arrears 180 days; exemptions for bad harvests are allowed, and exemptions of 30 additional days are often granted on nonagricultural loans. Many countries now recognize bad loans after arrears of 90 days, which is the proposed standard in the new Basel Capital Accords. Required initial provisions in India are 10 percent, lower than in most Latin American countries, and as loans deteriorate, required provisions are not increased very rapidly, especially compared to the low recovery rates through the judicial system. New RBI regulations will encourage restructuring by allowing restructured loans to be treated as performing, allowing existing specific provisions to be shifted to nonrestructured loans. However, unless borrowers' incomes actually improve, this new regulation simply temporarily postpones the need for provisions.

28. The difference may be even greater, because higher-level public sector employees often receive public sector-owned housing at less than market rates, and receive "other perks" that are not considered costs to the same degree as in private sector banks. Employees of public sector banks also may benefit from low-interest-rate loan schemes for employees (Hanson 2001).

29. Employees per billion Rs of assets in 1998 were 136 for the public sector banks, 106 for the old private banks, 14 for the new private banks, and 22 for the foreign banks (Indian Bankers Association). There is some evidence that the public sector banks have much higher ratios of lower-level employees to assets than the private or foreign banks (Sarkar 1999).

30. Entry-level salaried positions in the private banks appear to pay 2.5–3 times as much as in the public sector banks, with the differences widening to 6–10 times at the top levels of management. Comparisons are complicated, however, by free housing and allowances and by bonuses (for private sector employees).

31. Another factor in the low profit rates of public sector banks is the form that their recapitalization took—nonmarketable government bonds paying 10 percent. The average market rates on government bonds during the decade has been much higher. However, the recent decline in interest rates has reduced the importance of this factor somewhat.

32. A recent study of seven centralized asset recovery agencies (Klingebiel 2000) found recovery was effective and quick only in industrialized countries, where assets were easily sold (real estate), transparent procedures used, political interferences minimized, and adequate bankruptcy and foreclosure laws in place. In the developing countries that were studied, where these conditions were not in place, asset recovery com-

panies did not work effectively. In the Indian context, there would almost certainly be additional problems in setting up a centralized Asset Recovery Corporation: (1) NPLs would probably increase as bankers try to clean their books and debtors attempt to switch to what they are likely to perceive as an easier regime given their experience with the BIFR; (2) problems could easily develop in the switch-over of the more than 1.4 million cases in existence, given the already poor documentation of loans and collateral, the incentives for error, and the lack of accountability of public sector bank officers; (3) legal challenges would probably delay the process; and (4) the corporation would likely start slowly and be underfunded, based on the experience with BIFR and the debt tribunals.

33. S. S. Tarapore has recommended turning weak banks into narrow banks to limit new losses on bad loans. See Tarapore 1997, 1999.

34. Perhaps the best known example is the *unit desa* program of Bank Rakyat Indonesia. However, other units of the bank were unsuccessful in applying this model and have suffered large NPLs.

35. Demirguc-Kunt and Detragiache (2000) find that across countries deposit insurance tends to increase banking system instability, providing empirical support for the importance of moral hazard.

Works Cited

Ahluwalia, M. 1997. Governance issues in India's economic reforms. Paper presented at Workshop on Governance Issues in South Asia, Yale University. Mimeographed.

Barth, J., G. Caprio, and R. Levine. 2000. *Banking systems around the globe: Do regulation and ownership affect performance and stability?* Policy Research Working Paper 2325. Washington, D.C.: World Bank.

Caprio, G., J. Hanson, and P. Honohan. 2001. Introduction and overview: The case for liberalization and some pitfalls. In *Financial liberalization: How far, how fast?* edited by G. Caprio, P. Honohan, and J. Stiglitz. Cambridge: Cambridge University Press.

Caprio, G., P. Honohan, and J. Stiglitz, eds. 2001. *Financial liberalization: How far, how fast?* Cambridge: Cambridge University Press.

Demirguc-Kunt, A., and E. Detragiache. 2000. *Does deposit insurance increase banking system stability? An empirical investigation*. Policy Research Paper 2247. Washington, D.C.: World Bank.

Hanson, J. A. 2001. Indonesia and India: Contrasting approaches to repression and liberalization. In *Financial liberalization: How far, how fast?* edited by G. Caprio, P. Honohan, and J. Stiglitz. Cambridge: Cambridge University Press.

Hanson, J. A., and S. Kathuria. 1999. *India: A financial sector for the twenty-first century*. Delhi: Oxford University Press.

Joshi, V., and I. M. D. Little. 1994. *India: Macroeconomics and political economy, 1964–1991*. Washington, D.C.: World Bank.

Klingebiel, D. 2000. *The use of asset management companies in the resolution of banking crisis: Cross country experiences*. Policy Research Working Paper 2284. Washington, D.C.: World Bank.

La Porta, R., F. Lopez Silanes, and A. Schleifer. 2000. Government ownership of banks. Cambridge: Harvard University. http://post.economics.harvard.edu/faculty/laporta/papers.html.

Narasimham Committee. 1991. *Report of the committee on the financial system*. Mumbai: Reserve Bank of India.

———. 1998. *Report of the committee on banking sector reforms*. Mumbai: Reserve Bank of India.

Reddy, Y. V. 1999. Financial reform: Review and prospects. *Reserve Bank of India Bulletin* 52 (1): 33–94.

Reserve Bank of India. 1998. *Report on trend and progress of banking in India 1997–98*. Mumbai: Reserve Bank of India.

———. 1999a. *Report on trend and progress of banking in India 1998–99*. Mumbai: Reserve Bank of India.

———, Department of Banking Supervision. 1999b. Some aspects and issues relating to NPAs in commercial banks. *Reserve Bank of India Bulletin* 52 (7): 913–36.

———. 1999c. *Report on currency and finance 1998–99*. Mumbai: Reserve Bank of India.

———. 2000. *Report on trend and progress of banking in India 1999–2000*. Mumbai: Reserve Bank of India.

Sarkar, J. 1999. Indian banking: Preparing for the next round of reform. In *India: A financial sector for the twenty-first century*, edited by J. A. Hanson and S. Kathuria. Delhi: Oxford University Press.

Sen, K., and R. R. Vaidya. 1997. *The process of financial liberalization in India*. Delhi: Oxford University Press.

Shah, A., and S. Thomas. 1999. Developing the Indian capital market. In *India: A financial sector for the twenty-first century*, edited by J. A. Hanson and S. Kathuria. Delhi: Oxford University Press.

Tarapore, S. S. 1999. Indian banking: Preparing for the next round of reform. In *India: A financial sector for the twenty-first century*, edited by J. A. Hanson and S. Kathuria. Delhi: Oxford University Press.

Tarapore, S. S. (Chairman). 1997. *Report of the committee on capital account convertibility*. Mumbai: Reserve Bank of India.

Vasudevan, A. 1999. *Committee on technology upgradation*. Mumbai: Reserve Bank of India.

World Bank. 2000. *India: Reducing poverty, accelerating development*. Delhi: Oxford University Press.

Comment
Threats to the Indian Financial Sector

K. V. Kamath

With the advent of financial sector reforms in the 1990s, the Indian financial system has been exposed to global best practices in banking as well as prudential regulation. However, one of the macroeconomic factors that has affected the banking system is the high fiscal deficit run-up by the government in the last few years. Banks per force have to keep 25 percent of their net demand and time liabilities in the form of low-yielding government securities under the statutory liquidity ratio stipulation. Secondly, the issue of non-performing loans (NPLs) has afflicted banks perceptibly in the last five years or so. The average net NPL ratio for the system was 6.8 percent in FY 2000, which is quite high considering that the norm for recognizing an NPL is more liberal in the Indian context.

While in most domains ballooning NPLs are becoming a strong threat to the survival of banks, in India it would appear that there are other potential problems that have a far greater impact on the health of the financial sector. The issue of bank NPLs should not be overemphasized in the Indian context, since, unlike in the East Asian nations that were affected by the 1997 meltdown, Indian banks have shown great resilience in times of crises. By being compelled to invest in low-risk government securities, the banking system's credit-to-GDP ratio is low, which makes the economy less susceptible to a crisis. The bank credit-to-GDP ratio was about 24 percent in FY 2001, while it was as high as 180 percent in Thailand, 125 percent in Malaysia, and 69 percent in Korea at the peak of the crisis in 1997. Further, bank lending to volatile sectors like real estate is virtually nonexistent. Capital account convertibility exists only to a limited extent in India, and short-term external borrowings are very low. Therefore, while there is need to reduce the level of NPLs, there is an inbuilt cushion that prevents the issue from escalating to a crisis.

Paradigm shifts in the way technology is used in the banking sector appear to be a more tangible threat. New realities are driving the future of Indian banking given the state of the economy and direction of reforms. Banking is driven today by four factors, which have become synonymous with success. These are human resources, technology, capital, and speed. The financial services industry is being driven by technology, and the business of banking is getting customer-centric. Technology is a building block for improving efficiency and cutting costs and has to be leveraged successfully. But the role of technology has transcended operational efficiency with the widespread adoption of customer-relationship management tools. Banks need to reach out to the customer by offering a wide array of customized products and must extract value from existing customer relationships through the cross selling of other financial products. This necessitates investment in developing a unique brand identity that the customer can trust to deliver high-quality financial services.

The challenge of effectively leveraging technology and brands is accentuated by the need for capital to meet prudential guidelines. Banks that do not adapt to changing market dynamics will find it increasingly difficult to access the capital required for growing their businesses. This would inevitably lead to greater consolidation in the Indian financial sector. The global heads of large international banks have publicly stated their intent to acquire Indian banks. Meanwhile, mergers among leading Indian private sector banks have helped them become a force to reckon with.

In a competitive environment, where there is a premium attached to being the innovator, speed is of crucial importance, and the bank that acts first and fast is the winner. Human capital has thus emerged as a key driver of success. There is a need for a lean and talented human resources team, which can take on the challenge of a hypercompetitive business environment and come out on top.

Public sector banks, which have thus far dominated the banking sector, are trying to get past the shackles of being state owned. However, issues such as productivity and prevalence of unionization would impede their progress. Their ability to harness the power of technology and recruit people with requisite skill sets has been called into question. The will of the public sector banks to adopt global best practices and their ability to adapt to changing industry paradigms will be tested. In the interim, a few nimble private sector banks and foreign banks could completely alter the dynamics of the marketplace with their ability to leverage technology and attract human as well as financial capital.

In this scenario there will emerge a stratified setup, based on competency, and banks have to balance the twin issues of capital and technology. Banks need to have both these strengths to be successful. And above all, "speed capital" is of essence to remain ahead in an increasingly competitive setup. Thus the challenges before the public sector banks would not be restricted to the conventional threat of asset quality alone but would encompass broader issues pertaining to capital, technology, and human resources.

4

POLICY ISSUES IN THE INDIAN SECURITIES MARKET

❖

Ajay Shah and Susan Thomas

1. Introduction

Market-oriented economic reforms in India began in 1991. With the removal of administrative controls on bank credit and the primary market for securities, the capital markets came to occupy a larger role in shaping resource allocation in the country. This led to a heightened interest among policy makers in the institutional development of securities markets. The efforts toward empowering the securities market regulator (SEBI, Securities and Exchange Board of India) and the first efforts toward attracting foreign portfolio investment began early in the reforms process. Almost immediately after the reforms began, there was a prominent scandal on the fixed income and equity markets, which was exposed in April 1992.

This set the stage for an unusual policy intervention: the establishment of a securities exchange, the National Stock Exchange (NSE), by the government (Section 2). Contrary to most expectations, the NSE succeeded, becoming the largest equity market in 1995. The NSE pioneered many important innovations in market design in India. The most important of these included nationwide electronic trading (1994), the clearing corporation as a central counterparty (1996), and paperless settlement at the depository (1996). The NSE was a pioneer among securities exchanges in the world in using a "demutualized" structure, where brokerage firms do not own the exchange.

Nationwide trading energized financial market participation from all over the

We are grateful to Anne Krueger, Raghuram Rajan, Jim Hanson, John Echeverri-Gent, Tom Glaessner, Raghavan Putran, Ashok Jogani, Rajesh Gajra, Ruben Lee, Ashish Chauhan, and D. Balasundaram for ideas and assistance.

country, as opposed to being concentrated in Bombay. *Electronic trading* gave a high degree of transparency and sidestepped the difficulties associated with supervision of market makers. The *central counterparty* made anonymous electronic trading across the country possible, by eliminating counterparty credit risk. Electronic settlement at the *depository* sharply reduced costs at settlement and eliminated the flourishing criminal activities in theft and counterfeiting of share certificates. The *demutualized* structure helped in keeping the NSE focused on the needs of investors as opposed to the profit maximization of brokerage firms, and was critical in obtaining sharp improvements in enforcement as compared with other securities exchanges in the country.

The creation of the new exchange, clearing corporation, and depository were important accomplishments of institution building. The pressure of competing with the NSE, and access to the services of the depository, helped existing exchanges also transform their functioning. Roughly speaking, these changes gave a tenfold improvement in market liquidity—the one-way transactions cost faced by retail trades is estimated to have dropped from 5 percent to 0.5 percent.

Yet, some important structural defects in market design persisted (Section 3). Through this period, India's equity market was unique, by world standards, in featuring leveraged futures-style trading on the *spot* market. There was a mismatch between the extent of leverage and the risk management and governance capacity found at securities exchanges and the SEBI. These difficulties helped generate a steady stream of crises on the equity market. The typical crisis involved price manipulation on the secondary market and payments problems at one or more exchanges. The more prominent of these crises were highly visible disruptions of the smooth functioning of the equity market.

As a consequence, from 1996 onward, debates about policy issues on the equity market were dominated by questions about the role for leveraged trading. On one hand was a conservative position, which supported the status quo. On the other hand was the proposal to have a spot market based on "rolling settlement" (where leverage is limited to intraday positions only). In this vision, access to leveraged trading would be obtained through trading in financial derivatives. From 1996 to 2001, the SEBI broadly supported the conservative position, and the functioning of the equity market was unchanged.

In 2001, a major crisis broke on the equity market. It involved numerous elements: large leveraged positions that went wrong, accusations of market manipulation, a payments crisis at the Calcutta exchange, fraud in the banking system, accusations of collusion between institutional investors and collusive cartels, ethics violations at the Bombay Stock Exchange, and revelation of large-scale incidence of fraudulent contract notes with *badla*.

This crisis was valuable in breaking this five-year deadlock (Section 4) and moving on with reforms. In June 2001, trading in index options commenced. In July 2001, all major stocks moved to rolling settlement and options trading commenced on the most liquid stocks. These were large changes from the viewpoint of investors and securities firms; market liquidity fell sharply when the new regime first came about. However, within a matter of weeks, liquidity had improved sharply.

One of the most important questions before policy makers concerns the interfaces between the banking system and securities markets. Policy makers traditionally favored a highly restricted set of interactions between banking and securities. However, there are important gains in efficiency and risk management, for both securities markets and the banking sector, if the interplay between the two is enlarged through appropriate mechanisms.

The first aspect of the interface between banks and securities markets concerns the payments system (Section 5.1). Over the 1990s, the equity market became a nationwide platform with real-time capability for trading and settling stock transactions. However, comparable improvements in the infrastructure for funds transfer in the country have not taken place. Weaknesses in the payments infrastructure are now a critical bottleneck hindering further institutional development of the securities markets.

The central bank (RBI) has had proposals for building an improved payments system for many years, but little progress has been made in its implementation. This motivates a search for partial solutions that allow securities markets to make progress. One such solution could be to harness the subset of new banks that are well equipped with modern information technology to provide real-time funds transfer for post-trade activities on securities markets.

The second aspect of the interface between banks and securities markets concerns loans given out by banks, backed by securities as collateral (Section 5.2). Securities are ideal collateral owing to (a) publicly observed prices that can be used for marking to market of collateral value, and (b) publicly accessible markets through which collateral can be readily liquidated. These attributes enable the creation of sound risk-management systems at banks. This is in contrast with opaque collateral, such as real estate or plant and machinery, where marking to market is not possible and liquidation involves large risks and transactions costs. It is important to note that the key issue in the successful operation of these risk-management systems is the *transparency* of collateral, and not its *volatility*. The imperfect understanding of these issues in India has led to many flaws in policy formulation.

Beyond technical questions of market design, the most important concerns about the securities markets today are questions of governance and policy formulation (Section 5.3). Securities markets have made significant progress in terms of exploiting modern trading technology and modern financial instruments. However, the regulatory capacity on the part of both exchange institutions and the SEBI is highly limited.

In the case of the NSE, there is a need for a well-developed set of incentives and governance mechanisms that ensure that it continues to foster innovation, cost-efficiency, and avoid the ills that have afflicted numerous other public sector organizations in India. In the case of the market regulator, the SEBI, recent years have revealed important gaps in human capital, operational efficiencies, and political independence. Policy makers should focus on addressing these difficulties.

2. Changes in the Indian Equity Market in the 1990s

In this section, we summarize the important changes that took place in the design of the equity market in the decade of the 1990s. Table 4.1 shows the dates for some of the prominent events. Our treatment is organized around securities exchanges (Section 2.1), risk management of counterparty credit risk (Section 2.2), and improvements in settlement (Section 2.3).

2.1 The Securities Exchanges

Equity trading in India was dominated by floor-based trading on India's oldest exchange, the Bombay Stock Exchange (BSE), up to late 1994. This process had several problems. The floor was nontransparent and illiquid. The nontransparency of the floor led to rampant abuse, such as investors being charged higher prices for purchases as compared with the prices actually traded on the floor. It was not possible for investors to cross-check these prices.

The BSE did not sell new memberships and barred corporate entities or foreign brokerage firms from obtaining memberships. Investors were forced to pay high brokerage fees to undercapitalized individual brokers, who had primitive order-processing systems.

The BSE was located in Bombay. The primitive state of telecommunications in India, coupled with the use of floor-based trading, greatly limited market access to investors outside Bombay. It also generated inferior liquidity for the market as a whole, by failing to harness the order flow from outside Bombay.

This situation was transformed by the arrival of the new National Stock Exchange (NSE) in 1994. The NSE was owned by a consortium of government-owned financial institutions. The NSE built an electronic order-matching system, where computers matched orders without human intervention. It used satellite communications to make this trading system accessible from locations all over the country. The NSE used a new organizational structure, where the exchange is a limited liability firm with brokerage firms as franchisees. Hence there was no incentive to restrict membership, and the NSE freely admitted new brokerage firms, including corporate and foreign brokerage firms.

TABLE 4.1
Major Events in Indian Equity Markets

Date	Event
1876	Birth of Bombay Stock Exchange (BSE).
27 June 1969	Notification issued by government under SC(R)A prohibiting forward or futures trading.
January 1983	Regulatory permissions obtained for *badla* trading, a mechanism to carry forward positions.
2 January 1986	Computation of BSE "sensitive" index commenced.
12 April 1988	SEBI created.
1992	Fixed income and equity markets scandal.
30 June 1994	Start of electronic debt trading at National Stock Exchange (NSE).
3 November 1994	Start of electronic equity trading at NSE.
13 December 1994	Ban on *badla*.
25 January 1995	SC(R)A amended to lift the ban on options trading.
14 March 1995	Start of electronic trading on a few stocks at BSE.
3 July 1995	Electronic trading of all stocks on BSE.
5 October 1995	Ban on *badla* reversed.
April 1996	National Securities Clearing Corporation (NSCC) commenced operations.
8 November 1996	National Securities Depository Ltd (NSDL) commenced operations.
1999	Securities law modified to enable derivatives trading.
12 June 2000	Start of equity index futures trading.
4 June 2001	Start of equity index options trading.
2 July 2001	Major stocks moved to rolling settlement; start of stock options market.

Trading in equities commenced at the NSE in November 1994. From October 1995 onward (11 months after commencement), the NSE has been India's largest exchange. There are few other parallels to this episode internationally, where a second exchange displaced the entrenched liquidity on an existing market within a year (Shah and Thomas 2000).

The competition between the NSE and the BSE is a unique one by international standards, where both exchanges are in the same city and have the same trading hours. All major stocks trade on both exchanges, so the exchanges compete for *order flow* and not just listings. The rise of the NSE has proved to be a powerful spur to reforms at the BSE. Months after the NSE started operations, the BSE also launched electronic trading and improved rules governing admission of corporate and foreign brokerage firms. Today, the BSE also uses an open, electronic, limited-order book market, using satellite communications to reach locations outside Bombay.

2.2 Risk Management of Counterparty Credit Risk

Electronic trading plays a role in reducing the search cost associated with finding a counterparty. Once a trade is agreed upon, and until a trade is settled, there are significant risks of malfunction. When two economic agents L and S agree on a transaction on an exchange, each could be exposed to the risk that the other will default. The extent to which a securities market is vulnerable to this "counterparty credit risk" is important for two reasons:

1. When economic agents are exposed to the risk that transactions might fail because the counterparty defaults, it raises the cost of transacting. One response that commonly comes about is for economic agents to retreat to transacting only within small clubs. This is harmful insofar as it impedes market liquidity and broad-based market access.
2. If the failure of *L* affects the failure of *S*, it offers a mechanism through which the failure of one economic agent imposes an externality upon counterparties. These externalities are a mechanism for "contagion," and it is possible to have a failure by some important entities leading to a systemic crisis. Hence, a key goal for designers of securities settlement systems is to ensure that when individual economic agents fail, there are no externalities imposed upon counterparties.

The extent of counterparty credit risk is determined by two factors: (a) the extent to which positions are leveraged, and (b) the time horizon over which price volatility impacts upon the position. Leveraged positions are more vulnerable to failure, and price fluctuations over longer periods can generate larger losses.

Both these aspects are strongly influenced by the method through which securities trading is organized, of which there are two: account-period settlement or rolling settlement.

Account-Period Settlement

Under account-period settlement, trading takes place for the "account period" (which could be a week or a fortnight). Trades are netted through the account period, and the net outstanding position at the end of the settlement period goes to settlement a few days later. Account-period settlement is exactly like a futures market, where positions are netted until expiration date, and only open positions as of expiration date go on to settlement. For this reason, account-period settlement is also called "futures-style settlement." Many ideas and principles that normally apply for futures markets are quite applicable to a *spot* market that uses futures-style settlement.[1] With account-period settlement, as with futures markets, positions are *leveraged,* insofar as the capital required in order to adopt a given position is a small fraction of the position size.

Rolling Settlement

Rolling settlement is the same as account-period settlement where the netting period is shrunk to one day. With rolling settlement, trades are netted through the day, and all open positions at the end of the day are settled *n* days later. This is called T + *n* rolling settlement, to denote settlement *n* days after T, the day of the trade.

Rolling settlement is attractive because on the settlement date all open positions are settled. This is in contrast with futures-style settlement, where large leveraged positions can be present and do not normally unwind. Systemic risk is reduced when the delay between trade date and settlement date is small, and rolling settlement with a small *n* is the vehicle through which this delay can be brought down to values like five working days and less. The minimum international recommendations of the Group of 30 and IOSCO have argued in favor of T + 3 rolling settlement, and many countries are now in the process of moving to T + 1.

India adopted account-period settlement as part of the inheritance of equity market design from England.[2] The extent of leverage associated with spot market trading on the Bombay Stock Exchange (BSE) was exacerbated by a peculiar mechanism, called *badla*. *Badla* allows deferment of settlement obligations into the next settlement period.[3] With *badla*, the market was like a futures market without a stated expiration date. Since settlement could be deferred indefinitely, the counterparty risk was commensurately larger (as described above). Therefore, with *badla*, it became even more important to have strong risk containment practices in place. Unfortunately the exchanges were largely deficient in these practices. The difficulties with *badla* were further exacerbated by a lack of enforcement capacity at the SEBI.

These considerations led the securities regulator, the SEBI, to ban *badla* in 1993. However, the political economy forced a reintroduction of *badla* in weak form in 1995 and a further weakening of prudential regulation in 1997.

On traditional exchanges, brokerage firms were bound by family and ethnic ties. These ties were exploited in reacting to systemic crises. When the NSE admitted new brokerage firms into equity trading, in the absence of bonds based on ethnicity or kinship, the problem of counterparty risk was present with a greater intensity. This motivated the NSE to create a new credit enhancement institution, which performed the function of a futures clearing corporation, called the National Securities Clearing Corporation (NSCC). As with all futures clearinghouses, the NSCC performs novation; the NSCC is the legal counterparty to the net settlement obligations of all brokerage firms This blocks the externalities associated with defaults: the failure of one leg of a transaction does not affect the other leg. The NSCC protects itself using a risk-containment system, which is a combination of online real-time risk monitoring, an initial margin, and the daily mark-to-market margin.

The NSCC has been successfully performing novation since June 1996, through periods containing some of the highest market volatility in Indian history. The NSCC is justly criticized for being overly conservative in margin calculations, but it has produced an unprecedented reliability in the operation of market processes.

Apart from the NSE, none of the other securities exchanges in India made progress in the establishment of a central counterparty. This failure of institution building on the part of the exchanges is also, in part, a failure of the SEBI, which supported exchanges in using inferior risk-management mechanisms called "trade guarantee funds." The limitations of these inferior mechanisms were exposed in the payments problems, which were experienced at the Bombay and Calcutta exchanges at several points in recent years, most notably in 2001.

2.3 Electronic Settlement

In the early 1990s, the use of physical share certificates in India was the cause of elevated back-office costs, a high incidence of failed trades, and vulnerabilities associated with large-scale theft and counterfeiting of shares.

This situation changed with the commencement of the National Securities Depository Limited (NSDL), a depository based on dematerialization. The NSDL was created by two major domestic financial institutions and the NSE. The NSDL commenced functioning in 1996, and within five years roughly 99 percent of equity settlement in India was done through the NSDL. With the depository, back-office costs, the incidence of failed trades, and issues like theft or counterfeiting all dropped to near-zero levels. This was an important success of institution building in the financial sector.

3. *Vulnerability to Crises*

Despite all the changes in the equity market, there have been some spectacular cases of fraud and market manipulation on the securities markets in the 1990s. In the decade of the 1990s, the equity market suffered from a series of crises, major and minor. The most important of these were the four crises of 1995, 1997, 1998, and 2001:

- In 1995, the Bombay Stock Exchange closed for three days in the context of payments problems on M. S. Shoes.[4]
- In 1997, there was a scandal where CRB Mutual Fund defrauded its investors, which cast doubts upon the supervisory and enforcement capacity of the SEBI and RBI.[5]
- In summer 1998, there was an episode of market manipulation involving three stocks (BPL, Sterlite, Videocon). In this case, a variety of questionable methods were employed at the BSE to avoid a failure of settlements. The actions partly led to the dismissal of the BSE president by the SEBI.

- Finally, the most recent crisis, in March 2001, led to a second dismissal of a BSE president, the dismissal of all elected directors on the Bombay Stock Exchange and the Calcutta Stock Exchange, and payments failures on the Calcutta Stock Exchange (Thomas 2001).

Each of these crises hit the front pages of newspapers and distorted stock prices and liquidity. The crises had significant negative ramifications for economic agents directly involved in them. This steady stream of crises may have helped preserve the traditional image of securities markets as dangerous investment avenues for uninformed investors, and thus helped elevate risk premiums demanded by households.

By 2001, the most important concern among policy makers was this vulnerability to crises. In order to accurately address this concern, we need a clear diagnosis identifying the elements of market design that generate this vulnerability to crisis. Unfortunately, a parsimonious explanation that captures the essence of *all* the crises on the securities markets in the decade of the 1990s does not exist. The crises range over a diverse set of issues, ranging from regulations of the primary market to supervision of mutual funds.

However, it appears that leveraged market manipulation may have played an important role in numerous crises. In particular, it appears to have played a significant role in the most important four crises listed above. In each of these crises, investigations have revealed manipulative cartels that appear to have built up large leveraged positions on the secondary market. A detailed examination of these crises reveals many situations where the administrators of the securities exchanges failed to enforce stated rules, or explicitly violated rules. These lapses played a crucial role in generating these crises. Thus, it appears that the limited institutional capacity at the exchanges was unable to obtain a sound functioning under conditions where the spot market featured highly leveraged positions.

After each of these crises, the question of moving away from futures-style settlement and *badla* toward rolling settlement was debated in India. However, the political economy of this question was dominated by the interests of incumbent financial intermediaries, and the SEBI chose to leave the basic structure of the market intact. Indeed the constituency opposed to reforms was so effective that from 1995 to 1997 the reforms were rolled back even as important new crises unfolded on the market: after the M. S. Shoes crisis in 1995, the SEBI reversed the ban on *badla*, and after the CRB scandal of 1997, the SEBI substantially weakened the prudential regulation of *badla*.

Derivatives trading was widely seen in India as an alternative vehicle for obtaining leveraged positions, and hence seen as a threat to the traditional technology of leveraged positions adopted on the spot market with *badla*. In response to these concerns, the SEBI took five years to get from the first proposals for exchange-traded index futures trading to the onset of index futures trading, which took place in June 2000.

4. Policy Responses in 2001

The crisis of 2001 proved to be extremely prominent in the public eye. The revelation of a wide variety of malpractices by securities exchanges, listed firms, and institutional investors in this episode helped to undermine the effectiveness of conservative voices. An extremely important set of reforms came about in June 2001:

- *A spot market without leveraged positions.* Trading in all major stocks moved to rolling settlement in July 2001. It was also decided that trading in all stocks would move to rolling settlement in January 2002. All variants of *badla* ceased to exist in July 2001.
- *Derivatives trading* in stock index futures had commenced in June 2000. In June 2001, the universe of derivatives where trading was permitted was expanded to include index options. Options on individuals stocks started trading for 31 companies in July 2001.

The transition into these new regimes was smooth, in the sense that these new market mechanisms had reached high levels of liquidity within a few weeks after they were put into place. Empirical evidence about market efficiency and vulnerability to crises under this new regime is not yet available.

5. Policy Issues

In this section, we focus on the key policy issues that now confront the securities markets. We deal with the payments system (Section 5.1), the prudential regulation of banks in connection with loans backed by securities as collateral (Section 5.2), and questions of governance and policy formulation (Section 5.3).

5.1 The Payments System

The securities industry is an intensive and performance-sensitive user of the payments system. This takes place at two levels: movement of funds between securities firms and the clearing corporation (which utilize the wholesale payments system) and movement of funds between individuals and securities firms (which utilize the retail payments system).

In India, both these systems suffer from severe deficiencies, which inhibit settlement procedures that seek to achieve short-time intervals between the trade date and the settlement date. In particular, the lack of real-time interbank funds transfer and of access for the clearing corporation to the central payments systems has had a crippling effect upon equity settlement procedures.

The minimum international standard for the equity market as of 1989 was considered to be T + 3 rolling settlement. In 2001, India was at T + 5 settlement. This gap is exclusively caused by the inferior payments infrastructure in the country. Roughly speaking, this may imply that the payments infrastructure in India is at least 12 years behind international standards.

The RBI has thus far been the systems operator with regard to the payments system. While the RBI has tried to obtain improvements in the payments system for many years, the existing prognosis for improvements in this regard is not promising.

In recent years, a small set of roughly 10 banks has pioneered high-quality technology, which makes it possible for them to move funds at high speed across locations in India. The defining feature that characterizes these banks is internal technology infrastructure, which connects up all branches and ATMs in a computer network, with a single *national* database of client accounts.[6] This implies that these banks exhibit an interface to the user where there is a single bank account, regardless of geographical location. For these banks, clear funds in a bank account are instantly usable at any location in the country. Hence, these banks have come to play a prominent role in settlement-related functions on the equity market.

It may be possible to obtain significant progress on the payments infrastructure associated with the securities markets by exploiting these banks. We can think of dividing all banks in India into two groups: "Class A banks," which have the above infrastructure, and "Class B banks," which do not. A small electronic payments system could be rapidly established between all the Class A banks.[7] This would not be a comprehensive nationwide electronic funds transfer system; however, it would be a major advance compared with the existing situation. The RBI would have to extend limited support to such an effort in order to ensure that interbank clearing takes place in central bank funds, thus eliminating the risk of possible failure of any of these banks.

In such a scheme, every securities firm in the country would have to use one of the Class A banks for the purpose of clearing and settlement functions. This is not a constraint, since every securities firm is already doing so.

5.2 Loans Against Securities

The second major aspect where there is an interplay between banking and securities lies in bank loans that are backed by securities as collateral. There are two ways in which this can be motivated: from the perspective of access to limited leverage on the spot market (Section 5.2.1) and from the perspective of credit-risk management by the bank (Section 5.2.2). We evaluate the RBI's policy position (Section 5.2.3) from these two perspectives.

5.2.1 The Role for "Margin" Trading on the Spot Market

With rolling settlement, leveraged positions are limited to intraday positions as far as the core securities market infrastructure is concerned. Outside India, economic agents obtain multiday leveraged positions in a world with rolling settlement, using a mechanism called "margin trading." Margin trading may be summarized as follows:

1. The buyer puts up 40 percent of the funds.
2. The moneylender brings in 60 percent.
3. Shares are purchased, and immediately pledged to the lender of the funds, through the depository.
4. "Marking to market" is done frequently, to collect all losses made on the position, and to ensure that the funds put up by the buyer do not drop below 40 percent.

Margin trading is a relationship between a financier (e.g., a bank) and the customer. A key feature of margin trading is that the cash market remains a cash market—all open positions turn into delivery and payment from the viewpoint of the clearing corporation.[8] Through margin trading, leveraged positions become available without generating credit risk for the lender, though they involve a lot less leverage than is presently observed with futures-style settlement, with or without *badla*.

5.2.2 Risk Management for Loans Against Securities

The major concern faced by policy makers in the area of banking is the poor success of Indian banks in dealing with credit risk. The "nonperforming assets" of Indian banks are large in absolute terms, and particularly when compared with the equity capital available for financing them.

Most bank loans in India utilize physical assets, such as commodities, land, or machinery, as collateral. These assets are termed "opaque collateral" owing to the difficulties faced in observing prices (required for marking to market of collateral value) and in selling off the assets given the lack of a transparent, liquid secondary market. The difficulties with credit-risk management that Indian banks have faced suggest that their risk-management systems are unable to ensure collateral adequacy, and are unable to liquidate collateral when the borrower is delinquent.

In this context, loans using securities as collateral are an important avenue through which banks can extend loans in greater safety. The key difference here lies in the fact that securities are "transparent collateral"—the secondary market provides prices that can be used for marking to market of collateral value, and the secondary market supports swift liquidation of collateral. There are three issues here:

1. *Continuous valuation*. The securities market provides a continuous valuation of these shares, which can be used for daily marking to market of collateral. Once systems for revaluing collateral daily are in place, the focus of risk management becomes the one-day drop in collateral value.

   This is unlike real estate, plant and machinery, and so on where a lack of transparent prices prevents marking to market.
2. *Calculation of collateral requirements*. Securities prices and liquidity have been well understood by the research community, to a point where a fair degree of knowledge is available for computing value at risk (Jorion 2000; Thomas and Shah 1999) on a one-day horizon, integrating price risk and liquidity risk. This is unlike collateral in the form of real estate, plant and machinery, and so on where the models for measuring price risk and liquidity risk are lacking.
3. *Liquidation of collateral*. When the collateral is deemed inadequate to back a given loan, a bank would send out a request for additional capital. If the borrower does not comply, the bank can harness the liquidity of the stock market and liquidate collateral within minutes. This harnesses the liquidity of the exchange. This is unlike collateral in the form of real estate, plant and machinery, and so on where liquidation takes weeks or months, which (in turn) generates liquidity risk and price risk.

A modern bank would have processes for these steps (valuation, risk assessment, and collateral liquidation) functioning through an IT system, which would produce reliable and highly automated operations.[9] This is in sharp contrast with the human frailties that afflict the typical bank loan.

In summary, the traditional wisdom in India about the need to constrain loans against securities is inconsistent with the realities of risk management.

This discussion has been phrased in terms of the role for *securities* in banking. These arguments are essentially unaffected by the identity of these securities. The essential feature is trading in public marketplaces, with liquidity and transparency. Once this is present, the publicly visible price makes marking to market possible, and reliable liquidation procedures can be put into place. Neither of these can be done with opaque assets.

Once liquidity and transparency are found, the distinction between debt and equity instruments, or spot and derivative instruments, does impact upon the technical implementation of value-at-risk systems at banks. However it does not affect the character of prudential regulation. Hence, banking policy needs to have only one consistent policy framework that deals with all securities.

5.2.3 A Critique of the RBI's Policy Position

The reasoning presented above is quite unlike the traditional stance of policy makers in India. Traditionally, loans against shares were viewed as "unproductive" as compared with loans that went into the real economy. In recent years, the fears of policy makers have been focused upon risk management, in the light of the volatility of share prices.

We analyze and critique the policy position as of May 2001 as one concrete example of one policy statement by the concerned regulators.[10] The details of policy positions do change from time to time; however, the basic policy stance of banking regulators has shared many elements of this position across more than a decade.

1. Policy statement: *The "exposure of a bank to the equity market" is defined as the sum of direct investments, loans against shares, loans to stock broking firms, and bank guarantees to stock broking firms. However, loans against shares where the borrower utilizes the loan for purposes unrelated to the stock market are excluded from this definition. The revised guidelines require that the exposure of a bank to the equity market is capped at 5 percent of the bank's total advances.*

   By our arguments, loans against equities should be backed by a sound risk-management system. The goal of prudential regulation should be to ensure that this risk-management system has the required technical attributes. If the risk-management system is sound, then a cap of 5 percent is irrelevant, and the extent to which a bank engages in loans against shares could easily be much larger. If the risk management system is weak, then even a level of 5 percent is insufficient protection.

   There *is* a role for prudential regulation in requiring minimum *capabilities* of the risk-management system. Once this is done, the extent to which banks choose to lend against shares is a legitimate *market outcome;* it should not be specified by regulators.

   By this same reasoning, the end use of funds does not affect the credit risk faced by the bank. The policy position that "loans against shares *for purposes unrelated to the stock market* are exempt from the 5 percent limit" is illogical. Since money is fungible, this position gives incentives to agents to disguise their utilization of loans.
2. The policy position: *Loans against shares should be over-collateralized by 40 percent.* Our arguments above suggest that the collateral required for a loan should reflect the frequency of marking to market, the delays in asset liquidation of the bank's risk-management system, the value at risk of the portfolio, and the mean and variance of asset liquidity. A flat rule requiring 40 percent ignores these nuances.

3. The policy position: *Banks are forbidden from engaging in arbitrage or lending to firms which do arbitrage.*

   Arbitrage consists of trading strategies that involve near-zero risk. For instance, a bank may choose to buy the index on the spot market and sell it off on the futures market when the cost of carry embedded in the index futures market is sufficiently attractive. On both sides, the bank would face the clearing corporation as a legal counterparty (through novation) and hence face near-zero credit risk.

   The above policy position forces banks to avoid deploying resources into this riskless activity and thus adopt higher risks through other forms of lending that involve higher credit risk.

4. The policy position: *Banks are required to do marking to market of collateral every week, but daily marking to market is recommended.*

   Given contemporary IT systems, it is a trivial matter for any bank to engage in daily marking to market of collateral. Every bank can, and should, have risk-management systems that do daily marking to market, issue margin calls, and automatically liquidate collateral when the collateral is inadequate. One-day risk is much smaller than one-week risk, and the marginal cost of moving from weekly to daily marking to market is zero, so daily marking to market yields improved risk management at zero cost. The RBI's requirement that marking to market be done weekly underexploits the possibilities from modern IT systems.

5.3 Governance and Policy Formulation

At a *technical* level, India's equity market fared very well in the decade of the 1990s. Starting from extremely primitive conditions, policy makers at the SEBI, the Finance Ministry, and the NSE were able to create complex, technology-intensive market infrastructure that transformed the mechanics of trading securities. This is a nontrivial achievement, and the outcomes could easily have been less encouraging. For example, the government bond market presents a striking contrast where a different set of policy choices, made at the RBI, yielded very little change in market mechanisms and liquidity over the same decade where the securities exchanges experienced revolutionary changes.

At the same time, the experiences of recent years throw up important concerns about governance and policy formulation. Given the successes that have been experienced in the technical questions of market design, the agenda for policy formulation in the future should involve a greater focus upon questions of enforcement, incentive-compatible institutional mechanisms, and political economy.

The basic character of political economy of policy formulation with securities markets is the same as that seen in most parts of economic policy making. Policy reforms yield diffused gains to economic agents in the economy at large. However, these same reforms yield focused losses to some groups of economic agents, who then have strong incentives to actively lobby against reforms.

From the viewpoint of market efficiency and costs of financial intermediation, financial markets function best when markets are transparent and competitive and financial products are commoditized. These are often the conditions under which the profit rates of financial intermediaries are lowest. Hence, the interests of financial intermediaries are often contrary to those of efficient financial systems. This reasoning helps explain numerous aspects of the competing political forces affecting financial sector reforms in India.

This perspective predicts that brokerage firms and mutual funds, which have much to gain or lose from alternative policies and market designs, will intensively expend efforts in lobbying with the SEBI. Similarly, on the government bond market, this perspective predicts that banks and primary dealers will expend efforts in lobbying with the RBI in favor of nontransparent market mechanisms, entry barriers in financial intermediation, and so on. Both these predictions prove to be broadly accurate.

5.3.1 SEBI

In its early years, the SEBI was remarkably distant from stockbrokers and formulated policies based on an independent vision about where India's capital markets should be headed. A reforms program that focuses on markets and not intermediaries is inevitably unkind to intermediaries. The early success of reforms in the stock market (in 1993 and 1994) led to a halving of the price of a BSE card, a reduction of Rs 20 million of the net worth of each BSE broker. Applied to the set of 600 member firms, this was a substantial loss of wealth of Rs 12 billion to the universe of BSE members.

From a political economy perspective, these early years of the SEBI were not an equilibrium, since the reform program was under attack from a constituency (market intermediaries) that had clear self-interest to engage in political actions. This is a sharp incentive for intermediaries to mobilize politically.

Hence, from this political economy perspective, it is not surprising to see that in recent years, the SEBI has been substantially co-opted into the interests of the brokerage community. The debates about *badla* are an interesting litmus test that highlight the extent to which the SEBI shared the worldview of brokerage firms. The SEBI was concerned about the consequences of *badla* from 1992 onward, and explicitly banned *badla* in 1993. However, from 1995 onward, the SEBI worked toward the resuscitation of *badla* and the easing of margin requirements and other restrictions upon it.

This suggests that while the SEBI may have started out as a reformist organization that took a detached view of securities markets, it seems to have been co-opted into sharing the worldview of intermediaries to a greater extent in recent years.

From a policy perspective, this suggests that special efforts should be undertaken so that the viewpoint of economic agents in the economy at large bear upon the decision making of the SEBI. This is difficult insofar as the specialized knowledge of the securities industry is normally found only among market practitioners. However, there *are* many avenues through which individuals and organizations, who have knowledge about securities markets but not these conflicts of interest, can be brought into the SEBI's decision making to a greater extent.

5.3.2 NSE

The decision at the NSE to use a "demutualized" structure was an important innovation. If the NSE had been owned by brokerage firms, it would have had greater incentives to maximize the profit rates of brokerage firms. Instead, the fact that large institutional investors owned the NSE helped ensure that the prime goal that the NSE worked toward was the reduction of transactions costs, even if it involved reduced profit rates for brokerage firms.

While the NSE has been an extremely successful organization, there are two important areas of concern when we visualize its functioning in the future:

1. *Capture.* The governance of the NSE suffers from important vulnerabilities that flow from its being a public sector organization. Now that the NSE is the most important securities exchange in the country, there is likely to be significant interest on the part of political actors to capture the NSE and derive rents from it. The constituency that benefits from a well-functioning securities exchange (households engaging in saving across the country) has too little at stake to engage in political actions that favor a soundly run NSE.
2. *Cost minimization and innovation.* It increasingly appears that the NSE faces little competitive pressure from other securities exchanges in India. Given the public sector ownership of the NSE, there is a real possibility that the NSE may be weak on cost minimization and innovation in the years to come.

Policy makers should be conscious of these two vulnerabilities about the NSE in the future. As with the SEBI, it is important to undertake special efforts to allow the diffused beneficiaries of sound securities markets to have a greater impact on decision making at the NSE.

In addition, *globalization* of India's financial sector is a powerful device that should be used to put competitive pressures upon the NSE. This can work in two directions:

1. *Indian products traded offshore.* As of today, Indian firms do list offshore, and index futures on the NSE-50 index do trade at Singapore. These offshore trading venues constitute some competition for NSE. For example, the transactions charges in NSE-50 futures trading at Singapore have been an important source of pressure for the NSE to lower charges for NSE-50 futures trading in India.
2. *Offshore products traded in India.* Conversely, international products traded at the NSE would also serve as competitive situations that could help governance and provide incentives for cost minimization at the NSE.

The extent to which the international financial system imposes competitive pressures upon the NSE today is quite limited. However, it can be substantially expanded in the future. This can play a valuable role in giving the NSE incentives in favor of innovation and cost minimization.

Notes

1. For example, Solnik (1990) documents the impact of the settlement date on the distribution of stock returns in Paris, where futures-style settlement is used on the equity spot market. This is reminiscent of the expiration-date effects that have been studied on futures markets.

2. Kyriacou and Mase (2000) and International Securities Consulting (2000) describe the impact of the move to rolling settlement in the United Kingdom in 1994.

3. The concept of *badla*, which was used to avoid settlement even at the end of a settlement period, was part of the transfer of securities exchange market design from England to India. It often went along with account-period settlement in Europe. For example, Williams and Barone (1991) describes the *riporti* mechanism in Milan, which is essentially like *badla*.

4. This crisis came about as a combination of weaknesses in regulations on the primary market and leveraged market manipulation on the secondary market.

5. This crisis was primarily about a failure of supervision of CRB Mutual Fund. However, it did have facets that involved leveraged market manipulation on the secondary market.

6. This is in contrast with traditional banks where information about clients is held at the level of the bank branch, and a person who holds an account at one bank branch cannot transact with any other branch of the bank.

7. Such an effort appears discriminatory in adversely affecting the revenues of Class B banks. However, any Class B bank could choose to improve its technological-logical capabilities and graduate to the status of the Class A bank. Hence, this proposal introduces no insurmountable entry barriers.

8. Margin trading is profoundly different from *badla* in many respects. With margin trading, we have an absence of netting *at the clearinghouse* between long and short posi-

tions. All longs who are unable to take delivery borrow funds (from moneylenders), and all shorts who lack securities borrow securities (from stocklenders). Distinct borrowing transactions take place at both legs, and both legs face positive interest rates. These features are all absent with *badla*.

9. These procedures require a high degree of market liquidity as a precondition. Hence, prudential regulation should exploit market impact cost in defining haircuts for a given portfolio of collateral.

10. This is the revised guideline governing "Bank Financing of Equities and Investments in Shares" released by the joint committee of the RBI and the SEBI on May 11, 2001.

References

International Securities Consulting. 2000. *Moving from account period settlement to rolling settlement.* Technical Report. Washington, D.C.: World Bank.

Jorion, P. 2000. *Value at risk: The benchmark for controlling market risk.* 2d ed. New York: McGraw-Hill.

Kyriacou, K., and B. Mase. 2000. Rolling settlement and market liquidity. *Applied Financial Economics* 32:1029–36.

Shah, A., and S. Thomas. 2000. David and Goliath: Displacing a primary market. *Journal of Global Financial Markets* 1 (1): 14–21.

Solnik, B. 1990. The distribution of daily stock returns and settlement procedures: The Paris Bourse. *Journal of Finance* 45 (5): 1601–9.

Thomas, S. 2001. *The anatomy of a stock market crisis: India's equity market in March 2001.* Technical Report. Mumbai: Indira Gandhi Institute of Development Research.

Thomas, S., and A. Shah. 1999. Risk and the Indian economy. Ch. 16 in *India development report, 1999–2000,* edited by K. S. Parikh. New Delhi: Oxford University Press.

Williams, J., and E. Barone. 1991. *Lending of money and shares through the riporti market of the Milan stock exchange.* Technical Report. Stanford, Calif.: Stanford University.

Comment
Some Issues on Securities Market Reforms

Ravi Narain

The securities market in India has seen considerable reform in the last five to seven years, aimed at making the market more efficient, fairer, and safer. The reforms in the securities market, for example, have far outstripped reforms in the banking sector. Yet, popular perception remains that not enough has been done in the securities market, and every market event, however small, gets magnified into a major issue. Part of the problem could well be that the market with its live stock-price tickers and volatile swings tends to attract more attention. However, part of the problem may also be due to inaccuracies in our definitions of the goals of public policy in this area.

Where Is Investor Protection Required?

Investors enter the market and invest in equities with a desire to earn a rate of return in excess of what they would typically receive from deposits or debt market instruments. Their choice of instrument, the timing and duration of their investment, and so on are driven by their perception of expected returns on the instruments. They understand that the risks in the equity market, for example, are different from those in the bank deposit or debt markets. They also understand that the risks from short-duration trading strategies (such as leveraged day trading) are different from those incurred when investing for a longer duration. The rational investor perceives that such strategies could yield high speculative returns but could equally well yield significant losses if one's assessment of the market proves to be wrong. We can make an argument that most such investors enter into such high-risk trading strategies with their eyes wide open.

Such trading strategies are clearly not advisable for every investor, and this certainly makes a strong case to expend greater resources toward educating those investors who may not fully understand these risks. It is difficult to make a case, however, that such investors need to be "protected" if they incur losses, or that in the absence of such protection they will not return to the stock market.

Investors certainly need to be assured that the market will throw up fair prices, that it is not prone to manipulation, that the settlement system functions reliably, and that investments are safe from broker defaults. I would argue that the possibility of short-term investors incurring losses in a volatile market should not by itself be a cause for concern for policy makers (just as there is no symmetric concern about the possibility that such investors could make profits when their investment decisions turn out right) unless the losses are a result of unfair prices, a manipulated market, or faulty securities market infrastructure.

The Settlement System

There is now reasonable experience in the securities market in India with the safety of settlements. Stringent risk-management systems (daily mark to market and other margins, and real-time exposure monitoring systems) and substantial settlement guarantee funds are now in place at the major exchanges. Modern financial economics has been brought to bear upon the computation of margins and exposure limits. This is done with regard to the past volatility behavior of stocks in such a manner that the margins are more than adequate to cover the one-day risk from having to close out the position of a broker facing financial difficulties. The risk measures are enforced through automated electronic systems, which leave a clear audit trail and are therefore difficult to abuse.

These systems ensure that broker defaults do not result in cascading risk from one broker to the next and that settlements are always completed. This is in contrast with the steady stream of "payments crises" that have marred the functioning of the equity market in the past. Moreover, customers of the defaulting brokers are compensated up to a limit of Rs 5 million per customer. This has brought considerable confidence to both investors and brokers participating in the market.

Crisis Management and Collateral Requirements

One issue of risk management that continues to trouble the market has to do with liquidity. The margins collected to ensure safety of settlements are based, in part, on the one-day risk of having to close out the open positions of a participant in financial distress. The assessment of such risk, in turn, is based on forecasts of volatility and liquidity.

There are two problems with this approach. First, existing models of risk management seem to fare poorly in episodes of market stress, where correlations between assets rise and market liquidity evaporates. Further, models that use recent information for forming value-at-risk estimates generally increase collateral requirements at a time of crisis. However, this is exactly the time that economic agents are overstretched and least able to bring forth additional capital. Prudential regulation based on value-at-risk models thus seems to generate a peculiar positive feedback where negative price shocks generate higher capital requirements, which generates fresh selling. This applies both for banks doing risk management for loans against securities, and for capital requirements at the clearing corporation.

These factors, in combination, seem to sharply reduce liquidity at times of market crisis, and perhaps require altogether different strategies for risk management when compared with rules that work in "normal times." It is important for policy makers to limit the extent to which prudential regulation hinders market liquidity in times of crisis. Ideally, we need to think of ways in which flexibility may be granted to relevant authorities, well ahead of an episode of market stress, to use alternate prudential norms and rules during the period of market stress.

Failure of Brokerage Firms Versus Failure of the Settlement System

It is important to make a distinction between a sound brokerage firm and a sound settlement system. A sound settlement system is one where the failure of one brokerage firm imposes no externalities upon other firms and cannot generate a systemic crisis. Once the institutional infrastructure for blocking this "contagion" is in place, the failure of one or more brokerage firms, while unfortunate, is a relatively less important event from a systemic point of view.

Yet, a perception lingers that broker defaults are bad and that a system that is unable to prevent these from occurring is weak. I would argue that this perception is incorrect and should not influence policy formulation. Indeed, a steady pace of entry and exit of brokerage firms would reflect a healthy, competitive brokerage industry. This is in contrast with many other sectors in India where there are significant barriers to exit. We can contrast the steady pace of exit among brokerage firms as opposed to the rigidities that afflict bank closure. The swift and clean fashion in which exit takes place today in the securities industry is an important source of efficiency and should be seen as a healthy feature.

Fairness of Prices

On market integrity (fairness of prices), the issue is quite complicated. Normally, the more liquid a security, the more difficult it is to manipulate the price of that security. Certainly, it would take far larger amounts of money to manipulate a highly liquid security than one that is fairly illiquid. Yet, certain events at times have left the market with the perception that it is precisely these securities (and some of them have witnessed enormous liquidity even by international standards, with thousands of trades emanating each day from all over the country) that were manipulated.

Part of this problem lies in the word "manipulation," which has incorrectly become a catchall for a variety of ills. We require careful thought in accurately defining the word "manipulation" and in applying a taxonomy for the other ills.

Of those ills, it is possible for us to be relatively precise in defining insider trading and front running. If we define manipulation in terms of collusive activity by a "small" group of market participants to rig the market up or down, then it is hard to apply this term to market activity (the so-called collusive activity) that involves thousands of investors trading in the same direction. This is not to argue that manipulation cannot and does not take place in this manner. However, under such conditions, it is hard to differentiate manipulative activities from the normal processes of speculative markets. To the extent that manipulation is indeed taking place under such an environment, it is certainly hard to detect.

The fact that the Indian market has multiple exchanges, with common brokers trading in common securities, further compounds the problem. The transactions emanating from these brokers are settled in a weekly cycle that differs across exchanges. The net result is that brokers and their customers routinely shift their positions from one exchange to the other in continual search of small arbitrageable opportunities or to avoid settlement. Given the "background noise" of a large number of such transactions, an investigative agency finds it quite difficult to separate genuine market activity from possible attempts at market manipulation.

The Gap in Disclosure

The area of corporate governance may actually hold the key to issues of insider trading and front running. Listed firms are required to provide investors with symmetric and continual disclosure of material events that are price sensitive. Decisions on selling a division or merging with another company are examples of such price-sensitive events. While many companies in India take this responsibility quite seriously, many others do not as yet have a strong reputation for corporate governance.

There is now a reasonable sense about the events that require a company to disclose information to the market. However, there is considerably less clarity on the timing of this disclosure. If information is released "too early," and the decision finally does not go through, the company could face charges of misleading the market. If the information is released "too late," the market invariably gets wind of the proposed events and charges of insider trading fly thick and fast. There are no definitive answers to this problem. However, industry forums will need to sit down with the exchanges and the regulators to develop some rules of thumb that could be used to guide disclosure policies of companies.

The second essential instrumentality to check insider trading and front running is, of course, the need to have a unique identifier for every investor that must form part of the information supplied to the trading system at the time of each trade. Improvements in computer technology now make this quite possible. Recently, regulators have announced that a unique ID number should be provided; however, the rules allow a choice between several such IDs (such as the income tax PAN number, the passport number, or the driver's license number). It would be helpful to have one unique mandatory ID, and expectations are that this should happen soon.

Difficulties with the Payments System

A brief reference was made earlier to the pace in reforms on the securities market outstripping the pace of reforms in the banking sector. A key area where the banking sector impinges on the securities market is the payments system. Until recently, few banks in India could boast of an electronic payments system to transfer funds electronically across their own branches. This significantly increased the risk faced by the exchanges in monitoring the swift collection of margins and funds for settlement.

The newer banks of India made a remarkable difference to this problem by setting up electronic funds transfer mechanisms that worked across all their branches. The NSE's clearing corporation began to appoint such banks as clearing banks. Once this was done, funds from across the country could be transferred efficiently to the NSCC, as long as it was done through one of these clearing banks.

While this addressed a significant subset of the payments problems faced in equity settlement, the clearing corporation remained unable to move funds from one clearing bank to another, since this is only done through physical checks that are written on the central bank. The reduction of systemic risk in the securities market (to achieve the international standard of "delivery versus payment"), as also some amount of product innovation, is now critically dependent upon the central bank pushing through an electronic funds transfer arrangement for the entire banking sector. In the interim, the securities market would be greatly assisted if clearing banks could obtain a dedicated electronic fund clearing cycle in the central bank for the purpose of secondary market settlement. This could be a first, rapidly implementable phase of the central bank's real-time gross settlement (RTGS) system project.

Loans Against Shares

Securities markets the world over offer leveraged trading in the form of access to borrowed funds or securities. Historically, banks in India have avoided loans backed by securities as collateral. This is partly based on a historical perception that such loans were somehow "unproductive." In addition, it was also driven by weaknesses in the real-time risk-management systems that are required as part of prudential regulation of loans against securities.

Given the starvation of loans from the formal financial system, the securities market has harnessed loans from the "informal," unregulated financial sector. This has had significant ramifications for the economy in terms of the lack of an audit trail for investigations, the mechanisms used by participating economic agents for contract enforcement, the incidence of a parallel economy, and so on.

One could easily argue that further growth of the securities market is dependent on the banking sector interfacing more closely with the securities market. Interestingly, this could also help the banking sector as banks' traditional sources of business (asset-based lending, etc.) come under pressure from falling margins and rising non-performing assets (NPAs). In fact, some of the newer private sector banks have begun to aggressively pursue business emanating from the securities market. If the success stories seen with a greater embrace of securities markets on the part of a few banks have to be scaled up across the banking system, it will require many changes. Perceptions and policies on the part of regulators and boards of banks will need to be thought afresh. The process engineering and human capital at banks, in the area of real-time risk management, will also need a major overhaul.

One hurdle to be faced with this kind of argument is the perception that banks, to some extent or the other, have been a part of many securities market frauds. However, this is an enforcement problem and should not really detract from the merits or otherwise of this proposition. In fact, all too often weaknesses in enforcement have influenced policy making without tackling the fundamental problem of weak enforcement. Today, judicious use of technology allows us to look afresh at problems of enforcement.

The International Dimension

Finally, the policy framework under which the securities market operates needs a review from the perspective of international competition. Historically, the Indian market has worried little about international competition due to foreign exchange restrictions. However, this is bound to become a more serious issue as the country moves closer to convertibility. The securities market policy framework, therefore, needs to take this into account and worry about the kind of structure that would position the securities industry to better withstand international competition. Undercapitalized intermediaries with a marked reluctance to invest in technology or multiple exchanges are some examples. Policies, in this context, that discourage consolidation, whether of market intermediaries or of exchanges, could be reviewed to encourage and accommodate efforts at consolidation.

Comment
Policy Issues in the Indian Equity Market

Raghuram G. Rajan

The authors start by documenting the various scandals that have recently hit the Indian stock market. They then ask why the market has been prone to scandals (though the authors do not say whether the frequency of such scandals is particularly high compared with the frequency in markets in countries at India's stage of development). Assuming, however, that scandals in the Indian stock market are overly frequent, the authors seem to suggest that archaic market design may be responsible. What I found especially illuminating was the authors' discussion of recent policy changes announced by the SEBI and the RBI. An important source of the problems, it seems to me, lies in the nature of regulation in India. It is on this aspect, which is hinted at but not fully discussed by the authors, that I will focus the bulk of my remarks.

Since there are a variety of different scandals ranging from corporate theft to theft at banks that are listed by the authors, let us take a specific scandal. I choose to focus on price rigging or market manipulation, and ask why the Indian market might be particularly prone to it.

Let me say at the outset that I do not believe that this has anything to do with the lack of liquidity in the markets. The authors show that liquidity (by their admittedly crude measures) seems to be comparable between the largest stocks on the NASDAQ and the BSE. Since many of the price-rigging accusations have focused on the manipulation of large capitalization stocks, lack of liquidity cannot be the source of the problem. Even theoretically, an illiquid stock may not be the best candidate for manipulation. Though its price moves substantially on a small amount of trade, it is hard for the manipulator to conceal his unusual trading activity. The less liquid a stock, the easier it is for other traders to divine who is manipulating it. Unless they are in cahoots with the manipulator, they should quickly make it unprofitable for the manipulator to rig (for instance, by selling heavily into his purchases).

The problem comes if everyone believes there is a sufficiently powerful cartel pushing the price of a stock. In that case, it may make sense for even honest traders to join the herd, hoping to get out before the bubble bursts. All the informed traders make money off the poor innocent individuals who are uninformed, or the public sector traders who are informed but corruptible. Manipulation is exacerbated, not by the lack of liquidity, but the lack of regulatory competence and backbone. If every serious market player knows someone is manipulating prices of particular stocks, surely the regulators should also know. Paraphrasing a famous quotation about the function of the Federal Reserve, the function of the stock market regulator is to take away the punchbowl just when the party for particular shares gets going.

There are two hurdles, however. First, the regulator has to have effective teeth to intervene. Second, the regulator has to have backbone. At least one of these seems to be missing in India.

Let us first distinguish effective teeth from rules. As the authors point out, the regulatory response in India to a new scandal often seems to be a new rule. Yet additional rules can be very counterproductive, more so if they are not enforced.

The reason, quite simply, is that when rules can be evaded, the unscrupulous figure out that the best way to do business is to ignore all rules, and to buy their way out in the remote eventuality that they are caught. By contrast, the honest businessman follows all rules, to the detriment of his business. Over time, the crooked have a comparative advantage, and are more successful. They will tend to survive in greater numbers, leading to a more corrupt business environment. Moreover, as my colleague Raaj Sah points out, when people see the substantial rewards to being crooked, and the low penalties of becoming so, the number of crooked people will increase. A vicious circle begins. Unenforceable, or unenforced, rules are indeed counterproductive!

The problem for stock market regulators is that there is no easy way to define market manipulation, and thus no easy way to write an enforceable rule. Suppose someone buys a stock in large quantities. Is he manipulating the price or simply buying on a hunch? Suppose someone sells in large quantities when a stock is being ramped up (and the SEBI did accuse some sellers during the recent Ketan Parekh scandal of manipulation). Are they getting out after manipulating the price, or are they getting out because they know the price is being rigged and want to escape before the inevitable collapse? Should they be condemned for their avarice or commended for their foresight? Unfortunately, no rule can be defined in such a manner as to be airtight and immune to legal challenge.

Because market manipulation is so difficult to prove, there is a great danger for the regulator in simply pointing fingers at a number of "usual suspects" and starting court proceedings against them. In general, the cases are unlikely to stick. More dangerous, if the cases are filed indiscriminately against the good and the bad, there is less and less stigma for a trader to have regulatory action taken against him. In fact, it becomes a badge of honor to join the elite who have been noticed by the regulator. Indiscriminate but ineffective action makes the regulator truly toothless.

So how does one proceed against a crime where everyone but the law recognizes the perpetrator? The regulator's strongest weapon is fear, fear that the transgressor will get caught, fear that he will be punished, and fear that he will lose business. The regulator has to cultivate this weapon by acting infrequently but with great effectiveness. The regulator cannot be seen to fail. This means the regulator has to constantly collect information, to lay traps for the crooked, and to use every means to punish them. The last statement is worth elaborating on. Michael Milken, the famous Drexel Burnham Lambert bond trader, was convicted of the technical transgression of "parking" securities even though he was suspected of far more. And the judge threw the book at him for that minor violation. It would do wonders for the Indian markets if regulators could get together and go after the major players in previous scandals, figuratively hanging them from the highest pole for all to see. Everyone knows who these players are. All it takes is the will to act. There must be some securities law they have violated, some tax they have not paid. It is not new rules India needs, but enforcement.

A common response to suggestions such as the one above is that the legal system is so tardy that no regulatory punishment can be meted out, at least in the lifetime of the prime accused. But this would suggest that regulators have recourse only to punishments through the law. Perhaps as effective, however, would be to deny transgressors the opportunity to conduct business, and to publicize widely the evidence on the basis of which this action is taken. For example, nothing requires the SEBI to allow everyone to trade. They could ban major manipulators from trading. Furthermore, if these manipulators try trading under various other fronts, regulators could proceed against those fronts too, making it harder and harder for the manipulator to do business. The regulator may face legal challenge, but this is where the tardiness of the judicial system helps rather than hinders.

Of course, in any such suggestions there is the danger that regulators will become a law of their own. Fortunately, however, there are limits to how much this can happen in a democracy. Regulators know their actions will be challenged as a matter of course in the legislature, especially because their targets are usually rich and well connected. Their only hope of making regulatory action stick is to have a record of unimpeachable integrity so that legislators are hesitant to interfere. This naturally makes the far-sighted regulator proceed carefully, and only against those who are widely known to have breached the law.

Some of this is being done, but the effects have been diluted. Well-known manipulators have been banned from trading but have managed to influence prices with impunity through a variety of indirect channels without being challenged. Some firms have been banned from issuing shares—it remains to be seen how long such a ban will last. The Vigilance Commission publicized the list of government officials who faced corruption charges, but the impact was diluted when it was shown that the list had not been adequately filtered. All these efforts are in the right direction, but much more is needed.

The far-sighted regulators will use not just the stick but also the carrot. They will create special privileges that are accessible only to those who are known to have abided by the rules. For example, they will allow only those investment houses that have an impeccable record to serve as specialists for the most liquid stock. They will include particular stocks in major indices (usually a boost to their liquidity) only if the promoters have a record of staying far from manipulation. The idea should be clear.

It thus seems to me that regulators can create their own teeth, and not just by promulgating new rules. Why, then, don't they? The answer that I increasingly lean to is that they do not have sufficient backbone to resist the pressures on them to treat manipulators lightly. For after all, there are strong interest groups, not just in India, who are happy to leave financial markets in their country underdeveloped. This is not, however, the place to develop that argument (see Rajan and Zingales 2001).

In summary, this is a very interesting essay. It asks the right questions. While it is appropriately cautious in addressing the question of why there have been so many regulatory failures, I have taken the liberty of speculating on the basis of the evidence in the essay.

Reference

Rajan, R., and L. Zingales. 2001. *The great reversals: The politics of financial development in the twentieth century.* Working Paper 8178. Cambridge, Mass.: National Bureau of Economic Research.

Comment
Political Economy of India's Fiscal and Financial Reform

John Echeverri-Gent

Although economic liberalization may involve curtailing state economic intervention, it does not diminish the state's importance in economic development. In addition to its crucial role in maintaining macroeconomic stability, the state continues to play a vital, if more subtle, role in creating incentives that shape economic activity. States create these incentives in a variety of ways, including their authorization of property rights and market microstructures, their creation of regulatory agencies, and the manner in which they structure fiscal federalism.

India has experienced two important changes that fundamentally have shaped the course of its economic reform. India's party system has been transformed from a single-party-dominant system into a distinctive form of coalitional politics where single-state parties play a pivotal role in making and breaking governments. At the same time economic liberalization has progressively curtailed central government *dirigisme* and increased the autonomy of market institutions, private sector actors, and state governments. These changes have shaped the politics of fiscal and financial sector reform. In particular, the details regarding changes in India's party system are important to how they have affected India's fiscal politics. Coalitional politics makes fiscal reform problematic but not impossible. The collective action problems presented by coalitional politics can be alleviated by mechanisms that coordinate different parties.[1] I will compare and contrast the efforts of the National Democratic Alliance government to implement fiscal reforms at the central and federal levels. I will then analyze the politics of reforming India's financial sector, giving special attention to the reforms of the capital market and the crisis in the spring of 2001. I conclude by pointing out the uneven progress of India's reforms, and I offer some preliminary explanations for the political causes of this unevenness.

India's Changing Party System

The decline of the Congress Party has left an increasingly fragmented party system in its wake. The number of parties contesting parliamentary elections averaged 42 from 1952 to 1989 and 165 from 1989 to 1999.[2] Parliament became more fragmented, as indicated by the number of "effective parties," which increased from an average of 2.1 for the period prior to 1989 to 5.0 from 1989 to 1999.[3]

The 1990s have seen an increase in political instability as a consequence of the fragmentation of parliamentary representation. The National Democratic Alliance (NDA) government that was formed in the fall of 1999 was the ninth government to rule India in the previous ten years. The challenge of cobbling together a coalition that would provide stability is dramatized by the formation of the NDA government. With Atul Bihari Vajpayee at the helm, the NDA government ascended to power with a 70-member cabinet, the largest in India's history. Its size was further increased during the following year.

Simply equating party system fragmentation with instability is misleading. Although the party system is as fragmented as ever, the Vajpayee government has good prospects for lasting its entire five-year term, as the party system becomes more bipolar. The NDA and Congress-led coalitions control an increasing number of parliamentary seats. Their share of the total has grown from 63 percent in 1996 to 78 percent in 1998 to 80 percent in 1999. BJP coalitions account for all of the increase, and their share has risen from less than 36 percent in 1996 to more than 55 percent in 1999. The share of parliamentary seats controlled by the Congress Party has marginally diminished from just less than 27 percent to 25 percent.

However, there have been other changes that affect coalitional politics and governmental stability. Party system fragmentation has been accompanied by the rise of single-state parties. These are political parties who win parliamentary elections in only one state. Single-state parties are either identified with a regional culture that does not transcend state boundaries, such as the Dravida Munnetra Kazhagam (DMK), or they are led by political leaders like Laloo Prasad Yadav, whose personal following forms the core of party support but does not transcend state boundaries. Parties controlled by regional leaders were usually formed when ambitious politicians defected from declining national parties like Congress. The share of seats in the Lok Sabha controlled by single-state parties has risen from a low of 7.2 percent in 1977 to 33 percent in 1999. At the same time the vote share of these parties increased from 13.1 percent to 35.6 percent.

The growing mobilization of India's lower castes has been an important factor in the rise of single-state parties. India is one of the world's rare democracies where the poor have higher voter participation rates than the wealthy. In the 1999 elections, voter turnout for members of scheduled castes and scheduled tribes were 2.2 percent and 0.4 percent above the national norm, respectively (Heath 1999). This process began with the mobilization of the "other backward classes" (OBCs). By the 1960s, single-state parties rode the support of the OBCs to power at the state level. As the process spread north from the southern state of Tamil Nadu, it bred defections from the Congress Party and led to the creation of new opposition parties.

The rise of single-state parties has contributed to the declining salience of national issues and the growing importance of state-level considerations in coalitional strategies. From 1971 to 1989 national parties framed their election campaigns in terms of national issues in order to mobilize the electorate and win national elections.[4] During this era the number of parliamentary seats and vote share of single-state parties reached their nadir, averaging 11.4 percent and 16.6 percent, respectively.[5] During the 1990s, state government performance became an important factor affecting national parliamentary outcomes. For instance, during the 1999 election, it is likely that poor performance by state governments run by the BJP and its NDA allies was more important in determining the outcome of parliamentary elections in Karnataka, Punjab, and Uttar Pradesh than national issues such as Kargil and Atal Bihari Vajpayee's attractive leadership qualities. In Andhra Pradesh, the good performance of the state government run by the Telegu Desam Party, an NDA ally, was crucial in determining the outcome.

The increasing importance of single-state parties has raised the national profile of state-level leaders and has important consequences for parliamentary coalitions. Under Indira Gandhi, state leaders served at the beck and call of national leaders even when, as in the case of Sanjay Gandhi, they held no elected office. During the 1990s, the support of state leaders was often crucial to making and breaking national governments. During the spring of 2001, the Trinamool Congress Party defected from the NDA because its leader, Mamata Banerjee, decided that it would provide advantages in the state-assembly elections in West Bengal. Conversely, the BJP has gained alliance partners whose support is essential to the NDA national government because parties such as the Telegu Desam are locked in state-level competition with rivals of the BJP at the national level.

The fragmentation of the national party system and the rise of single-state parties presents formidable challenges for economic reform. In the days of single-party dominance, the Congress Party served as a means for coordinating public policy across the ministries of the central government and between central and state governments.[6] This means of coordination is no longer available. National parties are often willing to sacrifice the interest of their units in particular states for the welfare of the party in the nation. Single-state parties have less incentive to sacrifice their state interests for the benefit of political constituencies in other parts of the nation. They often join national coalitions to gain control over ministries and influence over policies that provide them with resources to improve their position in their home state. For instance, until she left the NDA, Mamata Banerjee was notorious for using her position as railway minister to channel resources from the railways to her home state of West Bengal. These dynamics have important consequences for India's fiscal politics.

Fiscal Politics in India's Decentered Polity

In the era of coalition politics and the increased prominence of single-state parties, power and authority within India's polity have become "decentered."[7] The 1990s have seen a modest horizontal dispersion of power from the governmental cabinet to other central institutions such as the Supreme Court and the president (Rudolph and Rudolph forthcoming). Curtailing of industrial licensing and the relaxation of controls on foreign investment have greatly increased the mobility of private capital at a time when the share of private investment in gross domestic capital formation has increased from an average of 54 percent in the decade of the 1980s to 71 percent in 1997–98.[8] These changes have redistributed power among India's economic and political institutions in three ways. First, by increasing the mobility and autonomy of private industry, they have enhanced its power and influence over public policy. Second, in order to attract private investment and promote competition, the central government—sometimes in conjunction with the states—has created a new locus of authority through its establishment of independent regulatory agencies. Finally, the end of central government investment controls and the increasing mobility and importance of private investment have provided state governments with more autonomy and incentive to pursue their own developmental strategies. The changes in the party system and the decentering of India's polity create the need for new forms of coordination in order to maximize the effectiveness of Indian public policy.

Prime Minister Vajpayee initiated three important measures to improve strategic coordination and promote economic reform. In the wake of Finance Minister Yashwant Sinha's disappointing first budget announcement on June 1, 1998, Vajpayee shifted N. K. Singh from the Finance Ministry to the Prime Minister's Office (PMO). Singh, along with Brajesh Mishra, the high-profile prime secretary to the prime minister, has made the PMO an important force in advancing the government's economic reform program. Shortly after Singh's transfer, the PMO announced the formation of the Council on Trade and Industry, whose membership included 12 of the country's leading industrialists, and the Economic Advisory Council consisting of 10 high-powered, reform-minded economists. The two councils have contributed many of the ideas behind the Vajpayee government's economic reforms. Finally, the Vajpayee government has attempted to promote coordination within the cabinet by forming an estimated 35 "groups of ministers" on policy matters requiring cooperation between different ministries.

As many single-state parties join the NDA with the objective of securing more resources from the central government, the leaders of these parties are loath to see reductions in subsidies and the budgets of the central ministries that they control. Some of the most vociferous opposition to subsidy cuts has come from leaders of important coalition partners like Chandrababu Naidu, a single-state-party leader with a reputation for state-level reform. NDA partners such as Haryana's Om Prakash Chautala have succeeded in raising minimum support prices for food grains well beyond the recommendations of the Commission on Agricultural Costs and Prices and of the Ministry of Agriculture and Food, even while stocks of the Food Corporation of India rot away.

Privatization is an important element in the central government's strategy to reduce its fiscal deficit, but as is often the case, labor unions and opposition parties vehemently oppose privatization. After the NDA struck a deal to sell 51 percent of Bharat Aluminum Company Limited (Balco) to Sterlite Industries on March 2, 2001, 7,000 workers at Balco's production facility in Chattisgarh immediately went on strike to protest the sale and prevent the new management from operating the plant. The BJP's own labor federation, the Bharati Mazdoor Sangh (BMS), joined the strike, and BMS leader Dattopant Thengadi condemned the sale of Balco as "fraud committed by bureaucrats." Federalism can complicate matters when an opposition party rules a state. The Congress Party chief minister of Chattisgarh, Ajit Jogi, stoked the fire by charging that the NDA had grossly undervalued the Balco shares as the result of bribes to central government officials. Jogi offered that his state government would purchase Balco instead of Sterlite. The Supreme Court finally issued a decision that ended the two months of tumult by obliging a compromise that completed the ownership transfer.

More insidious opposition to privatization comes from political leaders supporting the ruling coalition. NDA ministers often oppose the privatization of public sector enterprises under their authority since it means losing control over capital, jobs, and prestige. The NDA created a Ministry of Disinvestment to advance the ambitious privatization objectives announced in each of its budgets. It has also convened the Cabinet Committee on Disinvestment to pressure reluctant ministers to acquiesce to privatization plans, but ministers still succeed in diverting privatization initiatives. For example, Shiv Sena leader Manohar Joshi has slowed efforts to privatize automobile manufacturer Maruti Udyog Ltd. NDA leaders at the state level also use their influence in the alliance in attempts to prevent privatization. Chief Minister Chandrababu Naidu has the reputation for promoting reform in Andhra Pradesh, but he single-handedly forced the government to postpone disinvestments of Rashtriya Ispat Nigam Ltd., a central-government-owned steel company based in his state. Similarly, M. Karunanidhi, as chief minister of Tamil Nadu, fought the privatization of Salem Steel.

The difficulties of securing the political cooperation necessary to reduce the fiscal deficit has led the NDA to attempt a strategy of debt reduction through the Fiscal Responsibility and Budget Management Bill. Introduced to Parliament in December 2000, this legislation would establish legally binding targets for the reduction of fiscal and revenue deficits. The central government would be required to eliminate its revenue deficit, now at 3.6 percent, by 2005–6. The legislation would require the central government to make proportionate reductions in disbursements should there be a revenue shortfall or an excess of expenditures over a stipulated level. The legislation has strong support from business associations such as the Confederation of Indian Industry and the Associated Chambers of Commerce and Industry of India. Nevertheless, the bill has been referred to the parliamentary standing committee for finance where strong resistance from the opposition has dimmed its prospects for passage (Manoj 2001).

Recent work on the politics of fiscal federalism argues that the increase in the influence of subnational politicians promotes the decentralization of control over fiscal resources.[9] In the last few years, the increasing power of single-state parties and their political leaders has seen the central government assert greater control over the finances of state governments by promoting reforms that make it easier for the center to monitor state finances and by setting up an incentive system that sanctions fiscal profligacy by state governments. Through its ability to direct additional revenues to state governments, the central government has also succeeded in promoting fiscal cooperation among the states in ways that promise to increase government revenues.

The state governments' fiscal problems are grounded in the manner in which India's system of federalism is designed. The central government controls the most buoyant revenue sources under Indian fiscal federalism, and two institutions redistribute central resources back to the states: the Planning Commission and the Finance Commission. The Planning Commission finances developmental projects proposed by state governments. The Planning Commission's assistance to the states is allocated on the basis of the "Gadgil formula," which accounts for the states' population, poverty, and revenue mobilization. The central government convenes a Finance Commission once every five years to redistribute tax revenues to the states. Until recently, they have taken a "gap-filling" approach that determines the distribution of funds to the states on the basis of the gap between their revenues and nonplan expenditures. The distribution of funding by the Planning Commission—along with the fact that the Reserve Bank of India has traditionally arranged for state governments to borrow at identical interest rates—has meant that that the cost of funding for development is unrelated to whether the funds are put to productive use. The "gap-filling" approach of the finance commissions creates incentives for the state governments to increase their nonplan expenditures without raising revenues.

It is within this institutional framework that populism came to dominate the terms of partisan competition at the state level. In their eagerness to win elections, populists made fiscally irresponsible campaign promises. State governments provided explicit and implicit subsidies amounting to an estimated 9.9 percent of GDP.[10] Most of these subsidies go to power, irrigation, transport, and higher education where user charges are low, collections are weak, and overstaffing and inefficiencies inflate costs. Particularly troubling is the power sector, where the losses of state electricity boards, responsible for the distribution of electricity, grew from 9.8 percent of state plan expenditure in 1992–93 to 18 percent in 1998–99. State subsidies encourage inefficiency, and they benefit the more affluent. Since state governments have been unwilling to improve their tax base, they have paid for these subsidies with growing fiscal deficits and reductions in spending on social and economic infrastructure.

The central government is not without responsibility for the states' fiscal problems. Efforts to bring fiscal discipline to the center have resulted in a decline in transfers to the states, which dropped from 4.8 percent of GDP in 1990–91 to 3.6 percent in 1998–99. The Planning Commission has routinely underestimated the support necessary to meet the demands on the states' revenue expenditures in the form of administrative costs and transfers that accompany the state plans. This, along with the costs imposed by centrally sponsored schemes, has contributed to the deterioration of the states' revenue accounts.

In view of the mounting fiscal problems of the states at the end of the 1990s, the central government began to take measures to alter the institutional incentives that shaped their finances. One of the first steps was taken in the spring of 1999, when the Ministry of Finance negotiated arrangements with a committee of the National Development Council. The Finance Ministry agreed to aid state governments under extraordinary fiscal stress in return for their signing a memorandum of understanding (MoU) that specified fiscal reforms creating greater discipline. Nine state governments eventually signed MoU's with the Finance Ministry.[11]

When the central government convened the Eleventh Finance Commission on July 3, 1998, it asked the commission to review state finances and suggest ways in which the states might restructure their finances to restore budgetary stability, as well as draw up a fiscal reforms program to reduce the revenue deficits of the states and recommend how implementation of a state's deficit-reduction program could be linked to the grants that the central government provided to cover the states' nonplan revenue deficits. The commission eventually did so in a supplemental report accepted at the end of 2000.

The supplementary report recommended reforms that begin to alter the institutional incentives of India's fiscal federalism. It urged that 15 percent of the revenue-deficit grants rewarded to 15 chronic revenue-deficit states be reallocated and combined with matching funds from the central government to create an "incentive fund" of Rs 106 billion to reward fiscal reform in all states. The objective was to eliminate all revenue deficits of state governments by 2004–5 and reduce the states' gross fiscal deficit to 2.5 percent of the GDP. In February 2001, the Ministry of Finance sent the states detailed guidelines about the incentive fund. It has also asked the states to make the reports on their finances more transparent and comparable with the financial positions of other states, and it set up the Expenditure Finance Commission to monitor the states' financial positions (Government of India 2001).

The central and state governments have achieved a remarkable degree of cooperation in resolving the collective-action problem of limiting tax concessions to lure investment and resolving the thorny issues involved in establishing a common value-added tax. Ever since November 1997 when the working group on state resources for the Ninth Five-Year Plan recommended a uniform floor on sales taxes for all states, the central government has taken steps to encourage states to cooperate in implementing a uniform sales-tax floor and ultimately moving to a VAT.

How has the central government achieved such progress in resolving state government fiscal problems when it has met with such strong resistance in advancing solutions at the level of the central government? No doubt, part of the answer is that India's fiscal federalism is more insulated from parliamentary politics than is central government fiscal policy. The central government may be more successful in promoting cooperation among state governments because it can grant them substantial rewards and impose substantial penalties. There is no comparable third party whose authority places it above the fray of fiscal politics at the central level. A final factor is that political leaders at different levels of government have disparate payoffs. This is especially true for leaders of single-state parties. Single-state party leaders join the central government largely to gain control over governmental resources that they can use to promote development and build political support in their state.[12] The interstate competition for private investment under market-preserving federalism creates incentives for state government leaders to pursue responsible fiscal policies in order to establish an attractive investment climate. Under these circumstances, central government intervention can be decisive in establishing a "race to the top" equilibrium instead of a "race to the bottom."[13]

Politics of Financial Reform

Economic reform has transformed India's equity markets more than any other sector of the economy. At the beginning of the 1990s, trading was conducted through an open outcry system that was monopolized by some 3000 brokers who closed membership to outsiders. Settlements were based on two-week account periods that were frequently extended to four or more weeks when brokers encountered financial problems. Registration of transactions was a time-consuming paper chase that was plagued by manipulation. Poor communications infrastructure fragmented the equity market into 23 regional exchanges. Public sector financial institutions dominated even the largest markets, especially the Unit Trust of India (UTI) a distinctive, public sector "mutual fund" (Joshi and Little 1996, 156; Government of India 1985, 10).

By the beginning of the new millennium, much had changed. All trading is conducted through an electronic order-book system matching orders according to time-price priority. The *dirigiste* Controller of Capital Issues was abolished, and the Securities and Exchange Board of India, the country's first independent regulatory agency, now regulated markets.

How did change come so rapidly to India's equity markets when it has been so slow in coming to other sectors of the Indian economy?[14] Finance Minister Manmohan Singh, who since the early 1980s had been eager to promote equity market development in order to enable private sector industry to meet its capital needs, now wanted to reform the markets to attract foreign investment.[15] At the same time, the volume of international resource flows was growing, the financial sector was experiencing rapid technological change, and the declining costs of informatics brought down the costs of cutting-edge securities market infrastructure.[16] Finally, international organizations have helped to promote standards for global best practices. The Financial Institution Reform and Expansion of the U.S. Agency for International Development was especially active in promoting the practices of American exchanges and regulation beginning in 1994. Paradoxically, the spread of these global norms for market-based practices empowered the Indian state to promote reform over the resistance of recalcitrant brokers by undermining their claim to a monopoly of knowledge about market practices (Echeverri-Gent 2000).

Financial globalization was not a sufficient condition for such rapid reform. Processes comparable to those shaping equity markets were also transforming banking. As the chapter by Hanson in this volume documents, progress has been more halting in the banking sector. Reforms have liberalized interest rates, enhanced competition, and improved capital adequacy, but the preponderant public sector banks have yet to experience a technological transformation comparable to that in the equities market, there remains a serious problem with non-performing assets, and the legal framework for recovering bad debt is in need of reform.

The Board for Industrial and Financial Reconstruction (BIFR) is an important element in the process of recovering non-performing loans to industrial companies. However, the priority it gives to the protection of the jobs of workers and proprietors from creditors makes debt recovery an inordinately time-consuming process that encourages proprietors to default on their financial responsibilities. Since 1993, the central government has convened three committees to reform the situation. The NDA convened the third committee headed by V. B. Eradi. Based on the committee's recommendations, the NDA has drawn up legislation that would repeal SICA and replace the BIFR with a National Companies Law Tribunal (NCLT), to be staffed by professional liquidators.

There is a growing consensus among central government officials, financial institutions, and business associations that the BIFR should itself be wound up,[17] but a political bottleneck remains. All trade unions have expressed vehement opposition to the proposed abolition of SICA. The vehemence of labor's opposition reflects its view that the repeal of SICA is part of a general attack on labor represented by the finance minister packaging the abolition of the BIFR with the reform of the Industrial Disputes Act to enable more firms to lay off workers.

Reforms of the capital market have not aroused formidable political opposition. The strongest opposition to important parliamentary legislation such as the Securities and Exchange Board Act of 1992 and the 1996 Depositories Act has come from the stockbrokers. However, they number only a few thousand, in large measure because until the mid-1990s they maintained rules that placed exclusionary restrictions on new membership.

To say that India's equity markets have undergone a dramatic transformation in the 1990s is not to say that they no longer suffer problems. The stock market crisis of the spring of 2001 demonstrates many of the remaining problems. The manner in which the government has subsequently responded highlights the political dynamics of the sector. The problems that contributed to the crisis fall into three issues: market microstructure, regulation, and moral hazard at Unit Trust of India, the public sector intermediary that is the biggest single intermediary in India's capital market.

In the spring of 2001, two elements of market microstructure combined to make Indian equity markets unique. Settlement was conducted through weekly account periods that were staggered across different days of the week on the country's 23 exchanges. Liquidity for speculation at the major exchanges for the 200 most actively traded stocks was provided by different versions of carry-forward finance that allow investors to carry forward their open positions from one settlement to another for up to 90 days. In combination, these features enabled intermediaries to assume positions that they could transfer from one exchange to another and across the settlements of a single exchange for long periods of time. In effect, they combined cash and futures markets, and they offered powerful leverage that might be used to manipulate market prices. Beginning in 1999, Ketan Parekh, through his 10 brokerages and network-associated brokers, used these facilities to speculate on and allegedly drive the boom in select information, communications, and entertainment stocks. His favorite scrips were widely referred to as the K-10 stocks. When the global decline in technology stocks put downward pressure on the K-10, Parekh attempted to maintain his positions. Ultimately, his efforts failed. Ten brokers who were part of Parekh's network defaulted after causing a payments crisis for three consecutive settlements in March 2001. Ketan Parekh, who became an object of multiple investigations, was arrested on charges of financial fraud on March 30.

The practices encouraged by the settlement and carry-forward features of market microstructure presented formidable demands on regulation of the stock exchanges. The March crisis reveals the areas where India's regulatory agencies were not up to the challenge. The first level of regulation occurs through the stock exchanges as self-regulatory organizations. Here, major flaws appeared at the CSE. As a center of trade in cash-based industries such as tea and jute, Calcutta has a large pool of floating cash available to finance the carry-forward system of the CSE. In fact, the brokers of the CSE are widely known to operate an "unofficial" carry-forward market as well as an official one. The brokers associated with Ketan Parekh increasingly resorted to the "unofficial market" to meet their obligations as they became more desperate to defend their positions. If the "unofficial market" was completely unregulated, the official CSE market was poorly regulated. The exchange did not collect margins or monitor exposures properly. Officials at the CSE admit the problem but pin the blame on flawed software ("CSE Crisis Unique" 2001). However, a history of lax regulation of margins and exposures at India's stock exchanges[18] along with the fact that the biggest defaulter, D. K. Singhania, was a prominent member of the CSE governing board, suggests that there was more going on than just faulty software, or that there were ulterior motives for using the flawed package for such an extended period.

Problems also appeared at the Bombay Stock Exchange (BSE) when Anand Rathi became the second consecutive president of the BSE to leave the post under a cloud of alleged improprieties. The controversy arose after a tape recording was made public of the BSE president calling the BSE surveillance department on March 2 to ascertain information on the outstanding positions of leading players in the market. Rathi—an active player through his five brokerage firms—allegedly leaked the price-sensitive information to other broker members of the BSE governing board who were sitting with him at the time of the call. In the wake of these charges, the Securities and Exchange Board of India (SEBI) forced all broker-members of the BSE governing board to resign.

The crisis incited strong criticism of the SEBI. The agency's earlier decision to permit the BSE to inaugurate a depository while the exchange management was under investigation for a 1998 scandal and the regulator's efforts to perpetuate carry-forward finance while delaying the introduction of rolling settlement left the impression that the SEBI was biased in favor of the brokers. The SEBI was criticized for tolerating the CSE's "unofficial" market and allowing its lax supervision of trading. The SEBI also neglected warning signs of market manipulation. Trading levels of K-10 stocks grew to extraordinarily high levels while deliveries remained at low levels, suggesting the possibility of circular trading. Leveraged trading on K-10 stocks to sustain long positions grew as prices steadily declined. Parekh's desperate search for finance to sustain his positions led to his illicit collusion with the management of Madhavpura Mercantile Cooperative Bank (MCCB). Together, they defrauded the bank of an estimated Rs 12 billion. They were exposed only after the MCCB was unable to make good on a pay order of Rs 1.4 billion that Parekh had presented to the Bank of India. The revelation embarrassed the Ministry of Finance and caused the minister of finance to face heavy criticism in Parliament. It was only after the SEBI felt intense pressure from the ministry that it took serious and, in some cases, misguided measures to investigate and rectify the situation.

The decline in the market that accompanied the Ketan Parekh scandal exacerbated long-standing problems in the Unit Trust of India's (UTI) flagship investment fund, US-64. The UTI was created by a 1963 act of parliament. It began US-64 the following year in order to mobilize investments throughout the country for India's capital markets. By the spring of 2001, US-64 was by far the country's largest fund, accounting for approximately 17 percent of all mutual fund assets. It attracted 4.5 million investors by offering high dividends and fixed redemption prices that held regardless of market fluctuations.[19] The decline in market prices during the first half of 2001 caused a growing gap between US-64's administered prices and its underlying value, and a stream of investors began to redeem their units. The situation deteriorated to the point where UTI Chairman P. S. Subramanyam suspended redemptions on July 2. His announcement caused furor that forced Subramanyam to resign two days later.

The causes underpinning US-64's problems were deeply rooted in its organization and relationship with the government. They were incisively analyzed by the Deepak Parekh Committee, which had been convened by the Ministry of Finance to recommend reforms as part of a bailout of Rs 33 billion in 1999.

The Parekh Committee recommended that US-64 be converted to net asset-value pricing within three years. It declared that management of US-64 should be transferred from the UTI to an asset management company. It urged that US-64's holdings be restructured to reduce its 70 percent holdings in equity to 40 percent, and it recommended that US-64 be brought under the supervision of the SEBI. More than two years after the bailout, the UTI had made virtually no progress on any of these recommendations. It missed the opportunity to easily convert to NAV (net asset-value) when the effective NAV of US-64 exceeded its administered price throughout most of the year 2000. US-64 continued to operate without the transparency associated with contemporary mutual funds. It lacked a clearly articulated investment strategy, and it informed the public about only 75 percent of its holdings. During the spring of 2001, the market was rife with rumors that the UTI had provided funds to bail out Ketan Parekh. On July 9, 2001, Finance Minister Yashwant Sinha announced that he was initiating an investigation of the UTI for insider trading.

The Ministry of Finance announced a series of reforms in the aftermath of the crisis. It was under tremendous political pressure, especially after a joint parliamentary committee (JPC) was formed to investigate the crisis. On March 13, the finance minister declared that he would introduce compulsory rolling settlement, strengthen the SEBI, and divorce brokers from exchange management by demutualizing the stock exchanges. On July 2, account-period settlement and carry-forward finance was terminated for the country's 200 most traded stocks, and rolling settlement was introduced with futures trading permitted on 31 scrips. The government announced on July 14 that it was ready to amend the SEBI Act to add four full-time members to the SEBI board, enhance the regulatory agency's investigative powers, and increase the penalties that it can levy. On July 15 the UTI initiated a plan to allow redemption at fixed prices until May 2003 for small investors holding less than 3000 units and to convert to NAV by January 2002 for new investors, while providing an option for current investors to switch to NAV prices.

Concluding Remarks

This examination of the political economy of reform in India's fiscal and financial sectors has highlighted the unevenness of the reform process. Our discussion of fiscal politics at the national level demonstrates how the fragmentation of the party system and the rise of single-state parties has impeded efforts to curb the central government's fiscal deficit. Remarkably, these changes in the party system have been less of an impediment to reforms of India's fiscal federalism. India's central government has achieved some surprising success in orchestrating the states' acceptance of incentives for greater fiscal discipline. It has also risen to the challenge of bringing about the coordination among the states necessary for establishing a value-added tax. While important changes have taken place in India's financial sector, reform has transformed India's equity markets more dramatically than its banking system. Strong resistance from labor has until now stifled efforts to reform India's bankruptcy policy for industrial corporations at least since 1993. At the same time, reforms have transformed India's equity markets in terms of its market microstructure and regulation.

India's political process is frequently lamented as a bottleneck to its reform process, especially with the fragmentation of the national party system.[20] However, there are pockets, such as equity markets, with substantial reforms. The unevenness of India's reforms suggests that it is useful to take a more nuanced view of the political process. An important explanation of unevenness may be that reform policies are more insulated from the parliamentary process in some sectors. Yet, in the relatively dynamic equity market sector, some of the most important changes, for example, the empowerment of the SEBI and the establishment of depositories, were accomplished through parliamentary legislation. The manner in which policies structure politics may be an important variable in the relative success of reforms. Policies that redistribute resources away from well-entrenched groups like organized labor will meet strong resistance until their opposition can be counterbalanced by other sources of support. Policies that redistribute resources from the leaders of single-state parties at the national level will require the coordination among the national political leadership to overcome the not-in-my-backyard mentality that often delays or stifles reforms. The reforms that have been implemented in India's fiscal federalism suggest that distributive policies that enable the central government to create incentives for reform by allocating resources in ways that reward reformers and penalize opponents may have more scope for success. Finally, the experience of India's equity markets suggests that developmental policies that make markets more efficient and equitable may be a politically viable path to reform. Economic reformers would do well to study how different policy types shape the incentives of political actors in their efforts to pilot reforms through the political process.

Notes

1. For more on strategic coordination and party systems, see Cox 1997.

2. All election data in this essay comes from Election Commission of India, *Statistical Report on General Elections*, for the general elections in 1999, 1998, 1996, and 1991. These documents are available on the Election Commission of India's Web site at http://www.eci.gov.in/. Data for elections prior to 1991 was collected from Butler, Lahiri, and Roy 1995.

3. The number of "effective parties" is now the standard measure of how concentrated legislative seats and vote shares are within a party system. It is the reciprocal of the Hirschman-Herfindahl index used in the industrial organization literature to measure how concentrated sales are in a given industry. If there are N parties in a parliament, and each party won an identical number of seats, the number of effective parties would be N. Different numbers of parties and different distributions of seats can arrive at the same number of effective parties. Formally the measure can be stated as $N = 1/\Sigma p_i^2$ where N is the number of effective parties by seats and p_i is the percentage share of seats won by party i. See Laakso and Taagepera 1979.

4. Indira Gandhi began this trend in 1971 with her "Garibi Hatao" (Remove Poverty) slogan. In 1977, the Janata Party removed Indira Gandhi after the authoritarian interlude that was the Emergency with its slogan "Janatantra Ya Tanashahi" (Democracy or Dictatorship). After the factional infighting of the Janata Party administration, Indira Gandhi returned to power with the slogan "Elect a government that works!" In 1984 it was the "sympathy wave" favoring the Congress after Indira Gandhi's assassination. Finally, in 1989, "Bofors"—referring to a deal between the national government and the Swedish arms manufacture in which close associates to Prime Minister Rajiv Gandhi were charged with taking kickbacks—was used to mobilize the anticorruption vote to oust the Congress Party.

5. Note that the periodization is slightly different from that for the development of coalition politics. I have altered it based on the inductive observation that "Bofors" was a national issue. If we stick to the previous periodization for the development of coalition politics, averages are as follows. The number of parliamentary seats and vote share won by single-state parties from 1971 to 1984 are 11 percent and 15.7 percent. The shares for 1989 to 1999 are 21.4 percent and 25.4 percent.

6. The early literature on the Congress Party stressed its integrative and coordinating functions. See Kothari 1964; Weiner 1967; and Kochanek 1968. Atul Kohli (1990) argues that power became so centralized under Rajiv Gandhi that it diminished the capacity of the Congress to coordinate political action.

7. For more on the decentering of India's political system, see Echeverri-Gent forthcoming.

8. Computed from Ministry of Finance, *Indian Economic Survey, 1999–2000*, Appendix: Statistical Tables, table 1.4, Gross Domestic Savings and Gross Domestic Capital Formation, as cited at http://www.nic.in/indiabudget/es99-2000/app1.5.pdf.

9. Garman, Haggard, and Willis 2001. The classic statement of this theory is Riker 1975.

10. The Ministry of Finance found that subsidies amounted to 14.4 percent of GDP in 1994–95. Nearly 69 percent of all subsidies come from state governments. See Lahiri, 2000, 1543.

11. Data in this paragraph is from Lahiri 2000, 1540–41.

12. Weingast 1995. For applications to India, see Parikh and Weingast 1997; Sinha 2000; and Saez 2000.

13. For an analysis of the race to the bottom versus the race to the top among India's states, see Rudolph and Rudolph 2001. I offer an extension of the Rudolphs' analysis that state governments may not view the new fiscal discipline as a burden because it is a way to defend their autonomy from local political pressures by contending that desire for autonomy is motivated by interstate competition for private investment.

14. Taiwan experienced extraordinary growth in value traded during the period. Its share of value traded in emerging markets jumped from 17.6 percent for 1980–82 to 76.8 percent in 1989–91. After removing this outlier from both time periods, India's share still declined from 23.8 percent to 10.3 percent.

15. Interview with Dr. Manmohan Singh, New Delhi, 20 July 1999.

16. Ajay Shah and Susan Thomas estimate that the costs of the core IT infrastructure necessary for an exchange, clearing corporation, and depository dropped from $100 million in the late 1980s to just $4 million by the end of the 1990s. (See Shah and Thomas 2001, 9.)

17. India's leading business associations, the CII and FICCI, have called for winding up the BIFR. The recommendations of the Andhyarujina Committee and the RBI Advisory Committee on Bankruptcy have also built support for reform of India's bankruptcy laws.

18. For official discussions of the lax regulation of margins and exposures, see Government of India 1995, 10; and Government of India 1985, 33.

19. It is widely stated in the press that US-64 has 20 million investors. In fact, it has 20 million unit holders, but since investors often own more than one account, the total investors number between 4 and 4.5 million.

20. For a valuable treatment that suggests that India's political process is more amenable to reforms than is commonly perceived, see Jenkins 1999.

References

Butler, David, Ashok Lahiri, and Prannoy Roy. 1995. *India decides: Elections 1952–1995*. 3d ed. New Delhi: Books & Things.

Cox, Gary W. 1997. *Making votes count*. Cambridge: Cambridge University Press.

CSE crisis unique. 2001. *Business Standard,* 11 July. Available at http://www.rediff.com/money/2001/jul/11cse.htm.

Echeverri-Gent, John. 2000. Economic governance regimes and the reform of India's stock exchanges. Paper presented at the International Political Science World Congress, 1–5 August, at Quebec City.

———. Forthcoming. Politics in India's decentered polity. In *India briefing 2002*, edited by Philip Oldenburg and Alyssa Ayres. New York: Asia Society.

Garman, Christopher, Stephan Haggard, and Eliza Willis. 2001. Fiscal decentralization: A political theory with Latin American cases. *World Politics* 53 (January): 205–36.

Heath, Oliver. 1999. The fractionalisation of Indian parties. *Seminar* 480 (August): 66–71.

Government of India. Ministry of Finance. 1985. Report of the High Powered Committee on Stock Exchange Reforms. New Delhi: Department of Economic Affairs. Mimeographed.

Government of India. Securities and Exchange Board of India. 1995. Report of the Committee on the Review of the Present System of Carry Forward Transactions [also know as G. S. Patel Committee Report]. Bombay: Securities and Exchange Board of India. Mimeographed.

Government of India. Planning Commission. 2001. Tenth five year plan (2002–2007). Accessed at http://planningcommission.nic.in/.

Jenkins, Rob. 1999. *Democratic politics and economic reform in India.* Cambridge: Cambridge University Press.

Joshi, Vijay, and I. M. D. Little. 1996. *India's economic reforms, 1991–2001.* Oxford: Clarendon Press.

Kochanek, Stanley A. 1968. *The Congress Party of India.* Princeton, N.J.: Princeton University Press.

Kohli, Atul. 1990. *Democracy and discontent.* Cambridge: Cambridge University Press.

Kothari, Rajni. 1964. The Congress "system" in India. *Asian Survey*, December, 1161–73.

Laakso, Markku, and Rein Taagepera. 1979. Effective number of parties: A measure with application to West Europe. *Comparative Political Studies* 12:3–27.

Lahiri, Ashok K. 2000. Sub-national public finance in India. *Economic and Political Weekly*, 29 April, 1539–49.

Manoj, C. L. 2001. Fiscal bill hits rough weather. *Statesman,* 12 May.

Parikh, Sunita, and Barry Weingast. 1997. A comparative theory of federalism: India. *Virginia Law Review* 83 (October): 1593–1615.

Riker, William Riker. 1975. Federalism. In *Handbook of political science*, vol. 5, edited by Fred Greenstein and Nelson Polsby. Reading, Mass.: Addison-Wesley.

Rudolph, Lloyd I., and Susanne Hoeber Rudolph. 2001. Iconisation of Chandrababu: Sharing sovereignty in India's federal market economy. *Economic and Political Weekly*, 5 May, 1541–52.

———. Forthcoming. Redoing the constitutional design: From an interventionist to a regulatory state. In *Against the odds: India's democracy at fifty*, edited by Atul Kohli. Cambridge: Cambridge University Press.

Saez, Lawrence. 2000. Globalization and market-preserving federalism: Evidence from China and India. Paper presented at the annual meeting of the American Political Science Association, 31 August to 4 September, at Washington, D.C.

Shah, Ajay, and Susan Thomas. 2001. *Securities market infrastructure for small countries.* Technical Report. Mumbai: Indira Gandhi Institute for Development Research.

Sinha, Aseema. 2000. India and the theory of market preserving federalism. Paper presented at the annual meeting of the American Political Science Association, 31 August to 4 September, at Washington, D.C.

Weiner, Myron. 1967. *Party building in a new nation: The Indian National Congress.* Chicago: University of Chicago Press.

Weingast, Barry R. 1995. The economic role of political institutions: Federalism, markets, and economic development. *Journal of Law, Economics, and Organization* 11 (April): 1–31.

Part III

FISCAL POLICY

5

PUBLIC SECTOR DEFICITS, MACROECONOMIC STABILITY, AND ECONOMIC PERFORMANCE

❖

Sebastian Edwards

Introduction

During the last few years, internationally related issues have dominated macroeconomic discussions in the emerging countries. Debates on currency crises, exchange-rate policy, the banking system, and the current account have abounded. Because of this emphasis on international aspects of macroeconomic policy, issues related to fiscal policy—including the evolution of public sector debt—seem to have taken a backseat in recent debates. And yet, fiscal policy remains fundamentally important for the emerging nations. Fiscal policy interacts in complex ways with other policies: it affects country risk assessments in international financial markets, and it plays a key role in determining long-run growth. Countries that run large and persistent fiscal imbalances will typically face a higher cost of capital in international markets; moreover, they will tend to grow at a slower pace on average. Additionally, countries that run "less than prudent" fiscal policies have a higher probability of facing a major currency crisis in the future.

Fiscal problems have been at the heart of recent macroeconomic upheaval in a number of emerging nations. The currency crises in Russia in 1998 and in Brazil in 1999, for example, were largely the result of unsustainable fiscal policies. More recently, the Argentine financial crisis of 2001 has been the direct result of stubborn fiscal imbalances both at the federal and provincial levels. Fiscal issues have also become important in high-performance countries. In Chile, for instance, the government has recently argued that maintaining a fiscal surplus of 1 percent of GDP is a key feature of its long-term development strategy. Fiscal policy issues have also become central in policy discussions in India during the last few years. In a recent study, Srinivasan (2000) points out that the aggregate fiscal deficit of India's nonfinancial public sector climbed to almost 11 percent of GDP during 1999–2000. These figures are similar to those posted by India in 1990–91, just before its balance of payments crisis.

The purpose of this chapter is to analyze, from a policy perspective, the effects of fiscal policy on economic performance and macroeconomic stability. The analysis covers both analytical as well as empirical aspects of the problem. I use a large comparative data set to analyze the way in which fiscal policy—broadly defined—has affected a number of key macroeconomic variables during the last three decades. More specifically I investigate the relationship between large fiscal imbalances and external crises. This type of comparative analysis will help put India's recent fiscal performance in perspective. In particular, it should help answer questions related to the dangers (if any) associated with the country's expansive fiscal stance. Fiscal policy is an extraordinarily broad subject, and in this chapter I make no effort to cover every angle or ramification. I concentrate on those aspects of the problem that I believe are particularly relevant in countries such as India. More specifically, I concentrate on the following issues:

- Sustainability of public sector debt and its implications for the primary fiscal balance.
- Fiscal policy and growth. Here I investigate several channels at work, and I discuss the existing empirical evidence.
- Fiscal deficits and external sector crises. The main emphasis of this analysis is to investigate the effect of fiscal imbalances on broadly defined currency crises.

The rest of the chapter is organized as follows: In Section 1 I focus on models of public sector debt sustainability. I emphasize the importance of the public sector primary balance, and I deal with some important dynamic issues. In illustrating the importance of debt sustainability I focus on the recent experience of Argentina. The discussion in this section is supplemented in the appendix, where I present a fairly complete fiscal sustainability model for poor countries such as India. In Section 2 I use a massive data set to analyze some of the most important aspects of fiscal policy behavior in the world economy during the last quarter century. Although there are some important comparability issues, the analysis presented in this section provides some evidence that helps put individual countries' experiences in a historical and international perspective. In this section I also discuss some preliminary evidence on the relationship between fiscal adjustment and economic growth. In Section 3 I analyze the connection between fiscal imbalances and external crises. In Section 4 I deal with the relationship between fiscal balances and economic performance. I analyze both the relationships between fiscal deficits and investment and fiscal deficits and GDP growth. Finally, Section 5 contains some concluding remarks.

1. Public Sector Debt Sustainability and Fiscal Balances: A Minimalist Approach

Modern policy analyses have emphasized the concept of *macroeconomic sustainability.* In particular, studies on the causes behind recent currency crises have focused on current account unsustainability. The main point of these studies is that the "sustainable" level of the current account is consistent with macroeconomic solvency. According to Milesi-Ferreti and Razin (1998), this means that the sustainable current account is that level at which "the ratio of external debt to GDP is stabilized." Analyses of current account sustainability have become particularly popular among investment banks. For instance, Goldman Sachs's GS-SCAD model developed in 1997 has become popular among analysts interested in assessing emerging nations' external sector vulnerability. More recently, Deutsche Bank (2000) has developed a model of current account sustainability, both to analyze whether a particular country's current account is "out of line" and to evaluate the appropriateness of its real exchange rate.

Similarly, fiscal sustainability is defined as a situation where the ratio of public sector debt to GDP is stable and consistent with the private sector demand—both domestic and foreign—for government securities (Buiter 1990). An important feature of public sector sustainability analyses is that they make a distinction between the total (or nominal) public sector balance and the primary balance, which excludes interest payments on the public sector debt. Public sector sustainability models allow us to calculate the *primary balance* that is compatible with a stable debt-to-GDP ratio. This "required" primary balance is, in fact, an increasingly important policy goal in macroeconomic programs. Most IMF adjustment programs, for example, include primary balance targets as disbursement conditions. Also, investment banks and independent analysts tend to look carefully at the primary balance when assessing a particular country's economic and financial prospects. Indeed, investment banks' country risk models tend to include fiscal performance indicators as determinants of the risk associated with doing business in different nations (Ades and Kaune 1997).

1.1 Public Sector Debt Sustainability and Primary Balances

Debt sustainability is achieved when the public sector's debt-to-GDP ratio stabilizes at a level compatible with the public's demand for government securities. We denote this ratio by λ:

$$(1) \quad D/Y = \lambda$$

where D is the nominal public sector debt expressed in domestic currency and Y is nominal GDP also expressed in local currency. D is assumed to be composed of debt issued in domestic currency (M) and debt issued in foreign currency (F). If E is the exchange rate, then

$$(2)\quad D = M + EF.$$

Public sector debt sustainability requires that λ is stable at a level compatible with the public's demand for government debt.[1] We can denote the sustainable public sector debt-to-GDP ratio as λ^*. Once the economy is at this sustainable level, it is necessary that $dD = (g + \pi)D$, where g is real GDP growth and π is domestic inflation. The increase in nominal debt (dD) is also equal to interest payments plus the primary deficit (P). Interest payments, in turn, are equal to the sum of payments on the domestic and foreign currency denominated debts. Assume that the following interest arbitrage conditions hold:

$$(3)\quad i^d = i^f + \delta,$$

$$(4)\quad i^f = i^* + \rho$$

where i^d is the interest rate on domestic currency debt, i^f is the interest rate paid by the public sector on foreign currency debt, δ is the expected rate of devaluation, i^* is an international benchmark rate (LIBOR, say), and ρ is a country risk premium. Equations (3) and (4) assume that there is free capital mobility between the country in question and the rest of the world. If, however, there are impediments to capital mobility, a term reflecting the tax equivalent of such impediments should be included in the analysis.

The above framework implies that, in order to maintain a stable debt-to-GDP ratio, the primary deficit as a percentage of GDP has to be equal to

$$(5)\quad P/Y = (-\lambda^*)[g + \pi - \delta\mu - (i^* + \rho)]$$

where μ is the proportion of the debt that is denominated in foreign currency.[2] According to equation (5), (P/Y) can be either positive—implying that the country in question can sustain a primary deficit—or negative, in which case the country will have to run a primary *surplus* in order to maintain a stable D/Y. Notice that if the nominal rate of growth of GDP ($g + \pi$) falls below the cost of borrowing in foreign currency ($i^* + \rho$), the country will *have to run a primary surplus*. The magnitude of such surplus will depend on the difference between these two variables, as well as on the expected rate of depreciation of the domestic currency.

In order to illustrate the implications of this analysis, consider the case of Argentina, a country that was engulfed in a serious macroeconomic crisis, rooted in fiscal imbalances, during most of 2000 and 2001. At the time of this writing (mid-2001) the public sector debt-to-GDP ratio (D/Y) in Argentina stood at approximately 0.53, a figure that, according to most analysts, corresponded to the absolute upper bound for the country. For the year 2002–3, analysts expect that real rate of growth (g) will be 4 percent at most, and that inflation will be equal to zero. Argentina has a fixed exchange rate—the peso is fixed to the dollar at a one-to-one rate—backed by a currency board. If the currency board and the fixed exchange rate are credible, the expected rate of devaluation (δ) in equation (5) is equal to zero.[3] If the benchmark international interest rate (i^*) is assumed to be 4 percent, and the average country risk (EMBI + spread) is 600 basis points,[4] Argentina should run a primary *surplus* equal to 3.2 percent of GDP in order to stabilize (D/Y).[5] If, on the contrary, a smaller surplus is attained, Argentina's public sector debt to GDP will tend to increase, generating a perverse dynamic. Naturally, if the 2001 level of (D/Y) of 0.53 is not sustainable, Argentina will have to run an even larger primary surplus during a transitional period. Indeed, after this chapter was presented as a paper at the conference on Indian economic policy reform held at the Center for Research on Economic Development and Policy Reform at Stanford University in June 2001, the Argentine authorities acknowledged the unsustainable debt dynamics of the country. In August 2001, Argentina sought IMF assistance to implement a new zero-deficit policy aimed at stabilizing (D/Y).

1.2 The Dynamics of the Public Sector Debt

There are times when the fiscal dynamics of a country are such that the debt-to-GDP ratio is not stable. Naturally, one such circumstance will arise if the country does not generate a primary surplus consistent with equation (5). An important question regarding the dynamics of fiscal policy is how the debt-to-GDP ratio will evolve through time. From equation (1) through (4), it is possible to derive the following expression for the evolution through time of the debt-to-GDP ratio:

$$(6)\quad d\lambda = [(P/Y) + (i^f + \delta\mu)\lambda - (g + \pi)\lambda].$$

In this equation (P/Y) is the actual primary *deficit*; if the country is running a primary surplus, the expression is negative.

Naturally, ($d\lambda$) can be positive for only a limited time. This is because, at some point, investors will be unwilling to accumulate further securities from the country in question. When this point is reached, the country will have to generate a primary balance consistent with a sustainable level of λ. This primary balance is given, precisely, by the expression derived in equation (5) above. If the authorities are unable to stabilize λ, a financial/currency crisis will become inevitable. These indeed were the cases in Russia in 1998 and Brazil in 1999. Moreover, as pointed out above, the inability to stabilize λ was at the heart of the Argentine crisis of 2000–2001. Whether the Argentine authorities will be able to avoid a major collapse is still an open question at the time of this writing. See the appendix for a more general model of the dynamic behavior of the public sector debt and primary balance.

The framework presented in this section is very simple and indeed constitutes a "minimalist" approach for analyzing fiscal policy sustainability. In the appendix I present a more complete model of fiscal policy sustainability for a low-income country such as India. That model assumes that, initially, the country in question receives grants and concessional loans from the international community. As times goes by, however, the country's reliance on soft loans diminishes, until in the steady state it becomes equal to zero.

2. *Fiscal Balances in the World Economy Since the 1970s*

In this section I provide a broad analysis of fiscal balances in both emerging and advanced countries. I am particularly interested in understanding, from a comparative point of view, the magnitude of fiscal deficits in different regions at different points in time, as well as the implications of these imbalances for growth and macroeconomic stability. The data set covers 105 countries during the years 1970–97, was obtained from the World Bank, and refers to the central government fiscal deficit. In principle these figures are comparable across countries. This first look at the data should help answer questions such as "From a historical point of view, is 3 percent of GDP a large fiscal deficit?" and "Historically, for how long have countries been able to run 'large' fiscal deficits?"

Throughout the analysis I have concentrated on the public sector *deficit* as a percentage of GDP; that is, in what follows, a positive number means that the country in question, for that particular year, has run a current account deficit. In order to organize the discussion I have divided the countries into six regions: (1) Industrialized countries; (2) Latin America and the Caribbean; (3) Asia; (4) Africa; (5) Middle East and northern Africa; and (6) eastern Europe. In Table 5.1 I present the number of countries in each region and year for which there are data available. This table summarizes the largest available data set that can be used in empirical work.

Tables 5.2, 5.3, and 5.4 contain basic data on current account deficits by region for the period 1970–97. In Table 5.2 I present averages by region and year. Table 5.3 contains medians, and in Table 5.4 I present the third quartile by year and region. I have used the data on the third quartile presented in this table as cutoff points to define "high deficit" countries. Later in this section I analyze the persistence of high deficits in each of the six regions.

A number of interesting features of public sector balance behavior emerge from these tables. First, in virtually every region average fiscal imbalances have experienced a declining trend during the 1990s. When we concentrate on the median (Table 5.3) this trend is less clear. Indeed, in some regions the median

TABLE 5.1
Number of Observations per Region Used in Public Sector Balance Analysis

Year	Industrialized Countries	Latin America	Asia	Africa	Middle East and Northern Africa	Eastern Europe	Total
1970	12	5	4	3	0	1	25
1971	13	7	4	8	0	1	33
1972	19	16	8	18	4	1	66
1973	21	19	12	23	5	1	81
1974	22	19	13	25	7	1	87
1975	23	20	15	27	8	2	95
1976	23	22	15	28	8	2	98
1977	23	22	15	30	9	2	101
1978	23	21	15	29	9	2	99
1979	22	23	15	29	9	2	100
1980	23	26	16	29	10	2	106
1981	23	24	16	27	10	3	103
1982	23	24	17	29	8	2	103
1983	23	24	17	28	8	3	103
1984	23	26	17	28	8	4	106
1985	22	27	17	29	9	4	108
1986	22	24	17	30	10	4	107
1987	22	21	16	28	9	4	100
1988	22	23	17	27	9	5	103
1989	21	23	16	28	9	4	101
1990	22	22	16	27	10	4	101
1991	24	23	16	26	10	7	106
1992	24	22	16	22	10	8	102
1993	24	23	16	21	11	10	105
1994	23	20	16	15	11	13	98
1995	22	17	15	15	10	14	93
1996	17	14	15	10	8	12	76
1997	10	9	11	5	5	8	48
Total	591	566	403	644	224	126	2,554

SOURCE: World Bank.

deficit has either remained roughly constant during the last few years, or it has increased slightly. The combination of a lower mean and an unchanging median suggests that, in most regions, two distinct groups of countries are emerging. While one group has moved toward greater fiscal "responsibility," the other one has maintained historical practices in terms of public finances. The data on third quartiles presented in Table 5.4 show that 25 percent of the countries in our sample had, at one point or another, a public sector deficit in excess of 5.92 percent of GDP. Naturally, as the table shows, the third quartile differs for each region and year, with the largest values corresponding to Africa and the Middle East. I use the third quartile data in Table 5.4 to define "large public sector deficit" countries. In particular, if during a given year a particular country's deficit exceeds its region's third quartile, I classify it as being a "high deficit country."

TABLE 5.2

Average Public Sector Deficit to GDP Ratios by Region, 1970–1997

Year	Industrialized Countries	Latin America	Asia	Africa	Middle East and Northern Africa	Eastern Europe	Total
1970	0.51	1.52	2.09	1.34		1.75	1.11
1971	0.81	1.77	2.13	3.98		2.51	1.99
1972	1.28	2.88	2.88	4.19	4.81	1.67	2.87
1973	1.13	2.93	3.26	3.61	5.99	1.43	2.88
1974	1.89	2.22	2.07	1.80	−0.52	1.42	1.76
1975	4.59	2.50	3.09	4.38	7.44	0.39	4.01
1976	3.59	3.92	3.40	6.12	9.49	0.49	4.78
1977	3.64	2.78	2.80	5.12	2.45	2.33	3.63
1978	3.97	2.74	2.94	6.10	5.88	1.59	4.30
1979	4.48	3.28	2.98	5.01	1.68	2.30	3.84
1980	4.16	3.56	4.81	4.44	0.04	1.29	3.75
1981	4.92	5.00	5.03	5.78	0.46	0.88	4.63
1982	5.60	7.94	4.92	6.51	6.34	−0.55	6.23
1983	5.52	6.28	4.90	5.68	8.26	0.32	5.70
1984	5.18	5.93	2.64	4.86	5.93	0.16	4.74
1985	5.02	5.21	4.14	4.79	3.63	1.50	4.62
1986	4.21	3.81	5.14	4.31	3.46	0.33	4.08
1987	3.61	3.67	3.94	5.19	5.68	0.19	4.17
1988	2.64	3.05	2.38	3.54	5.15	0.76	3.05
1989	2.89	1.95	3.03	2.94	4.55	−0.49	2.73
1990	2.89	2.15	3.19	2.19	3.77	2.38	2.66
1991	3.81	−0.39	3.00	4.80	3.49	2.11	2.88
1992	4.09	0.47	2.82	3.62	3.90	4.32	3.01
1993	5.03	0.98	2.33	4.47	3.19	3.69	3.30
1994	4.61	1.61	1.57	2.67	4.97	3.61	3.11
1995	3.96	0.56	1.29	2.66	4.45	3.30	2.65
1996	2.32	0.64	1.32	1.46	4.96	3.69	2.20
1997	2.52	0.51	1.46	3.65	2.84	0.69	1.75
Total	3.70	3.10	3.16	4.40	4.22	2.20	3.63

SOURCE: World Bank.

How does India fare in comparison to the rest of the emerging nations in the sample? In 13 out of 17 years between 1980 and 1997, the public sector deficit in India has been among the highest 25 percent in Asia. That is, according to our definition, India has had a high deficit during 72 percent of the years, including the last three years for which there are comparable data (1995–97). Interestingly, South Korea's public sector deficit is never among the highest 25 percent of Asia's deficits during this period. Although the data for China are limited to a few years, in not one of them is the fiscal deficit classified as high.

An important policy question refers to the frequency and circumstances surrounding fiscal adjustments. In particular, it is interesting to analyze historically how common major fiscal adjustments have been in different regions. Many critics of the IMF and of the so-called orthodox adjustments policies have argued that abrupt reductions in the fiscal deficit tend to result in major declines

TABLE 5.3

Median Public Sector Deficit to GDP Ratios by Region, 1970–1997

Year	Industrialized Countries	Latin America	Asia	Africa	Middle East and Northern Africa	Eastern Europe	Total
1970	0.56	0.97	1.75	1.43		1.75	0.76
1971	0.67	1.60	0.90	2.74		2.51	1.52
1972	1.30	2.32	2.24	3.22	7.84	1.67	2.03
1973	0.82	1.75	2.73	2.68	5.82	1.43	2.05
1974	1.25	1.44	2.15	2.02	4.67	1.42	1.92
1975	3.33	1.86	2.06	4.21	5.10	0.39	3.17
1976	3.25	2.42	2.50	4.91	8.44	0.49	3.49
1977	3.39	2.24	1.96	3.91	4.89	2.33	3.24
1978	3.54	1.47	2.95	4.63	8.52	1.59	3.34
1979	3.78	1.55	2.91	4.78	3.75	2.30	3.39
1980	3.45	2.61	3.01	3.91	8.06	1.29	3.11
1981	4.77	3.51	4.31	3.95	6.32	1.48	3.98
1982	5.50	4.22	5.13	6.16	6.97	−0.55	5.13
1983	5.93	3.56	3.95	5.13	7.85	0.71	4.82
1984	4.71	3.66	2.95	4.76	6.18	−0.56	4.18
1985	4.75	2.42	2.69	4.04	3.77	1.36	3.47
1986	4.26	1.81	4.83	4.45	5.17	1.39	3.80
1987	2.84	2.28	2.56	4.56	5.07	2.29	3.28
1988	2.46	1.67	2.15	3.68	7.64	2.27	2.58
1989	2.56	1.72	2.58	3.38	4.30	1.48	2.25
1990	2.28	0.23	3.46	1.78	4.43	1.10	2.10
1991	3.26	−0.05	2.19	3.35	3.39	3.73	2.26
1992	3.53	0.04	2.52	4.38	3.89	4.80	3.08
1993	4.23	0.21	2.10	3.91	0.47	2.85	2.51
1994	3.72	0.91	2.59	3.19	2.92	3.90	2.95
1995	3.86	0.60	1.75	3.01	3.40	3.47	2.37
1996	2.26	0.63	1.59	2.24	3.14	2.02	1.95
1997	1.52	1.03	2.17	3.99	2.60	1.23	1.38
Total	3.14	1.79	2.93	3.94	4.94	2.10	2.95

SOURCE: World Bank.

in growth. In order to investigate this issue I concentrated on episodes where the fiscal deficit was reduced by at least 3 percentage points of GDP in one year. Table 5.5 contains tabulations for adjustment episodes for the six regions considered in this study, as well as for the total sample. As may be seen, for the sample as a whole, little more than 10 percent (11.9 percent) of the country-year observations correspond to "fiscal adjustment" episodes. The frequency of adjustments varies across regions: it is highest in the Middle East and lowest in the industrial countries. In a way this is not surprising, since as reflected in the preceding tables, it is precisely in the Middle East where both the median and third-quartile deficit ratios have been largest. This suggests that those countries that run very large deficits are precisely the ones that have to implement major adjustments more frequently.

I next inquire whether economic performance is different in the "fiscal

Table 5.4

Third Quartile of Public Sector Deficit to GDP Ratios by Region, 1970–1997

Year	Industrialized Countries	Latin America	Asia	Africa	Middle East and Northern Africa	Eastern Europe	Total
1970	1.73	1.17	4.57	3.09		1.75	1.78
1971	1.56	2.36	4.40	5.59		2.51	2.71
1972	2.70	3.30	3.99	5.72	14.41	1.67	4.17
1973	2.49	3.89	5.40	5.66	13.87	1.43	5.13
1974	3.43	3.87	3.23	4.16	9.92	1.42	4.16
1975	5.65	4.60	5.50	7.59	12.95	1.04	5.65
1976	5.65	4.35	4.25	7.66	14.40	1.55	6.70
1977	5.71	5.15	4.59	6.45	13.35	4.82	6.10
1978	6.94	4.47	4.51	9.04	12.72	3.34	7.51
1979	7.11	6.47	3.85	8.74	7.63	4.79	6.78
1980	7.02	4.68	5.83	7.91	11.69	3.07	6.70
1981	8.86	6.73	7.11	9.82	7.89	2.83	7.57
1982	8.27	8.45	6.32	8.41	12.69	1.90	8.27
1983	8.34	6.55	8.75	7.96	9.73	3.48	8.09
1984	8.22	5.65	6.18	6.07	11.41	4.36	6.82
1985	7.10	6.23	7.25	7.28	7.58	3.79	7.20
1986	6.04	4.01	8.58	7.43	8.34	2.65	7.14
1987	6.68	6.27	7.19	8.77	7.11	3.22	7.26
1988	4.15	3.60	5.57	5.99	9.15	2.99	5.42
1989	3.75	2.74	7.36	6.04	5.80	2.60	4.57
1990	4.51	2.52	7.14	5.28	5.71	5.64	5.18
1991	5.47	1.33	6.46	5.84	6.79	5.03	5.03
1992	5.08	2.96	5.36	6.56	6.39	5.57	5.15
1993	6.69	2.29	6.23	6.89	7.75	5.99	5.99
1994	5.75	3.79	6.34	4.80	11.17	4.71	5.47
1995	6.00	1.35	4.91	6.01	6.14	4.53	4.91
1996	5.26	2.02	4.71	5.76	4.35	5.03	4.30
1997	3.50	1.32	4.86	5.50	5.49	2.25	3.95
Total	5.75	4.04	5.80	6.65	9.04	4.15	5.92

SOURCE: World Bank.

Table 5.5

Frequency of Major Fiscal Adjustment Episodes by Region, 1970–1997

	Episode Type			
	Non-adjustment		Adjustment	
Region (# episodes)	Frequency	%	Frequency	%
Industrialized Countries (591)	554	93.74	37	6.26
Latin America (566)	507	89.58	59	10.42
Asia (403)	367	91.07	36	8.93
Africa (644)	550	85.40	94	14.60
Middle East (224)	179	79.91	45	20.09
Eastern Europe (120)	105	87.50	15	12.50
Total Sample (2559)				

TABLE 5.6

*Tests of Equality of Means of Growth of GDP per Capita: Adjustment Countries vs. Non-Adjustment Countries**

	t Statistic—Contemporaneous	*t* Statistic—One-Period Lagged
Industrial countries	−2.66[a]	−1.41
Latin America and the Caribbean	−1.18	−0.27
Asia	−0.40	−0.53
Africa	−1.81	−0.86
Middle East and Northern Africa	0.42	−0.31
Eastern Europe	−0.82	−0.08

*The null hypothesis is that the two means are equal (or that the difference in the means is equal to zero).

[a]Significant at the 95% level.

adjustment countries"—that is, those countries that reduced the deficit by at least 3 percent of GDP—than in nations that did not go through this type of process. In order to address this issue I computed a series of nonparametric tests on the equality of means (*t* statistic), medians (χ^2 test), and the distribution (χ^2) of GDP growth per capita. Since the (potential) negative effect of fiscal adjustment may take some time to manifest itself, I computed these tests both contemporaneously, as well as with a one-period lag. In Table 5.6 I present the results corresponding to the equality-of-means test—the other tests give a similar picture, and have been omitted for space considerations. As may be seen from this table, the hypothesis that growth of GDP per capita is lower in "fiscal adjustment" countries than in the rest of the nations is rejected, both contemporaneously and with a lag, for every one of the emerging nations regions. The only case where this hypothesis cannot be rejected is for industrial countries.[6] These results are quite interesting and contradict the popular notion that countries that undertake a fiscal adjustment tend to suffer from a period of substandard economic performance. In the rest of this chapter I analyze several aspects of the relationship between fiscal balances and economic performance.

3. *Fiscal Deficits and Currency Crises: Is There a Link?*

In this section I use a previously analyzed panel data set for 1970–97 to analyze whether fiscal deficits have been empirically related to financial crises in the world economy. The section is organized as follows: In subsection 3.1 I deal with the definition of crisis. In subsection 3.2 I report some empirical results, obtained using panel-data econometric techniques, on the relationship between fiscal deficits and financial crises. I argue that there is persuasive evidence suggesting that larger fiscal deficits indeed increase the probability of a country facing a financial crisis.

3.1 Defining a Crisis

In the introduction to an NBER volume, Paul Krugman has recently said that "there is no generally accepted formal definition of a currency crisis, but we know them when we see them" (Krugman 2000, 1). While some authors, including myself (Edwards 1989; Edwards and Santaella 1993), have defined a currency crisis as a very significant depreciation of the currency (see also Frankel and Rose 1996; Milesi-Ferreti and Razin 2000), others have defined a crisis as a situation where a country's currency is depreciated and/or its international reserves are seriously depleted (Eichengreen, Rose, and Wyplosz 1996, Goldstein, Kaminsky, and Reinhart 2000).

In this chapter, and in order to cast a very wide net in the empirical analysis, I have used a rather broad definition of currency crisis. More specifically, in my definition of crisis I have included situations where the country in question has experienced a large currency depreciation, or has experienced a significant loss in reserves. In constructing this variable—which I call *acrisis*—I followed a three-step procedure:

1. I created a weighted average index of monthly rate of change of the exchange rate ($\Delta e/e$), and of reserves ($\Delta R/R$), so that both components of the index have equal sample volatility: $I_t = \Delta e/e - (\sigma_e/\sigma_R)(\Delta R/R)$.
2. I define a crisis (C_t) to have taken place when the index exceeds the mean of the index plus 3 standard deviations:

$$(7)\quad C_t = \begin{cases} 1 & \textit{if} \quad I_t \geq mean(I_t) + 3\sigma_I \\ 0 & \qquad\qquad \textit{otherwise} \end{cases}$$

3. I annualized the crisis index by considering each year as a June to June period. In other words, a year t is assigned a crisis (= 1), if any month between June of year t and June of year $t + 1$ is a crisis.[7]

How frequent have currency crises been, according to these indicators? This is addressed in Table 5.7, where I present tabulations for the six regions and for the complete sample. As may be seen, the frequency of "crises" goes from 6 percent to 11 percent of the country-year observations. In terms of the distribution across regions, the highest incidence of crisis takes place in Latin America, with over 10 percent of the observations corresponding to crisis episodes.

3.2 Fiscal Imbalances and Currency Crises: A Formal Analysis

In a recent and influential paper, Frankel and Rose (1996) empirically analyzed the determinants of currency crashes. Their data set included 105 countries for the period 1970–91, and their definition of crisis was confined to devaluations in excess of 25 percent. The results from their probit regression analysis indi-

TABLE 5.7
Frequency of Currency Crises by Region

	Episode Type			
	Non-crisis		Crisis	
Region (# episodes)	Frequency	%	Frequency	%
Industrialized countries (674)	632	93.77	42	6.23
Latin America (879)	790	89.87	89	10.13
Asia (480)	432	90	48	10
Africa (1230)	1123	91.30	107	8.70
Middle East and Northern Africa (303)	281	92.74	22	7.26
Eastern Europe (120)	132	90.41	14	9.59
Total Sample (3821)				

cated that a number of variables were good predictors of a currency crash. These included the fraction of the debt obtained in concessional terms, the FDI-to-GDP ratio, the reserves-to-imports ratio, the rate of growth of domestic credit, the country's rate of growth, and international interest rates. In terms of the present chapter, what is particularly interesting is that in Frankel and Rose (1996) the fiscal deficit was not significant, and in some of the regressions it even had the *wrong* sign. This led the authors to conclude that, "curiously, neither current account nor government budget deficits appear to play an important role in a typical crash" (365).[8] It is important to emphasize, however, that Frankel and Rose use a different, and stricter, definition of crisis than the one I am using in this chapter.[9]

In order to investigate this issue further, I estimated a series of probit models of currency crisis. I am particularly interested in understanding whether an increase in the fiscal deficits has a significant effect on a crisis occurring either in the same year or a year later. I thus define $Crisis_t$ as a variable that takes a value of 1 if there is a currency crisis—as defined in equation (7) above—in either period t or in period $t + 1$. I am interested in estimating the following probit equation:

$$(8)\quad \text{Prob}(Crisis_t = 1) = \Phi(x, \beta)$$

where $\Phi(\ )$ refers to a normal distribution, x is a vector of determinants of *Crisis,* and β represents parameters to be estimated.

In the benchmark estimation of the currency crisis model, I used the following regressors:[10]

- Fiscal deficit as a percentage of GDP (*deficit*)
- Ratio of public and publicly guaranteed foreign debt to GDP (*pubdebt*)
- Percentage of the foreign debt that is short term (*shortd*)

- The ratio of (gross) international reserves to GDP (*resgdp*)
- Deviations of the real exchange rate from PPP (a measure of "overvaluation") (*over*)
- Rate of growth of domestic credit (*cre_gro*)
- Foreign direct investment flows as a percentage of GDP (*fdigdp*)
- Current account deficit as a percentage of GDP (*cagdp*)

In the estimation, outliers for both the current account and the deficit variables were excluded. In reporting the regressions, I follow the tradition of presenting the effects of a unitary change in the independent variables on the probability of a crisis. In all of the regressions I report robust standard errors, which correct for heteroskedasticity. The benchmark results are in Table 5.8. In Table 5.9 I report the estimation results obtained when year dummies are included in the regression. The results are quite interesting and suggest that, with other things constant, higher fiscal deficits increase the probability of a currency crisis occurring in period t or $t + 1$. A higher public sector foreign debt also increases the probability of a currency crisis, as does an increase in the foreign debt that is contracted as short-term debt. The results indicate that higher FDI flows reduce the probability of crisis, a result also obtained by Frankel and Rose (1996). A higher degree of overvaluation increases the probability of crisis, as does a higher rate of domestic credit creation. The estimated coefficient of the

TABLE 5.8

Probit Estimates of Currency Crises, Benchmark Results, 1975–1997

Number of observations	1022
Wald statistic, $\chi^2(8)$	57.75
Probability $> \chi^2$	0.0000
Pseudo R^2	0.0902
Log likelihood	−458.40287
Observed p	0.1947162
Predicted p	0.1781506
Dependent variable	*acrisis*

Variable	dF/dx	Robust Standard Error	z	$p > \|z\|$	x-bar	Lower Bound, 95% CI	Upper Bound, 95% CI
deficit	0.008158	0.002962	2.71	0.007	3.422560	0.002353	0.013963
pubdebt	0.132857	0.032801	4.10	0	0.416889	0.068568	0.197146
shortd	0.002624	0.001048	2.49	0.013	15.303600	0.000569	0.004679
fdigdp	−0.020250	0.007725	−2.58	0.010	1.181120	−0.035393	−0.005113
cagdp	0.004811	0.002130	2.25	0.024	−3.937980	0.000636	0.008986
cre_gro	0.000472	0.000208	2.32	0.020	38.242000	0.000064	0.000880
resgdp	−0.001400	0.000795	−1.76	0.079	12.822600	−0.002960	0.000154
over	0.250949	0.065028	3.82	0	0.014391	0.123497	0.378402

NOTE: z and $p > |z|$ are the test of the underlying coefficient being 0.

TABLE 5.9

Probit Estimates of Currency Crises, Year Dummies Included, 1975–1997

Number of observations	1022
Wald statistic, $\chi^2(8)$	116.46
Probability $> \chi^2$	0.0000
Pseudo R^2	0.1393
Log likelihood	−429.87773
Observed p	0.1986028
Predicted p	0.1659814
Dependent variable	*acrisis*

Variable	dF/dx	Robust Standard Error	z	$p > \|z\|$	x-bar	Lower Bound, 95% CI	Upper Bound, 95% CI
*deficit*1	0.008990	0.003181	2.78	0.005	3.466140	0.002756	0.015224
pubdebt	0.074353	0.030799	2.43	0.015	0.422549	0.013988	0.134719
*shortd*1	0.002870	0.001021	2.77	0.006	15.354700	0.000869	0.004872
*fdigdp*1	−0.020640	0.007624	−2.65	0.008	1.192880	−0.035585	−0.005701
cagdp	0.001911	0.002331	0.82	0.411	−3.991060	−0.002660	0.006480
*cre_gro*1	0.000477	0.000204	2.40	0.017	38.599100	0.000077	0.000878
*resgdp*1	−0.001450	0.000821	−1.75	0.080	12.730300	−0.003050	0.000164
*over*1	0.326831	0.071651	4.55	0	0.015152	0.186397	0.467265
d★	−0.133600	0.041706	−1.69	0.090	0.017964	−0.215345	−0.051861
d★	−0.121750	0.049937	−1.48	0.138	0.027944	−0.219620	−0.023870
d★	−0.177290	0.028024	−2.82	0.005	0.080838	−0.232210	−0.122360
d★	0.029227	0.117597	0.26	0.795	0.042914	−0.201260	0.259712
d★	−0.154190	0.026941	−2.70	0.007	0.043912	−0.206993	−0.101385
d★	−0.151990	0.028552	−2.63	0.008	0.047904	−0.207947	−0.096024
d★	−0.134060	0.037622	−2.11	0.035	0.049900	−0.207793	−0.060318
d★	−0.113380	0.047943	−1.61	0.107	0.047904	−0.207340	−0.019410
d★	−0.039300	0.076011	−0.48	0.634	0.049900	−0.188280	0.109683
d★	−0.043130	0.075364	−0.52	0.602	0.049900	−0.190840	0.104582
d★	−0.024800	0.083147	−0.28	0.776	0.051896	−0.187770	0.138160
d★	0.023194	0.098362	0.24	0.807	0.051896	−0.169590	0.215979
d★	−0.049210	0.074364	−0.59	0.553	0.049900	−0.194960	0.096540
d★	−0.073790	0.066045	−0.92	0.355	0.048902	−0.203240	0.055655
d★	−0.098040	0.055256	−1.33	0.184	0.050898	−0.206340	0.010257
d★	−0.077820	0.064947	−0.98	0.328	0.049900	−0.205110	0.049476
d★	−0.084920	0.061181	−1.10	0.272	0.046906	−0.204840	0.034988
d★	−0.091970	0.058495	−1.21	0.227	0.046906	−0.206620	0.022682
d★	−0.006490	0.088113	−0.07	0.942	0.046906	−0.179190	0.166203
d★	−0.053920	0.073834	−0.64	0.519	0.040918	−0.198630	0.090791
d★	−0.141790	0.037116	−2.03	0.042	0.042914	−0.214537	−0.069043
d★	−0.137270	0.037737	−1.98	0.048	0.034930	−0.211237	−0.063309

NOTES: ★dF/dx is for discrete changes of the dummy variable from 0 to 1. z and $p > |z|$ are the test of the underlying coefficient being 0.

international reserves variable is negative, as expected, and significantly different from zero. The coefficient of the current account deficit is significantly positive in Table 5.9. Notice, however, that when the year dummy variables are introduced into the probit regression, the coefficient of the current account deficit is no longer significant.

The results presented in Tables 5.8 and 5.9 were obtained using a data set that covers every region. In order to investigate whether these findings depend on a specific region, I reestimated the probit equations, excluding one region at the time. The results obtained—not reported here due to space considerations—indicate that the results are robust to the data set used.

4. *Fiscal Imbalances and Economic Growth: A Comparative Analysis*

The results in the previous section indicate that fiscal imbalance—in the form of larger deficits or larger public sector foreign debt—increases the probability of the country in question facing a currency crisis. In this section I go one step further and investigate the way in which fiscal policy is related to economic growth. I focus on two variables: GDP growth and the investment ratio. The analysis proceeds in stages. I first analyze whether currency crises—whose probability of occurrence is positively affected by fiscal imbalances—have an effect on GDP growth. In order to address this issue I estimate a series of growth equations using panel data. Second, I investigate whether deficits have an effect of their own—that is, independent of crises—on GDP growth. The third and final stage deals with deficits and investment. The question here is whether, on average, deficits have been used (at least partially) to finance increases in investment.

4.1 Currency Crises and GDP Growth

In this subsection I analyze whether currency crises have affected economic growth. I investigated this issue by estimating a number of basic growth equations in the tradition of Robert Barro and his associates. My basic regression equation is

$$(9)\quad \text{GROWTH}_{tj} = \beta_1 \text{ INVGDP}_{tj} + \beta_2 \text{ POP\_GROWTH}_{tj} + \beta_3 \text{ GOVCON}_{tj} + \phi \text{ TRADE\_OPEN}_{tj} + \theta \text{ LOGGDP0}_j + \gamma \text{ CRISIS}_{tj} + \xi_{tj}$$

where GROWTH_{tj} is growth of GDP in country j during year t, and LOGGDP0_j is the initial level of GDP (1970) for country j. INVGDP_{tj} is the investment ratio, POP_GROWTH_{tj} is the rate of growth of population and is used as a proxy for labor force growth. TRADE_OPEN_{tj} measures trade openness, and is defined as imports plus exports over GDP. Crisis is our *acrisis* dummy variable, and takes a value of 1 if the country in question was subject to a currency crisis in that particular year. As Barro and Sala-i-Martin (1995) and others have pointed out, the coefficient of government consumption ($GOVCON_{tj}$) is expected to be negative, while that of openness is expected to be positive. If there is a catching-up in growth, we would expect the estimated coefficient of the logarithm of 1970 GDP per capita to be negative. The main interest of this analysis is the coefficient of CRISIS. If a currency crisis has a negative effect on investment, we would expect the estimated γ to be significantly negative. The error ξ_{tj} is assumed to be heteroskedastic, with a different variance for each country (panel). Thus, assuming k panels (countries):

$$(10) \quad E\,[\xi\xi'] = \begin{bmatrix} \sigma_1^2\mathbf{I} & 0 & \dots & 0 \\ 0 & \sigma_2^2\mathbf{I} & \dots & 0 \\ . & . & \dots & . \\ . & . & . & . \\ 0 & 0 & \dots & \sigma_k^2\mathbf{I} \end{bmatrix}$$

Equation (9) was estimated using the feasible generalized least squares procedure (FGLS) suggested by Beck and Katz (1995) for unbalanced panels. The samples in the different estimations were determined by the availability of data on the different regressors. The data were obtained from the World Bank and from the Summers and Heston data set; year dummy variables were also included.

The results from the estimation of equation (9) using heteroskedastic feasible least squares on a *common support sample* are reported in Table 5.10. As can be seen, all coefficients have the expected signs and are significant at conventional levels. What is particularly important for this chapter is that the coefficient of CRISIS is significantly negative, indicating that nations that experience a currency collapse experience a reduction in GDP growth. A possible problem in estimating equation (9) is that, since currency crises are not drawn from a random experiment, the $CRISIS_{tj}$ dummy is possibly correlated with the error term. Under these circumstances the estimated coefficients in equation (9) will be biased and misleading. In order to deal with this problem I follow the procedure recently suggested for estimating "treatment interventions" models (see Heckman, Ichimura, and Todd 1997; Blundell and Costa 2000).

This procedure consists of estimating the equation in question using observations that have a common support for both the "treated" and for the "non-treated." In the case at hand, countries that experience a currency crisis are considered to be subject to the "treatment intervention." From a practical point of view, a two-step procedure is used: (1) The conditional probability of countries facing a reversal—this is the *propensity score*—is first estimated using a probit regression. (2) The equation of interest is estimated using only observations whose estimated probability of crisis falls within the interval of estimated probabilities for countries with actual crises. In estimating the propensity scores I used the

Table 5.10

GDP Growth and Currency Crises Estimated Using Heteroskedastic Feasible Least Squares, Panel Estimation, 1975–1997

(Common Support Sample)

Estimated covariances	110
Estimated autocorrelations	0
Estimated coefficients	29
Number of observations	1497
Number of groups	110
Observations per group, minimum	1
Observations per group, average	17.26052
Observations per group, maximum	23
Wald statistic, $\chi^2(28)$	505.13
Probability > χ^2	0.0000
Log likelihood	−3917.454
Dependent variable	*growth*

Variable	Coefficient	Robust Standard Error	z	$p > \|z\|$	Lower Bound, 95% CI	Upper Bound, 95% CI
invgdp	0.192281	0.013029	14.76	0	0.166744	0.217818
pop_growth	0.353835	0.089235	3.97	0	0.178937	0.528732
trade_open	0.007039	0.003504	2.01	0.045	0.000172	0.013906
loggpp0	−0.359650	0.106042	−3.39	0.001	−0.567490	−0.151810
govcon	−0.054990	0.013337	−4.12	0	−0.081130	−0.028850
acrisis	−0.996730	0.260505	−3.83	0	−1.507310	−0.486150
d	−1.984960	0.712857	−2.78	0.005	−3.382130	−0.587780
d	1.573768	0.708483	2.22	0.026	0.185166	2.962370
d	−0.710230	0.732202	−0.97	0.332	−2.145320	0.724861
d	1.106007	0.531534	2.08	0.037	0.064218	2.147795
d	0.248633	0.712344	0.35	0.727	−1.147540	1.644802
d	−0.812520	0.707345	−1.15	0.251	−2.198890	0.573854
d	−1.362590	0.695223	−1.96	0.050	−2.725200	2.25E-05
d	−2.484360	0.699275	−3.55	0	−3.854910	−1.113800
d	−1.354220	0.696869	−1.94	0.052	−2.720060	0.011622
d	0.354727	0.693940	0.51	0.609	−1.005370	1.714823
d	−0.118030	0.692738	−0.17	0.865	−1.475770	1.239715
d	0.277319	0.692353	0.40	0.689	−1.079670	1.634305
d	0.030413	0.693760	0.04	0.965	−1.329330	1.390157
d	0.986182	0.695350	1.42	0.156	−0.376680	2.349044
d	0.223332	0.697385	0.32	0.749	−1.143520	1.590180
d	−0.063380	0.695344	−0.09	0.927	−1.426230	1.299472
d	−1.302380	0.691753	−1.88	0.060	−2.658190	0.053429
d	−0.710060	0.691183	−1.03	0.304	−2.064750	0.644637
d	−0.787120	0.680803	−1.16	0.248	−2.121470	0.547230
d	0.747757	0.701152	1.07	0.286	−0.626480	2.121990
d	0.546641	0.727326	0.75	0.452	−0.878890	1.972173
d	0.191554	0.727485	0.26	0.792	−1.234290	1.617398
_cons	2.362496	1.133068	2.09	0.037	0.141723	4.583269

NOTE: Coefficients were computed using generalized least squares; the panels are assumed to be heteroskedastic, with no autocorrelation.

TABLE 5.11

Estimation of CRISIS Coefficient, Stratification Procedure

	Lowest Support Stratum[a]	Middle1 Support Stratum[a]	Middle2 Support Stratum[a]	Highest Support Stratum[a]
Estimated coefficient of CRISIS	−0.69	−1.52	−2.17	−0.88
t statistic	−1.52	−3.17	−2.10	−2.52
Number of observations in stratum	626	153	19	724

[a]Each stratum was defined according to the estimated probability of facing a crisis. The lowest stratum included predicted probabilities in the interval (0.07, 0.3025); the second stratum in the interval (0.3025, 0.535); the third stratum in the interval (0.535, 0.7675), and the highest stratum in the interval (0.7675, 1.00).

panel data probit results reported above in Table 5.8. Table 5.11 contains the estimated coefficient of the CRISIS coefficient for four different segments of the common support, its *t* statistic, and the number of observations in that stratum. As can be seen, the results obtained from the stratification analysis confirm those reported above, and indicate that crises indeed result in a lower rate of GDP growth. The simple average of the CRISIS coefficients using this stratification method is −1.33; on the other hand, the weighted average (using relative number of observations to calculate the weights) is −0.88.

4.2 Fiscal Deficits and Investment

In the vast majority of countries a proportion of public sector expenditures is devoted to investment. This means, then, that in many nations fiscal deficits are used, at least partially, to finance investment. This, of course, means that in principle, and through this channel, deficits could have a positive effect on growth. In this section I estimate a number of aggregate investment equations to investigate how important fiscal deficits have historically been as determinants of investment in a large group of countries. The recent empirical literature on investment, including that of Attanasio, Picci, and Scorcu (2000), indicates that investment exhibits a strong degree of persistence through time. This suggests estimating equations of the following type:[11]

$$(11)\quad \text{INVGDP}_{tj} = \beta\, \text{INVGDP}_{t-1j} + \phi\, \text{TRADE\_OPEN}_{tj} + \gamma\, \text{DEFICITS}_{tj} + \omega_{tj}$$

where INVGDP is the investment-to-GDP ratio, and TRADE_OPEN is an index that captures the degree of openness of the economy. And DEFICITS refers to the fiscal deficit-to-GDP ratio. Finally, ω is an error term, which takes the following form:

$$\omega_{tj} = \varepsilon_j + \mu_{tj}$$

where ε_j is a country-specific error term, and μ_{tj} is an iid disturbance with the standard characteristics. The estimation of equation (11) using panel data presents a potential problem, however. It is well known from early work on dynamic panel estimation by Nerlove (1971) that if the error contains a country-specific term, the coefficient of the lagged dependent variable will be biased upward. There are several ways of handling this potential problem. Possibly the most basic approach is using a fixed-effect model, where a country dummy (hopefully) picks up the effect of the country-specific disturbance. A second way is to estimate the instrumental variables procedure recently proposed by Arellano and Bond (1991) for dynamic panel data. This method consists of differentiating the equation in question—equation (11) in our case—in order to eliminate the country-specific disturbance ε_j. The differenced equation is then estimated using instrumental variables, where the lagged dependent variable (in levels), the predetermined variables (also in levels), and the first differences of the exogenous variables are used as instruments. The results obtained, using the Arellano and Bond method on a panel sample of 64 emerging nations and including year dummies, are reported in Table 5.12. Surprisingly, perhaps, the results suggest that, on average, higher deficits have had no effect (positive or negative) on aggregate investment in these 64 nations—remarkably the z statistic has a value of -0.00. The reason for this result has to do with the crowding-out effect that fiscal deficits have on *private investment*. Indeed, in the estimation of an equation for *private investment*, the coefficient of the fiscal deficit was significantly negative, with a point estimate of -0.29. According to this equation, an increase in the deficit in 1 percent of GDP results, on average, in a decline in private investment 0.4 percent in the long run.[12]

4.3 Fiscal Deficits and Growth: Is There a Direct Effect?

The final question is whether larger fiscal deficits have a direct effect on economic performance. That is, I am interested in understanding whether larger deficits have an effect on growth once we control for the CRISIS variable and by investment. The results obtained, summarized in Table 5.13, suggest that larger fiscal deficits have a very small direct negative effect on GDP growth. The point estimate indicates that, with other things given, an increase in the deficit in one percentage point of GDP will result in a reduction in GDP growth of 0.4 percent. This effect will take place over and above the deficit impact on the probability of a crisis, and compound the negative effect that fiscal imbalances have through a higher crisis probability.

5. Concluding Remarks

The main question addressed in this chapter is whether fiscal imbalances matter. The empirical analysis presented here, using a massive comparative data set, sug-

TABLE 5.12

Investment Equations Estimated Using Arellano-Bond Instrumental Variables, 1975–1997

Number of observations	686
Group variable (i)	*imfcode*
Number of groups	64
Wald statistic, $\chi^2(24)$	345.03
Time variable (t)	*year*
Minimum number of observations	1
Mean number of observations	10.71875
Maximum number of observations	22
Dependent variable	*invgdp*

Variable	Coefficient	Robust Standard Error	z	$p > \|z\|$	Lower Bound, 95% CI	Upper Bound, 95% CI
invgdp(−1)	0.531827	0.106446	5	0	0.323197	0.740457
deficit	−0.000250	0.070908	0	0.997	−0.139230	0.138727
trade_open	0.103345	0.040176	2.57	0.010	0.024602	0.182088
d77	1.214919	0.943716	1.29	0.198	−0.634730	3.064569
d78	1.272927	0.964692	1.32	0.187	−0.617830	3.163689
d79	1.256432	2.283532	0.55	0.582	−3.219210	5.732073
d80	1.148696	3.236638	0.35	0.723	−5.195000	7.492391
d81	3.405595	3.704153	0.92	0.358	−3.854410	10.665600
d82	2.699096	4.302400	0.63	0.530	−5.733450	11.131640
d83	2.577969	4.888475	0.53	0.598	−7.003270	12.159200
d84	3.007125	5.578877	0.54	0.590	−7.927270	13.941520
d85	3.818864	6.168774	0.62	0.536	−8.271710	15.909440
d86	5.229215	6.794528	0.77	0.442	−8.087810	18.546240
d87	6.367428	7.463031	0.85	0.394	−8.259850	20.994700
d88	7.806686	8.078155	0.97	0.334	−8.026210	23.639580
d89	8.057905	8.752531	0.92	0.357	−9.096740	25.212550
d90	8.960823	9.285110	0.97	0.335	−9.237660	27.159300
d91	9.325863	9.837763	0.95	0.343	−9.955800	28.607520
d92	10.222720	10.419080	0.98	0.327	−10.198300	30.643740
d93	12.012620	11.051300	1.09	0.277	−9.647530	33.672770
d94	11.759490	11.655100	1.01	0.313	−11.084100	34.603080
d95	11.938370	12.331440	0.97	0.333	−12.230800	36.107560
d96	12.738900	12.945580	0.98	0.325	−12.634000	38.111780
d97	14.057170	13.537140	1.04	0.299	−12.475100	40.589480
_cons	−0.694130	0.616056	−1.13	0.260	−1.901580	0.513318

NOTE: Arellano-Bond dynamic panel data. Arellano-Bond test that average autocovariance in residuals of order 1 is 0:

H0: no autocorrelation $z = -3.53$ $Pr > z = 0.0004$

Arellano-Bond test that average autocovariance in residuals of order 2 is 0:

H0: no autocorrelation $z = -0.89$ $Pr > z = 0.3718$

gests that the answer is yes: larger imbalances increase the probability of currency crises, reduce aggregate GDP growth, and have no discernible effect on aggregate investment. It is important to note, as was stated in the introduction, that I have not attempted to tackle every aspect of fiscal policy in the emerging economies. Indeed, dealing with every angle of the fiscal problem would require a treatise of several volumes. A particularly important aspect of fiscal policy not

TABLE 5.13

Fiscal Deficits and Economic Growth Estimated Using Heteroskedastic Feasible Least Squares, 1975–1997

Estimated covariances	110
Estimated autocorrelations	0
Estimated coefficients	30
Number of observations	1497
Number of groups	110
Observations per group, minimum	1
Observations per group, average	17.26052
Observations per group, maximum	23
Wald statistic, $\chi^2(28)$	535.61
Probability > χ^2	0.0000
Log likelihood	−3915.371
Dependent variable	*growth*

Variable	Coefficient	Standard Error	z	$p > \|z\|$	Lower Bound, 95% CI	Upper Bound, 95% CI
invgdp	0.192679	0.012774	15.08	0	0.167643	0.217715
pop_growth	0.303243	0.089749	3.38	0.001	0.127338	0.479148
trade_open	0.005678	0.003532	1.61	0.108	−0.001250	0.012602
loggpp0	−0.411010	0.105454	−3.90	0	−0.617700	−0.204330
govcon	−0.045160	0.013451	−3.36	0.001	−0.071520	−0.018800
acrisis	−0.929670	0.262082	−3.55	0	−1.443350	−0.416000
deficit	−0.041240	0.017378	−2.37	0.018	−0.075300	−0.007180
d75	−1.883380	0.714420	−2.64	0.008	−3.283610	−0.483140
d76	1.654678	0.709666	2.33	0.020	0.263758	3.045597
d77	−0.625290	0.733526	−0.85	0.394	−2.062980	0.812392
d78	1.115332	0.530930	2.10	0.036	0.074729	2.155935
d79	0.334518	0.713838	0.47	0.639	−1.064580	1.733615
d80	−0.733730	0.708715	−1.04	0.301	−2.122780	0.655328
d81	−1.251980	0.697742	−1.79	0.073	−2.619530	0.115567
d82	−2.347400	0.702310	−3.34	0.001	−3.723900	−0.970890
d83	−1.259970	0.698403	−1.80	0.071	−2.628810	0.108878
d84	0.450692	0.695439	0.65	0.517	−0.912340	1.813727
d85	−0.049240	0.693586	−0.07	0.943	−1.408650	1.310159
d86	0.330444	0.692794	0.48	0.633	−1.027410	1.688296
d87	0.078326	0.694194	0.11	0.910	−1.282270	1.438922
d88	1.009920	0.695432	1.45	0.146	−0.353100	2.372942
d89	0.265034	0.697817	0.38	0.704	−1.102660	1.632731
d90	−0.035190	0.695610	−0.05	0.960	−1.398560	1.328185
d91	−1.259800	0.691981	−1.82	0.069	−2.616050	0.096463
d92	−0.682770	0.691268	−0.99	0.323	−2.037630	0.672090
d93	−0.712930	0.676588	−1.05	0.292	−2.039020	0.613155
d94	0.819786	0.702025	1.17	0.243	−0.556160	2.195730
d95	0.615416	0.728216	0.85	0.398	−0.811860	2.042693
d96	0.222706	0.727666	0.31	0.760	−1.203490	1.648904
_cons	2.837671	1.143997	2.48	0.013	0.595478	5.079865

considered in this chapter refers to the intergenerational transfers implied by alternative fiscal stances. A detailed treatment of the issues related to intergenerational accounting can be found in Auerbach, Kotlikoff, and Leibfritz (1999). Additionally, I have not dealt with issues related to public sector "contingent liabilities" stemming from insolvent social security systems, or from implicit public social insurance schemes.

The results from the empirical analysis reported in this chapter are directly relevant to India's current situation. Specifically, the findings presented here indicate that India's current fiscal imbalances—of the order of 10–11 percent of GDP—are very large from an international comparative perspective. Indeed, very few countries in our sample have posted those kinds of figures. Our analysis suggests that the type of imbalances that India is running can, indeed, lead to a severe currency crisis, with its concomitant costs in terms of reduced economic activity.

Appendix
Debt Sustainability and Fiscal Policy in a Poor Country

An Analytical Framework

Fiscal policy sustainability is attained when the ratio of public sector debt to GDP is stable and consistent with the demand—both by domestic and foreign residents—for government securities. An important feature of public sector sustainability analyses is that they make a distinction between the total (or nominal) public sector balance and the primary balance, which excludes interest payments on the public sector debt. Public sector sustainability models allow us to calculate the *primary balance* that is compatible with a stable debt-to-GDP ratio.

Standard models are not completely suitable for the case of poor countries such as India, however. This is because a large percentage of poor countries' public sector debt is in concessionary terms. In this appendix I develop a general sustainability approach to provide guidance with respect to fiscal policy in poor countries. The model can also be used to analyze the cases of countries whose debt is being reduced under the HIPC initiative. As will be shown, the traditional steady-state results are a special case of our more general analysis. Moreover, the approach followed in this appendix is not restricted to the steady-state equilibrium; in fact, our approach allows us to concentrate on the *sustainable dynamic path* of fiscal policy.

Consider the case of a country's government that has two types of public sector debt:

- Concessionary debt, *DC*.
- Debt issued on commercial terms, *DD*, and denominated in dollars. In principle, both domestic and foreign investors can purchase this debt. In what follows we call this debt "domestic debt."

For now we will ignore issues related to the currency composition of the debt, and will assume that both types of debt are in foreign currency (U.S. dollars). We later, however, assume that changes in the real exchange rate introduce valuation complications into the analysis. At any moment in time total debt in the country is the sum of *DC* and *DD*; also, at any time *t*, the net increase in total (nominal dollar denominated) debt is equal to the sum of the increase in these two types of debt.

$$\text{(A.1)} \quad \Delta D_t = \Delta DC_t + \Delta DD_t$$

From the "uses" side, net debt increases (ΔD_t)are equal to interest payments plus the primary balance (*pb*), minus seignorage. More specifically:

$$\text{(A.2)} \quad \Delta D_t = (r_t^C DC_{t-1} + r_t^D DD_{t-1}) + pb_t - \Delta B_t$$

where r_t^C and r_t^D are nominal interest payments on each type of debt. ΔB_t, in turn, is the change in the monetary base; this corresponds to seignorage, and its actual magnitude will depend on the rate of domestic inflation, as well as on the ratio of the monetary base to nominal GDP. Notice that in equation (A.2) we have assumed that interest payments are made on the basis of last period's stock of debt. This assumption, which appears to be quite harmless, turns out to be very important in actual computations of the sustainable fiscal path. From (A.2), and after some manipulations, we can write the following expression for the primary balance:

$$\text{(A.3)} \quad pb_t = [DC_{t-1}(\Delta DC_t/DC_{t-1})] + [DD_{t-1}(\Delta DD_t/DD_{t-1})] - (r_t^C DC_{t-1} + r_t^D DD_{t-1}) - \Delta B_t.$$

This equation summarizes the evolution through time of the primary balance (a positive number is a primary deficit) as a function of interest payments, the net increases in both types of debt, and seignorage. We are interested in computing the primary balance consistent with macroeconomic "sustainability." That is, we are interested in the value of pb_t that is consistent with changes in the debt level that are on a sustainable path. A sustainable path of the debt is defined, in turn, as a situation where increases in each type of debt are in line with the pace at which creditors want to accumulate the country's debt. This means that, in order to compute the sustainable primary balance in period *t*, we need to know the "sustainable" rates of growth ($\Delta DC_t/DC_{t-1}$) and ($\Delta DD_t/DD_{t-1}$) in equation (A.3).

Without loss of generality, we assume that going forward the donor community is willing to increase the country's concessional debts at an annual rate of θ. Likewise, we assume that holders of the country's domestic debt are willing to accumulate it at a rate equal to β. An important constraint in the longer run is that neither the concessional nor the domestic debt-to-GDP ratio grows without limit. In other words, in the longer run these ratios should be bounded. If we denote the real rate of GDP growth by g, and the rate of dollar inflation by π^*, these constraints can be written as the following (remembering that, for now, we are abstracting from issues related to valuation that may arise from changes in the real exchange rate):

$$\text{(A.4)} \quad \theta \leq (g + \pi^*),$$

$$\text{(A.5)} \quad \beta \leq (g + \pi^*).$$

As will become clear from equation (A.6) below, these conditions are required to assure convergence of pb through time. With regard to seignorage, we assume that inflation will be maintained constant at a rate of π through time, and that the income elasticity of demand for money is unity. After manipulating equation (A.3) and using the sustainable rates of growth of both types of debt, we can write the primary balance that is consistent with debt being on a sustainable path in the following way:

$$\text{(A.6)} \quad (pb_t/Y_t) = [(\theta - r_t^C)(DC_0/D_0)e^{(\theta - g - \pi^*)(t-1)} + (\beta - r_t^D)(DD_0/D_0) \cdot e^{(\beta - g - \pi^*)(t-1)}][1/(1 + g + \pi^*)] - (g + \pi)(B_0/Y_0).$$

where Y_t is nominal (dollar denominated) GDP in year t. (DC_0/Y_0) is the ratio of concessional debt to GDP immediately after the HIPC debt reduction is actually implemented. Likewise, (DD_0/Y_0) is the domestic debt-to-GDP ratio immediately after the post-HIPC period. Finally, π is the (target) rate of domestic inflation and (B_0/Y_0) is the initial ratio of base money to GDP. It is clear from equation (A.6) that θ—the rate at which concessional debt evolves through time —is a key parameter in determining the sustainable level of the primary balance.

In order to organize the discussion, three possible cases with respect to donors' behavior are considered:

CASE A: The donor community is willing to provide sufficient concessional funds to maintain the DC-to-Y ratio at the immediate post-HIPC level. This is the case where

$$\text{(A.7)} \quad \theta = (g + \pi^*).$$

We also assume that the rate of growth of domestic debt is equal to (this assumption is maintained throughout the three scenarios)

$$\text{(A.7}'\text{)} \quad \beta = (g + \pi^*).$$

In this case the sustainable primary balance is given by equation (A.8):

$$(A.8)\quad (pb/Y) = (D_0/Y_0)[(g + \pi^*) - r^C(DC_0/D_0) - r^D(DD_0/D_0)] \cdot [1/(1 + g + \pi^*)] - (g + \pi)(B_0/Y_0).$$

CASE B: The donor community is willing to provide sufficient concessional funds as to maintain the real dollar value of the concessional debt at its current level. In this case, $\theta = \pi^*$. As in the previous case, we assume that $\beta = (g + \pi^*)$. Under this scenario, the sustainable dynamic path of the primary balance is given by equation (A.9) below.

$$(A.9)\quad (pb_t/Y_t) = [(\pi^* - r_t^C)(DC_0/Y_0)e^{-g(t-1)} + (g + \pi^* - r_t^D) \cdot (DD_0/Y_0)][1/(1 + g + \pi^*)] - (g + \pi)(B_0/Y_0).$$

Clearly, in this scenario it is more appropriate to talk about a "sustainable dynamic path" for *pb*. Whether on the *sustainable dynamic path* described by equation (A.9) we are in the presence of a primary deficit or surplus will be determined by the value of the different parameters in equation (A.9). An interesting feature of this equation is that the dynamic behavior of the primary balance through time will be greatly affected by the relationship between the international rate of inflation (π^*) and the nominal rate of interest on soft loans (r_t^C). Indeed the sign expression ($\pi^* - r_t^C$) will depend on whether concessional loans have a positive or negative *real* rate of interest. Interestingly enough, if $\pi^* = r_t^C$, there are no dynamics in equation (9). In the steady state, when $t \rightarrow \infty$, equation (A.9) becomes (A.10), which is a very standard expression for calculating a sustainable primary balance and is very similar to equation (5) in the body of this chapter:

$$(A.10)\quad (pb/Y) = (g + \pi^* - r^D)(DD_0/Y_0)[1/(1 + g + \pi^*)] - (g + \pi)(B_0/Y_0).$$

Notice that according to equation (A.10) in the steady state ($t \rightarrow \infty$), the country in question would have no concessional debt. This is, indeed, a very attractive feature of this Case B, since it is difficult to believe that any country will continue to receive concessional assistance into the indefinite future. Notice, in fact, that equation (A.10) corresponds to the traditional expression used by investment banks and other private sector analysts to evaluate fiscal sustainability in emerging countries.

CASE C: In this scenario the donor community is even stricter, and is willing to roll over only the concessional debt that matures at any point in time. That is, the nominal *value* of concessional debt is maintained constant. No net funds (in nominal dollars) are provided. As in the two previous scenarios, we assume that $\beta = (g + \pi^*)$. In this case $\theta = 0$, and the sustainable primary balance is given by equation (11) below.

$$(A.11)\quad (pb_t/Y_t) = [-r_t^C(DC_0/Y_0)e^{-(g+\pi^*)(t-1)} + (g + \pi^* - r_t^D) \cdot (DD_0/Y_0)][1/(1 + g + \pi^*)] - (g + \pi)(B_0/Y_0).$$

The steady state primary balance ratio is the same as in Case B:

$$(A.10')\quad (pb/Y) = (g + \pi^* - r^D)(DD_0/Y_0)[1/(1 + g + \pi^*)] - (g + \pi)(B_0/Y_0).$$

The main difference between Cases B and C is that in the latter the primary balance reaches the steady state faster. This is because under Case C, the donor community is less generous and rolls over only the nominal value of the maturing debt.

The sustainability exercises presented above assume that the real exchange rate remains constant at its initial level in the indefinite future. Naturally, this need not be the case. Indeed, it is perfectly possible that initially the real exchange rate is overvalued with respect to its equilibrium value. This situation would affect the calculations of the primary balance sustainable path. (The steady state value of the primary balance is not affected, however). More specifically, in this case the equation for the sustainable primary balance in period t becomes:

$$(A.12)\quad (pb_t/Y_t) = [(g/2 + \pi^* - r_t^C)(DC_0/Y_0)e^{[(d\,\mathrm{rer}/\mathrm{rer})-(g/2)](t-1)} + (g + \pi^* - r_t^D)(DD_0/Y_0)e^{(d\,\mathrm{rer}/\mathrm{rer})(t-1)}] \cdot [1/(1 + g + \pi^*)] - (g + \pi)(B_0/Y_0),$$

where $(d\ \mathrm{rer}/\mathrm{rer})_t$ is the change in the real exchange rate in period t. The real exchange rate, in turn, is assumed to evolve through time according to the following equation:

$$(A.13)\quad \mathrm{rer}_t = \mathrm{rer}^* + (\mathrm{rer}^* - \mathrm{rer}_0)e^{-\gamma t}.$$

Here, rer* is the equilibrium real exchange rate and γ is the rate at which real exchange rate disequilibria are eliminated through time.

Notes

1. Rigorously speaking, λ must be nonincreasing.
2. In deriving this expression I made use of the fact that there are country and currency risk premiums.
3. In mid-2001 the credibility of the currency board was rather low, and the expected rate of devaluation in Argentina—as reflected in interest rate differentials—was significant.
4. During late May/early June 2001, the spread was above 900 basis points.
5. In the particular case of Argentina it is not clear whether, under these particular

circumstances, private investors—both domestic and international—will be willing to accumulate further Argentine securities.

6. It should be noted that the "control group" is rather large and composed of countries that have rather different characteristics from those of the "fiscal adjustment" countries. This problem can be dealt with by implementing a "treatment" type of test, where the control group is corrected using the propensity score obtained from a logit (or probit) estimation of a fiscal adjustment equation. For an application of this type of methodology in the context of fiscal policy analyses, see the discussion in Section 4 of this chapter.

7. It should be noted that the results are robust with respect to the number of standard deviations (two or three) used to define a crisis episode.

8. This finding is not affected by any of the sensitivity tests undertaken by the authors.

9. An alternative line of inquiry would be to focus on banking—or more broadly "financial"—crises. It is significantly difficult to find reliable data on these crises, however. The most serious problem is that there are some data on banking crises that have resulted in bank failures and bailouts. No data are available, however, on crises that are resolved without a failure.

10. Most, but not all, of these regressors were used by Frankel and Rose (1996). The results reported here are not directly comparable to Frankel and Rose (1996), since the data sets are somewhat different. All independent variables are lagged one period.

11. On recent attempts to estimate investment equations using a cross section of countries, see, for example, Barro and Sala-i-Marti (1995) and Attanasio, Picci, and Scorcu (2000).

12. The estimated coefficient for lagged public investment is 0.4.

References

Ades, Alberto, and Federico Kaune. 1997. *A new measure of current account sustainability for developing countries.* New York: Goldman Sachs, Emerging Markets Economic Research.

Anderson, T. W., and Cheng Hsiao. 1981. Estimation of dynamic models with error components. *Journal of the American Statistical Association* 76:598–606.

Arellano, Manuel, and Stephen Bond. 1991. Some tests of specification for panel data: Monte Carlo evidence and an application to employment equations. *Review of Economic Studies* 58:277–97.

Attanasio, Orazio P., Lucio Picci, and Antonello E. Scorcu. 2000. Saving, growth, and investment: A macroeconomic analysis using a panel of countries. *Review of Economics and Statistics* 82 (2):182–211.

Auerbach, Alan J., Laurence J. Kotlikoff, and Willi Leibfritz, eds. 1999. *Generational accounting around the world.* Chicago: University of Chicago Press.

Banco de Mexico. *The Mexican Economy* (various issues). Mexico City: Banco de Mexico.

Barro, Robert J., and Xavier Sala-i-Martin. 1995. *Economic growth.* Cambridge, Mass.: MIT Press.

Beck, Nathaniel, and Jonathan N. Katz. 1995. What to do (and not to do) with time-series cross-section data. *American Political Science Review* 89 (3): 634–47.

Blundell, Richard, and Monica Costa Dias. 2000. Evaluation data for non-experimental data. *Fiscal Studies* 21 (4): 427–68.

Buiter, W. H. 1990. *Principles of budgetary and financial policy.* Cambridge, Mass.: MIT Press.

Corsetti, Giancarlo, Paolo Pesenti, and Nouriel Roubini. 1998. *Paper tigers? A model of the Asian crisis.* Working Paper 6783. Cambridge, Mass.: National Bureau of Economic Research.

Deutsche Bank. 2000. *Global market research,* March. London: Deutsche Bank.

Edwards, Sebastian. 1989. *Real exchange rates, devaluation, and adjustment.* Cambridge, Mass.: MIT Press.

Edwards, Sebastian, and Julio Santaella. 1993. Devaluation controversies in the developing countries: Lessons from the Bretton Woods era. In *A retrospective on the Bretton Woods system: Lessons for international monetary reform,* edited by Michael Bordo and Barry Eichengreen. Chicago: University of Chicago Press.

Eichengreen, Barry, Andrew K. Rose, and Charles Wyplosz. 1996. *Contagious currency crises.* Working Paper 5681. Cambridge, Mass.: National Bureau of Economic Research.

Fischer, Stanley. 1988. Real balances, the exchange rate, and indexation: Real variables in disinflation. *Quarterly Journal of Economics* 103 (1): 27–49.

Fischer, Stanley. 1994. Comments on Dornbusch and Werner. *Brookings Papers on Economic Activity* 1:304–9.

Fleiss, J. L. 1981. *Statistical methods for rates and proportions.* 2d ed. New York: Wiley.

Frankel, Jeffrey A., and Andrew Rose. 1996. Currency crashes in emerging markets: An empirical treatment. *Journal of International Economics* 41 (3): 351–56.

Goldstein, Morris, Graciela Kaminsky, and Carmen Reinhart. 2000. *Assessing financial vulnerability: An early warning system for emerging markets.* Washington, D.C.: Institute for International Economics.

Harberger, Arnold. 1950. Currency depreciation, income, and the balance of trade. *Journal of Political Economy* 58 (1): 47–60.

Heckman, James J., Hidehiko Ichimura, and Petra Todd. 1997. Matching as an econometric evaluation estimator: Evidence from evaluating a job training programme. *Review of Economic Studies* 64 (4): 605–54.

———. 1998. Matching as an econometric evaluation estimator. *Review of Economic Studies* 65 (2): 261–94.

Johnson, Harry G. 1955. Economic expansion and international trade. *Manchester School of Economic and Social Studies* 23:95–112.

Kamin, Steven B. 1988. *Devaluation, exchange controls, and black markets for foreign exchange in developing countries.* International Finance Discussion Paper 334. Washington, D.C.: Board of Governors of the Federal Reserve System.

Krugman, Paul. 2000. *Currency crises.* Chicago: University of Chicago Press.

Loser, Claudio. 1998. Aftermath: An IMF perspective. In *Mexico 1994: Anatomy of an emerging market crash,* edited by Sebastian Edwards and Moisés Naím. Washington, D.C.: Carnegie Endowment for International Peace.

Machlup, Fritz. 1943. *International trade and international income multiplier.* Philadelphia: Blakiston.

Milesi-Ferretti, Gian Maria, and Assaf Razin. 1996. *Sustainability of persistent current account deficits*. Working Paper 5467. Cambridge, Mass.: National Bureau of Economic Research.
———. 1998. Sharp reduction in current account deficits: An empirical analysis. *European Economic Review* 42 (5): 897–908.
———. 2000. Current account reversals and currency crises: Empirical regularities. In *Currency crises*, edited by Paul Krugman. Chicago: University of Chicago Press.
Nerlove, Marc. 1971. Further evidence on the estimation of dynamic economic relations from a time series of cross-sections. *Econometrica* 39 (2): 359–82.
Obstfeld, Maurice, and Kenneth Rogoff. 1996. *Foundations of international macroeconomics*. Cambridge, Mass.: MIT Press.
Radelet, Steven, and Jeffrey Sachs. 2000. The onset of the East Asian financial crisis. In *Currency crises*, edited by Paul Krugman. Chicago: University of Chicago Press.
Srinivasan, T. N. 2000. India's fiscal situation: Is a crisis ahead? Paper presented at the Stanford University Conference on India, at Stanford University, Calif.
Summers, Lawrence H. 1996. Commentary. In *Volatile capital flows*, edited by Ricardo Hausmann and Liliana Rojas-Suarez. Washington, D.C.: Inter-American Development Bank.
———. 2000. International financial crises: Causes, prevention, and cures. *American Economic Review* 90 (2): 1–16.
World Bank. 1993. *Trends in developing economies*. Washington, D.C.: World Bank.
———. 1994. *Trends in developing economies*. Washington, D.C.: World Bank.

Comment
Sustainable Debt-to-GDP Ratios

Alan J. Auerbach

This is an interesting and well-written essay on an important subject. In my comments, I will review the essay's findings, discuss its implications, and consider alternative measures of fiscal balance that might be used to evaluate a country's position.

The empirical analysis Edwards presents proceeds in stages. In the first stage, he uses a panel data set for a large number of countries to determine the causes of currency crises, which he defines as periods during which a country has experienced a large currency depreciation or significant loss in reserves. Contrary to earlier work by Frankel and Rose (1996), Edwards finds that high budget deficits and levels of debt, relative to GDP, do help predict currency crises. In the next stage of his investigation, he finds that currency crises, defined the same way, appear to contribute to slower subsequent growth. Finally, his results suggest that deficits contribute separately to low growth, over and above their indirect effect through the channel of currency crises.

To interpret these empirical findings, it is useful to go back to the underlying theory. For a government's projected fiscal policy path to be feasible, its debt-to-GDP ratio must stabilize at a sustainable level. Otherwise, investors will understand that a default must eventually occur or some other measures undertaken that could make holding the country's currency unwise, such as an attempt to monetize the debt. Achieving a stable debt-to-GDP ratio is likely to require deficits small enough that there is a surplus if interest is excluded, that is, a primary surplus. High deficits, added to a high initial level of debt, make fiscal balance less likely, increasing the prospect of inflation and instability and, thus, prompting a currency crisis. Such instability can contribute on its own to a lower rate of growth, and this impact can be augmented by the further disruptions resulting from the currency crisis.

Given the essay's empirical evidence, and this theoretical explanation for it, what are the implications for a country seeking to avoid currency crises and economic disruptions? One simple answer is that governments should attempt to maintain a relatively low level of debt, so that those deficits that may occur periodically don't induce crises. But what is a "safe" level of debt or deficits? Edwards focuses on the average deficit-to-GDP ratio of around 3 percent, but this is more an empirical regularity that anything based on theory. And how should fiscal adjustment be made, if the government's current policy is not sustainable? Edwards provides evidence that fiscal adjustments—which are more likely if deficits are large—don't seem to reduce growth, alleviating one of the concerns that might accompany such a move.

Thus, Edwards's basic story is that large deficits have a negative effect on growth, both directly and through their impact on currency crises, and that eliminating them is not to be feared from a macroeconomic perspective. Based on the theory and evidence he presents, I have little quarrel with the spirit of this message, but would offer some cautions both with respect to the empirical evidence and the methods used to gauge when fiscal policy is responsible.

As to the empirical evidence, let me offer a standard caveat with respect to the interpretation of cross-country regressions. Countries vary in many respects, fiscal policy being one of them. It is likely that fiscal policy differences are correlated with other differences that may have an important impact on economic performance. Looking at panel data helps, for we can hope that the effects of persistent cross-country differences will be eliminated as we look at the effects of *changes* in policy over time. But there remains the problem of policy endogeneity. For example, when a country adopts a fiscal reform, why did it do so? If the reform was prompted by the accession of a government committed to other economic reforms as well, then subsequent changes in economic performance are hard to attribute solely to changes in fiscal policy. Although many clever minds have devoted considerable attention to this problem, there is generally no simple solution. Economists vary in the credence given to cross-country analysis. In my view, such regressions are helpful in identifying empirical regularities, but should be augmented by case studies and other analysis of the behavior underlying the observations.

As to how a well-intentioned government should behave, the details remain vague regarding what is responsible and what is not. To adopt a quotation that Edwards uses to define currency crises, it would be nice to say of irresponsible fiscal policies that "we know them when we see them." Unfortunately, this is not always the case. Deficit and debt levels typically provide helpful rule-of-thumb measures, but not always. As the essay discusses, certain basic adjustments to the deficit are needed to control for differences in macroeconomics conditions. For example, a higher existing rate of economic growth makes a larger deficit sustainable, all else being equal. Beyond this, deficits may overstate or understate a country's fiscal problem. On the one hand, deficits may be run in order to finance productive infrastructure investment, which itself is typically ignored in evaluating the government's fiscal position. On the other hand, measured deficits also ignore major spending commitments. For example, pay-as-you-go public pensions represent enormous implicit liabilities for many countries; with aging populations, generous unfunded pension commitments may be unsustainable, but this is not apparent in current deficits as measured.

To deal with such ambiguities, other measures of a country's fiscal position exist and may be utilized. First, the long-run fiscal gap (as used, for example, in Auerbach 1994 and 1997), provides an indication of how much of a permanent fiscal adjustment is needed to make a country's fiscal policy sustainable, using the same definition as Edwards. This measure takes into account the assets and unfunded commitments that may make current debt and deficit measures unreliable. A second approach, generational accounting, goes one step further, determining not only how large a country's fiscal imbalance is, but also the impact of various policy adjustments on different generations. Sometimes these augmented measures provide the same answer as an inspection of current deficits and debt levels, but sometimes they do not. For example, many of the European countries that satisfied the fiscal conditions outlined in the Maastricht treaty, notably the requirement of a 3 percent debt-to-GDP ratio, have enormous and unsustainable fiscal imbalances (Auerbach, Kotlikoff, and Leibfritz 1999). It would be interesting to see how the types of cross-country regressions presented in this essay performed based on these alternative measures of fiscal stability.

In conclusion, I find the message of this essay sound. At the same time, one should exercise some caution in interpreting its empirical results and should understand the limitations of current debt and deficit measures as indicators of fiscal stability. But these empirical and measurement ambiguities do not alter the evidence conveyed here that when fiscal policies cannot be sustained, markets will precipitate adjustments if governments do not.

References

Auerbach, Alan. 1994. The U.S. fiscal problem: Where we are, how we got here, and where we're going. In *NBER macroeconomics annual*, edited by Stanley Fischer and Julio Rotemberg, 141–75. Cambridge, Mass.: MIT Press.

———. 1997. Quantifying the current U.S. fiscal imbalance. *National Tax Journal*, September, 387–98.

Auerbach, Alan, Laurence Kotlikoff, and Willi Leibfritz, eds. 1999. *Generational accounting around the world*. Chicago: University of Chicago Press.

Frankel, Jeffrey, and Andrew Rose. 1996. Currency crashes in emerging markets: An empirical treatment. *Journal of International Economics* 41 (3): 351–66.

Comment
"Parking the Deficit"—The Uncertain Link Between Fiscal Deficits and Inflation-Cum-Devaluation

Arnold C. Harberger

It is my firm conclusion, after observing major inflationary episodes all around the world for close to 50 years, that nearly all of these episodes were caused by large fiscal deficits financed by government borrowing from the banking system. This generalization has filtered through to a wide economically literate public. But it has come through the filter with an unfortunate twist—the public thinks there is a tight link between fiscal deficits and inflation, whereas my experience suggests a much more subtle and certainly more uncertain link.

To put my story in a more positive frame, countries can often avoid the torments of inflation, even after quite a spate of fiscal deficits. This is because there are a number of avenues through which fiscal deficits can be financed in noninflationary ways. There is no strict hierarchy of these noninflationary havens, but I will list them in what appears to me to be a natural order, going from easiest to hardest.

1. *Foreign aid*. Donor countries commonly designate their foreign-aid money as loans rather than grants—but the loans are at low interest rates and for long periods, so they contain what we call a large "grant component."[1] As long as donor-imposed restrictions on the uses of these loans are not too great, they are the borrowers' first choice as a "parking place" for deficits.
2. *Borrowing from multilateral agencies on preferential terms*. Loans from the World Bank, the regional development banks, and the IMF often also contain a grant component.

3. *Multilateral loans on "commercial" terms.* Here the preference for multilateral agencies comes from the fact that they may be more lenient than strictly commercial lenders in accepting rollovers and renegotiations, especially in times of crisis and emergency.
4. *Borrowing on the "foreign market."* Such borrowing is sometimes from the major international banks, sometimes from the sale of bonds on the international market. Loans are typically denominated in dollars or some other major currency. When the borrowing country's credit is good, the interest rate can be quite low—say, 1, 2, or 3 points above LIBOR.
5. *Selling bonds to the country's own social security system.* Once a developing country starts to have its own social security system, there typically follows an extended period (while the system is "young") during which contributors greatly outnumber retirees. The system is thus a sort of "cash cow" that can be easily milked by the government. Governments often find ways of using this system as a parking place for government bonds that bear interest at less-than-commercial rates.
6. *Forcing bonds down the throat of the commercial banking system.* This is different from simply placing on the open market bond issues that the banks can then acquire on their own volition and in the amounts that they want. It is when governments deem such an option to be too costly that they look for cheaper ways to borrow. One such way is simply to require that commercial banks hold a specified fraction of their assets in the form of certain special issues of government bonds—issues that are distinguished by their carrying lower-than-market rates of interest. Sometimes this strategy is implemented by first raising the standard reserve requirements that banks have to meet, and then giving the banks the "opportunity" to earn interest on a certain fraction of their required reserves (through "investing" this fraction in the above-mentioned special bond issues).
7. *Reducing the financial support given to public enterprises and state and local governments.* This looks like simply shifting the location of the deficit from the central government to these entities, but they may respond by eliminating or reducing their deficits, and if they still borrow, they will most likely do so in noninflationary ways.
8. *Floating bonds in the local financial marketplace.* This is what most advanced countries do as a matter of course. If the central bank pursues a responsible policy, deficits financed in this way can be noninflationary. Without a doubt, however, this policy comes at the cost of crowding out private sector borrowing.

Once one realizes that all these "parking places" are at least potentially available to governments seeking to cover their deficits in noninflationary ways, one

TABLE C.5.1
Government Deficits and Their Financing

Year	Fiscal Deficit/GDP	Foreign Borrowing/ GDP	Borrowing from Banking System/GDP
El Salvador (devalued from 2.5 to 5.0 colones per dollar in 1986)			
1965–69	0.008	0.009	0.005
1970–74	0.008	0.016	0.005
1975–79	0.004	0.012	0.010
1980–84	0.050	0.038	0.019
Guatemala (devalued from 1.0 to 2.5 quetzales per dollar in 1986)			
1965–69	0.009	0.008	0.001
1970–74	0.017	0.012	0.008
1975–79	0.015	0.006	—
1980–84	0.045	0.006	0.033
Honduras (devalued from 2.0 to 5.4 tempiras per dollar in 1991)			
1965–69	0.007	0.008	—
1970–74	0.018	0.019	0.007
1975–84	0.066	0.049	0.022
1985–89	0.050	0.037	

begins to see why in actual fact we find relatively poor correlations between the fiscal deficit/GDP and the rate of inflation. Of course, some governments are more responsible than others, and some are not strong enough in political terms to make use of some of the parking places. So we do not in fact see a systematic resort to all the noninflationary parking places before the inflationary tap is turned on. But we do observe a quite clear-cut disjointedness between fiscal deficits on the one hand and the rate of inflation on the other.

The disjointedness is even more striking between fiscal deficits and the rate of devaluation. Here the Central American countries provide interesting case studies. All these countries except Costa Rica had long histories of fixed exchange rates with the dollar. Not surprisingly, these histories were supported by traditionally conservative fiscal and monetary policies. Somehow, this triad of conservative policies became unglued somewhere between 1975 and 1985, with fiscal policy leading the way. Table C5.1 shows how El Salvador, Guatemala, and Honduras all started out with fiscal deficits of less then 1 percent of GDP. But one by one they broke through this barrier—Guatemala and Honduras in the early 1970s, El Salvador a decade later. Honduras's deficit crossed 5 percent of GDP in the late 1970s, El Salvador's in the early 1980s, at the same time that Guatemala's also came close to the 5 percent mark.

Yet all through the mentioned periods, all three of these countries managed to maintain their long-standing fixed exchange rates with the dollar. How did they do so? By "parking" their deficits in noninflationary parking lots, of course.

The table shows that foreign borrowing (i.e., parking lots 1–4) was the preferred source of funds, but borrowing from the domestic banking system also grew through time, probably as a result of the foreign parking lots gradually filling up (i.e., foreign lines of credit being used to the limit).

In any case, increased government borrowing from the local banking system can only work itself out through three escape valves: (1) squeezing private sector credit, (2) expanding the broad (M2) money supply, and (3) a reduction in net foreign assets (typically through a fall in the central bank's international reserves). Central banks can hold the line on monetary expansion by mechanism #1, but its unpopularity increases with each successive squeeze. Moreover, it sooner or later has a depressive effect on the real economy. The combination of political pressure from the affected borrowers and the recessive forces that are felt economy-wide in the end tends to induce the central bank not to try to offset further increases in M2 caused by incremental government borrowing. This is when M2 starts to expand beyond what is needed to accommodate the normal growth of the economy, that is, escape valve #2. But when people have more monetary balances than they really want to hold, they tend to spend the excess. And part of this induced spending surely goes to buy tradable goods and services. This part will normally end up draining the international reserve holdings of the central bank (i.e., escape valve #3). The central bank can try to stop this loss of reserves by reverting to a squeeze on private credit. But when use of that escape valve has been carried to the point where the political and economic costs of further squeezes are judged to be simply too high, the authorities have little alternative but to let M2 rise to reflect the increased government borrowing.

This is when a serious drain on the country's international reserves begins—a drain that ultimately leads to a foreign exchange crisis and a big devaluation. In the cases treated in Table C.5.1 one can see that there was a "long and variable lag" between the first signs of a fiscal deficit problem and the final surrender of the authorities in the form of a major devaluation. In Guatemala and Honduras, the fiscal deficit crossed 1 percent of GDP in the early 1970s, yet Guatemala did not devalue until 1986, Honduras not until 1991. El Salvador, in contrast, held the fiscal line longer, not reaching the 1 percent point until the early 1980s. But when El Salvador and Guatemala caved in, they did so in grand style, as they moved right away to deficits averaging 5 percent of GDP in 1980–84, and had their major devaluations in 1986.

I should not close without mentioning another set of devices that help postpone devaluations in scenarios like those we have examined. These devices are ad hoc restrictions on imports, which are all too often employed by countries when they are desperately seeking to stem a drain on their international reserves. There is a whole panoply of tricks—surcharges (beyond the normal tariffs) on some or all imports, lists of prohibited imports, lists of permitted imports (with all others prohibited), restrictions on buying imports on credit, schemes of importation only under prior license, and so on. These devices typically succeed in stemming imports, but at a cost of introducing huge uncertainties and distortions into the whole fabric of a country's international trade. These are the kinds of restrictions that give rise to smuggling, to black markets, to massive overinvoicing of imports and underinvoicing of exports, and in the end to major flights of capital. Often the actual devaluation is precipitated by a general speculative "run on the currency" that represents the end of the trail.

What are the lessons to be drawn here? In the first place, there is a somewhat beneficent lesson—one can have fiscal deficits for a long time without their generating the huge monetary and fiscal disequilibria that lead to major devaluations. Hence one has lots of opportunity to correct dangerous habits before it gets too late. The second lesson is that along the path of continuing deficits, one should take pains to avoid policies that introduce major new distortions into the economy—the path of import surcharges, licensing, prohibitions, and the like has far more costs than benefits. My third and final lesson is drawn with a particular eye to contemporary India. Unquestionably there have been enormous deficits over a significant period of years. Yet the authorities appear to have little sense of alarm about these deficits. Does this represent a myopic and irresponsible vision, aimed at surviving the moment while passing an ever greater burden on to future governments and later generations? Or does it mean that the authorities have studied the problem well, and that today's deficits are being placed in convenient parking lots that still have plenty of unused capacity? These are questions that can be answered only on the basis of a thorough understanding of the facts. So what we need right now is a program of serious study of India's fiscal deficits. Where are they being parked? At what cost? And how much vacant parking space remains to be occupied before major problems emerge? These are important questions for India's policy makers, but they are also important for all of us who want to reach as accurate a diagnosis as possible of India's problems. They should therefore have a high place on the research agenda for those who are interested in India's economic policy and performance.

Note

1. The grant component is usually defined by using a free-market interest rate to get the present value of contractual loan payments (PVLP) and then measuring the grant percentage as (ILA − PVLP)/ILA, where ILA is the initial loan amount.

6

TAX REFORM IN INDIA

N. K. Singh

It is now widely recognized that the most important challenge facing the Indian economy is to reverse the growing fiscal deficit for both the central and state governments. Attempts over the past few years to effect a significant fiscal correction have yielded disappointing results, and urgent action is needed to address this concern. Fiscal reform requires action both in the areas of expenditure and revenue and, at the same time, the use of nontax revenues from a credible privatization program to bridge the growing financing gap. Many decisions in both areas depend on political consensus, in particular to withdraw tax exemptions to phase out nonmerit subsidies and to increase the application of user charges for nonpublic goods. Furthermore, many of these difficult decisions need to be taken by state governments, especially those involving the power sector reforms that are at the heart of any strategy to improve state finances.

While this chapter briefly discusses some of the much-needed expenditure reforms, it focuses mainly on the need for tax reform—manifested through further tax-rate rationalization, elimination of exemptions, and, most importantly, improved compliance through better tax administration—so as to increase the tax-to-GDP ratio and help alleviate the fiscal quagmire in which the economy increasingly finds itself.

The rest of the chapter is organized as follows: Section 1 sets the context for fiscal reform by describing the nature of India's fiscal imbalances and its consequent detrimental impact on macroeconomic stability and growth. Section 2 then focuses on the role that expenditure management can play in helping alleviate the country's fiscal imbalances. Section 3 and following sections cover the main focus of the paper—the need for tax reform. While Section 3 assesses the tax structure as of 1990, Section 4 analyzes the tax reforms of the 1990s—in-

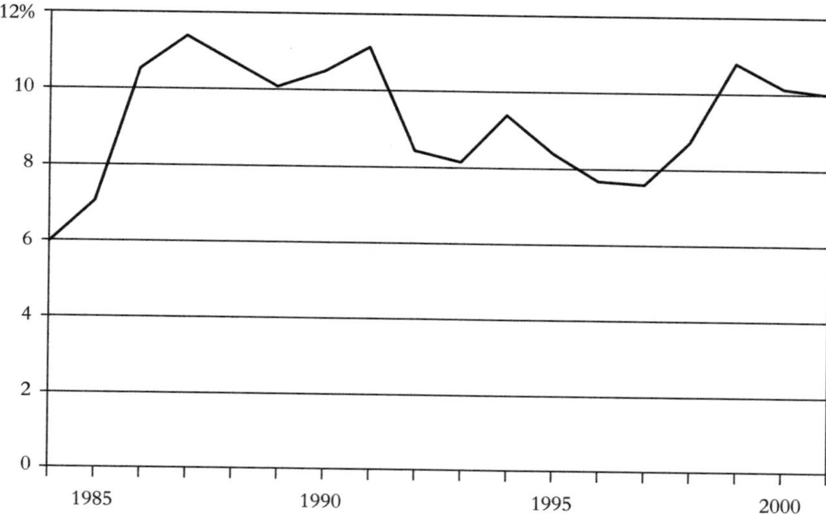

Figure 6.1. Consolidated Fiscal Deficit of Central and State Governments as Percentage of GDP.

SOURCE: CMIE.

cluding rate reductions, tax-base widening, and increased compliance. The impact of these reforms on the tax-to-GDP ratio over the decade of the 1990s, and in particular on the growth rate of direct taxes over the decade, is examined in Section 5. Sections 6 and 7 look ahead to assess the need for further tax reform (pointing particularly to the need for better enforcement of the country's tax laws) and also numerically estimate the impact that future reforms could have on revenues and deficits. Section 8 concludes.

1. *The Context*

The reform program, which began in 1991 when the consolidated gross fiscal deficit was 11.1 percent of GDP, initially obtained a modest fiscal adjustment, with the deficit dropping to 7.6 percent of GDP in 1997. But in subsequent years the fiscal deficit rose once more to about 10 percent of GDP (Figure 6.1). That is an astonishingly large fiscal deficit. It is hard to think of any country in the world that has sustained a gross fiscal deficit above 5 percent of GDP and where this did not negatively impact growth. These large fiscal deficits have led to a sharp increase in the liabilities of the central government (Table 6.1), which, in turn, has fueled concerns and debate about whether India is now in a debt trap (Buiter and Patel 1992; Lahiri and Kannan 2001).

TABLE 6.1
Central Government Liabilities

Fiscal Year	Liabilities (Billions of Rs)	% of GDP
1996–1997	6,754	49.36
1997–1998	7,780	51.10
1998–1999	8,915	51.19
1999–2000	10,207	52.90
2000–2001	11,767	56.36
2001–2002*	13,420	60.45
2002–2003*	15,125	59.59

SOURCE: Government of India.
*Forecasts as of mid-2002.

Going beyond the very serious implications for macrostability raised by persistent deficits, the size of the fiscal deficit has numerous other deleterious ramifications for economic policy formulation. It has decreased the ability of the government to engage in countercyclical fiscal policy. It has sharply circumscribed the ability of the government to initiate new spending programs that could produce highly beneficial public goods. It has served to crowd out private investment, and thus reduced GDP growth. Besides resulting in significant preemption of resources from the financial sector, it has also generated incentives to distort policies in that sector—thereby inhibiting banking reform and impeding the development of liquid markets.

For all these reasons, questions about fiscal adjustment policies in India are of the highest importance. It is well understood that there are many subtle policy ingredients in a fiscal adjustment program that need to be brought together—ranging from questions of taxation and reorientation of expenses into the production of public goods, to issues of user charges for infrastructure, pension reforms, subsidy reduction, and reforms in specific industries such as fertilizers. Shome (2000) and Srinivasan (2000) offer some recent perspectives on India's fiscal problems.

2. *What Role Can Cutting Expenses Play?*

In many countries, downsizing government or cutting government expenses has been central to fiscal adjustment. In the case of India, central government expenditure dropped from 18.9 percent of GDP in 1986 to 15.6 percent of GDP in 2001. These values do not appear to be particularly out of line by international standards, and are broadly consistent with the level needed to produce public goods of the required quality and quantity.

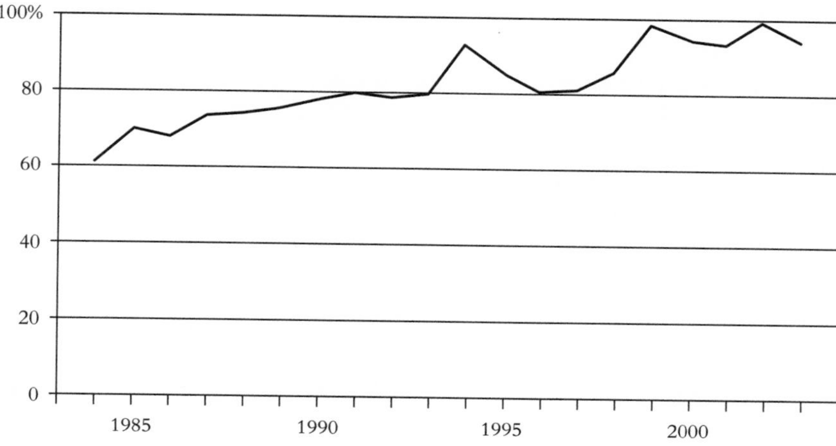

Figure 6.2. Interest, Defense, and Subsidies as Percentage of Tax Revenues.
SOURCE: CMIE.

2.1 Expenditure Management

Figure 6.2 shows how the three items of expenditure, that is, interest payments, defense expenditures, and subsidies, take up nearly 100 percent of tax revenues. Nonetheless, improving expenditure management is necessary to rein in the growing deterioration in the balance on current revenues (BCR) of both the central and the state governments. A credible expenditure reform policy would involve improving the quality of public expenditure and augmenting productivity of public assets. Specific initiatives would include the following:

- Restructuring the composition of public expenditure to focus attention on and give priority to the social sectors, with emphasis on investments in education, primary health care, water, and sanitation.
- Evolution of a national policy to regulate the pay and allowances of government employees. The last Pay Commission proved to be an unmitigated disaster for the finances of both the central and state governments. Overall finances of the central and state governments need to be borne in mind for determining the admissible level of emoluments of government employees for the future.
- Attrition in the number of government employees by at least 2 percent per annum. This could be accomplished through limiting fresh recruitment in all positions, except for those with technical responsibilities.
- Reduction in nonmerit subsidies, particularly in the areas of fertilizers, kerosene, and LPG (liquid petroleum gas). Effort should be made to

ensure that the benefits of the subsidies actually reach the small and marginal farmers.

- Improving the targeting of the public distribution system so that the subsidized goods reach the intended recipients—most importantly, those below the poverty line. The introduction of smart cards for the procurement of food grains needs to be explored.
- Public sector monopolies like the Food Corporation of India need to be made more efficient to avoid wasting excess food grains.

Power sector reforms are a high priority in view of their critical role in improving the finances of state governments.[1] These reforms must include a significant reduction in transmission and distribution losses (which now average 40 percent for the country as a whole, with some states significantly above the average) and a reduction/elimination of the large subsidy implicit in the pricing of electricity to farmers and some other consumers.[2] Cutting these losses would require the unbundling of generation and transmission, increased privatization at the distribution end, metering of electricity, energy auditing, and a system of market-based incentives. The implementation of these reforms should improve the cash flows of the state electricity boards and hence the state governments.

However, even with substantial cuts in expenditure, the larger burden of fiscal adjustment will fall on improving tax revenues. This is the focus of the present chapter. (Chelliah and Rao 2001 and Rao 2000 offer some ideas on related issues.)

3. *Tax Structure as of 1990*

As a starting point, it is useful to focus on the status as of 1990. Table 6.2 summarizes the tax collections from various sources as of 1990. The weaknesses of

TABLE 6.2

Structure of Tax Revenues in 1990

Source	Amount Collected (Billions Rs)	% of Total
Personal income tax	50.10	9.70
Corporate income tax	47.29	9.16
Customs taxes	180.36	34.93
Excise taxes	224.06	43.39
Other	14.55	2.82
Total	516.36	100.00

SOURCE: Government of India.

this regime may be broken down as follows. Almost 35 percent of tax collections came from customs. This is a distortionary tax that would have to fall to much lower levels as part of the economic reforms program, including trade liberalization in particular.

There was also an unhealthy reliance on indirect taxes (which added up to 78 percent of tax collections). This is inconsistent with the normative prescriptions that flow from public economics, and which favor direct taxes.

Personal income tax rates were extremely high, with a peak of 56 percent. While this was an improvement over the level of 77 percent from 1976 to 1977, it was still one of the highest rates of personal income tax in the world.

Customs and excise tariffs were extremely complex, with myriad rates, active political lobbying about each tariff line, and ground-level enforcement difficulties that are generally associated with a complex tax code.

Income tax rules were marred by numerous special cases and exemptions that simultaneously distorted financial markets and inhibited tax collections. The number of individuals who paid income tax was just six million.

The manufacturing sector bore the brunt of indirect taxation, even though manufacturing accounted for only 18 percent of GDP.

4. *The Tax Reforms of the 1990s*

The balance of payments crisis of 1991 was widely viewed as being integrally related to the large fiscal deficits that India experienced in the late 1980s. Hence, fiscal reforms were high priorities for policy makers in the early 1990s. These reforms may be divided into four broad categories: reduction of rates, improvements in the tax base, improvements in compliance, and simplification and rationalization.

In recent years, there has been an extensive effort to reduce the complexity of the tax system and remove glaring inconsistencies. This has helped reduce the costs of compliance for the economy, reduced the rate of noncompliance, and diminished the resources devoted by economic agents toward lobbying for favorable tax rules.

In the case of personal income tax, the number of rates was reduced to just three. The excise tax has been progressively converted from a specific tax into an ad valorem levy for most commodities. The facility of providing credit on input taxes under the MODVAT (modified value-added tax) program has been progressively extended to a larger number of commodities, reaching the present situation where over 80 percent of excise comes from commodities with MODVAT. MODVAT has further evolved into CENVAT (central value-added tax).

4.1 Reduction of Rates

There was a widespread recognition that the tax system in 1990 featured extremely high rates of taxation. This encouraged taxpayers to devote resources to tax avoidance, and distorted economic activities in the search for lower tax incidence. As a response to these concerns, in the 1990s rates have fallen sharply for income and customs taxes.

The peak personal marginal income tax rate fell from 56 percent in 1990–91 to 30 percent today. Corporate income tax rates were progressively reduced for both domestic and foreign companies to 35 percent and 40 percent, respectively. Both these rates are now at low levels by world standards.

In the case of customs, in 1990–91 the unweighted average nominal tariff was 12 percent and the peak rate was 355 percent. These were progressively reduced to a point where the peak rate is now 35 percent and the average rate has dropped below 20 percent. This is still one of the highest rates of tariff protection in the world, and needs to drop to near-zero levels as part of trade liberalization.

4.2 Widening in the Tax Base

One of the major weaknesses of the tax regime as of 1990 was the tiny base of individuals and firms that accounted for the entire tax revenue of the government (at relatively high tax rates). One of the central goals of tax reforms was to move toward low tax rates applied on a wide tax base. This effort has been particularly successful in the area of income tax.

In the case of income tax, in 1997, the government introduced four presumptive criteria to identify potential taxpayers. The criteria were (a) home ownership, (b) visit to a foreign country, (c) ownership of a telephone, and (d) ownership of a motor vehicle. Individuals who met any two of these four criteria were required by law to *file* a tax return regardless of the level of income.[3] This strategy has been highly successful in sharply increasing the number of individuals filing tax returns: an increase of 120 percent over 1997–2000. At the same time, it appears that roughly 50 percent of potential taxpayers continue to be outside the tax net.

The service sector has been an extremely fast growing sector and now accounts for around half of GDP. Hence, it was very important to add services into the tax base (Rao 2001). A "service tax" was introduced for some services in July 1994, and the list has been gradually expanded to cover more services.

The base for excise taxes was broadened by removing exemptions and levying excise at the lowest rate of 8 percent.

4.3 Improving Compliance

The foundation of successful tax collections, in the emerging environment with a simple and rational tax system, low tax rates, and a wide tax base, has to be a pervasive climate of compliance. Many elements of tax policy in the 1990s were designed to improve levels of compliance.

In particular, there were many concerns about how firms creatively exploited depreciation provisions to pay zero income tax. This led to proposals to use a minimum alternative asset-based tax (MAT). However, a minimum alternative tax implemented through assets has many flaws (Shah 1996; Rajaraman and Koshy 1996), and the implementation of the MAT in India avoided that route. From 1997 to 1998, a MAT was introduced for firms whereby a company with taxable profits less than 30 percent of its adjusted book profits (profits calculated under the Companies Act of 1956) would have to pay a minimum tax on 30 percent of the book profits at the tax rates in force.

5. What Have the Reforms Achieved?

Figure 6.3 shows the time series of the tax-to-GDP ratio. Many observers have pointed out that the tax-to-GDP ratio is still below its levels in the late 1980s. This observation, taken in isolation, is sometimes interpreted as implying a failure of tax reforms in India. However, this aggregate number masks important accomplishments in effecting change.

Table 6.3 summarizes changes in the *structure* of tax revenues from 1990 to 2000. The most important accomplishment was in the area of direct taxes, which grew by almost 600 percent over these 11 years, rising sharply from 19 percent of collections to 36 percent. This may be interpreted as a striking "Laffer curve" outcome, where a sharp reduction in rates was accompanied by an improvement in tax collections, by decreasing incentives for tax evasion and influencing labor supply decisions.

The average customs tariff fell sharply over this period (Figure 6.4). This reflects efforts to liberalize foreign trade during the period and resulted in the share of customs in overall tax collections falling from 35 percent to 25 percent. This constitutes a reduction in the vulnerability of public finance to tariff reforms, but at a quarter of tax collections it remains a substantial fraction. In coming years, India will need to obtain a correspondingly large increase in noncustoms revenues simply to replace the impact on the exchequer of the tariff reforms likely to take place.

The growth of excise collection over this period has been disappointing. In Figure 6.5 we examine excise collections, expressed as a fraction of the "tax base," which we may approximately define as the value added in manufactur-

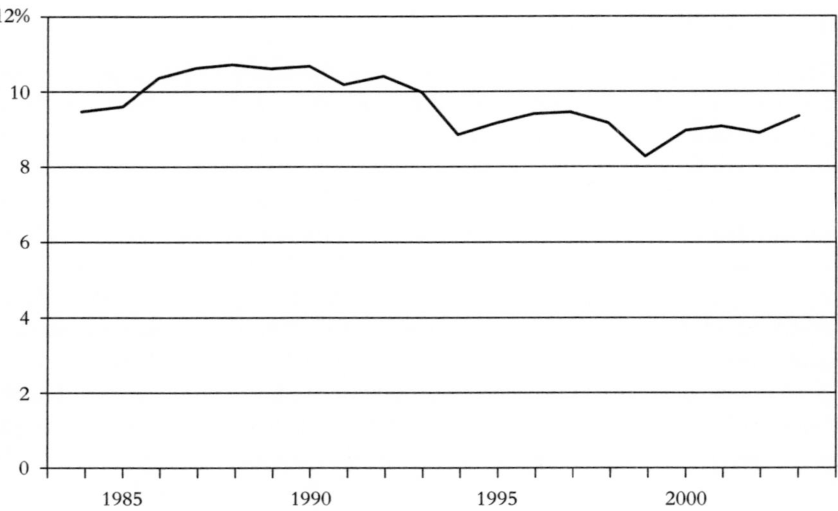

Figure 6.3. Tax-to-GDP Ratio (%).
SOURCE: CMIE.

TABLE 6.3
Structure of Tax Revenues in 2000

Source	Amount Collected in 2000 (Billions Rs)	Change from 1990 Amount Collected (Billion Rs)	% of Total Collected in 2000	Change from 1990 % of Total
Personal income tax	317.64	267.54	16.84	7.14
Corporate income tax	356.96	309.67	18.93	9.70
Customs taxes	475.42	295.06	25.21	−9.70
Excise taxes	685.26	461.20	36.33	−7.10
Service tax*	26.13	26.13	1.39	1.40
Other	24.63	10.08	1.31	−1.50
Total	1,886.04	1,369.68	100.00	(NA)

SOURCE: Government of India.

ing. By this measure, excise incidence fell sharply from 30 percent in 1991–92 to 20 percent in 1996–97.

In seeking to explain this decline, Shah (2002) observes that during the period reforms to excise rates and rules were broadly tax neutral. Over this period, it appears that excise collections from 4000 large firms rose from roughly 70 percent of all collections to above 90 percent. This may reflect a combination of (a) worsening of the quality of tax compliance for firms outside the largest 4000,

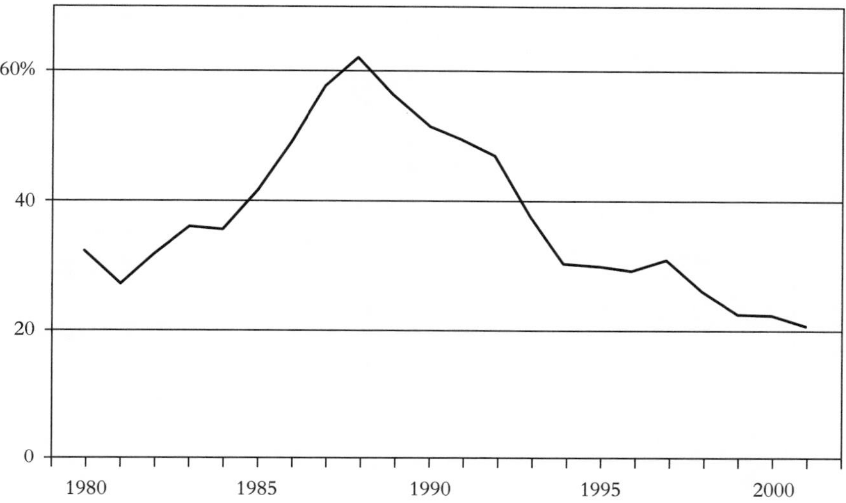

Figure 6.4. Customs Collections per Unit Gross Imports (%).
SOURCE: CMIE.

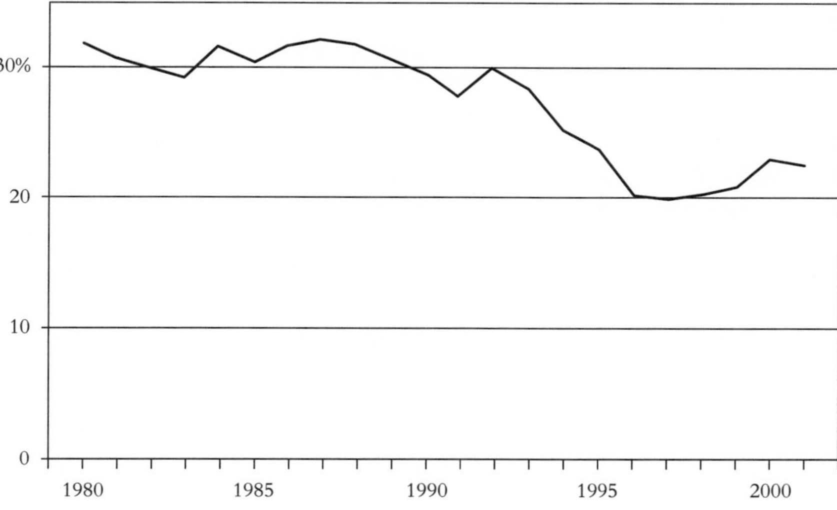

Figure 6.5. Excise Collections per Unit Manufacturing GDP (%).
SOURCE: CMIE.

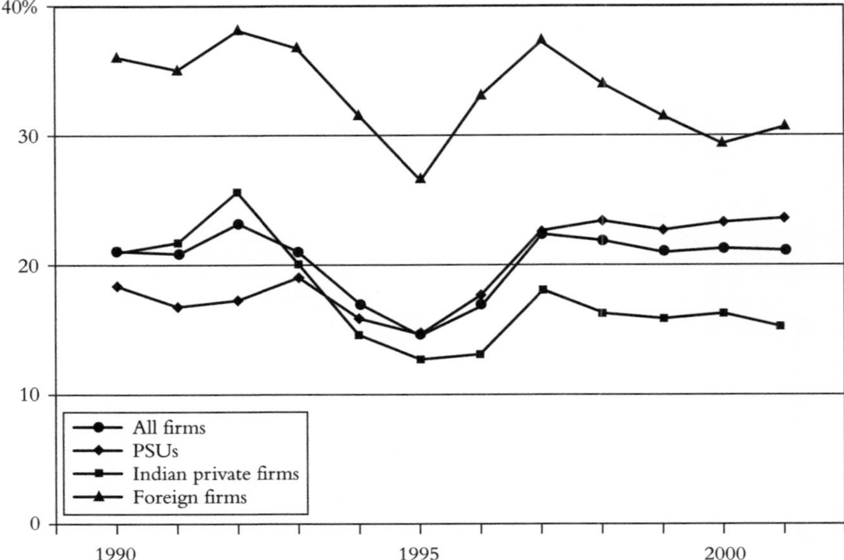

Figure 6.6. Average Income Tax among Profitable Firms in the CMIE Prowess Database.

SOURCE: CMIE.

and (b) changes to excise rules and exemptions that adversely affected tax collections, particularly from smaller firms. In particular, the extension of 100 percent MODVAT on capital goods and the misuse of MODVAT are likely to have been particularly serious among smaller firms.

Figure 6.6 gives us some insight into the quality of tax enforcement at the level of firms. The income tax faced by firms came down sharply during the period. At the same time, the overall average tax stayed roughly intact at 21 percent. There may be opportunities for substantial improvements in compliance here, given the fact that foreign firms and public sector firms seem to have much higher average tax rates when compared with private Indian firms.

6. Directions for Reforms

6.1 Structural Reforms

India has made enormous progress in rationalizing and simplifying the tax system. When compared with the tax regime in 1990, most of the first-order defects have been cured, but some issues still need to be addressed on this front:

Customs tariffs will have to drop sharply to much lower levels as part of the program of trade liberalization. There is a strong case for having a single flat customs rate of 10 percent or lower.

The central excise tax, the central service tax, the state excise tax, and the state sales tax need to be combined in a single, nationwide VAT (value-added tax) at a single rate.

Income tax continues to be plagued by significant exemptions, particularly distortions to the financial sector whereby certain financial instruments obtain different tax treatments than others. There is a need to move away from this paradigm toward one where all financial instruments are taxed equally.

Income tax is an area where simplification has not made progress on the same scale as in customs and excise taxes. There continues to be a strong case to replace the present Income Tax Act with a truly rational and simplified one.

These are important issues, which should perhaps be seen as the "last stretch of structural tax reforms" in the country. It is expected that policy makers will take up these issues as a priority in the coming two to five years.

The dominant issue in tax policy is that of enforcement and implementation.

6.2 Enforcement

The above discussion suggests that there is a need for a quantum leap in the quality of *enforcement* of tax laws. How can enforcement and implementation be transformed? One approach is that of tough policing. But, given the limited governance capacity in the country, there are serious limits to which the "inspector raj" can be used to obtain a substantial improvement in the tax-to-GDP ratio.

Hence, there is a need for a paradigm shift, in which the prime focus in enforcement is moved away from policing to being based on *a pervasive transparency of the operations and transactions of economic agents*. In an information-rich environment, where a great deal of data about the activities of economic agents is visible to tax authorities in electronic form, it is easy to detect inconsistencies associated with tax evasion. This suggests that the stance of policy should be based on three elements.

First, tax authorities should harness existing publicly available databases about firms and individuals, and seek to obtain an integrated perspective about the activities of taxpayers. These publicly available databases include the CMIE Prowess database (which has comprehensive information for about 6000 large firms), the CMIE DCA database (which has limited information for about 150,000 firms), securities transactions information from the NSDL, and transaction-level information from banks. Tax authorities should *integrate* information flowing from all these channels in order to build a composite picture of the activities of each taxable entity.

Second, the focus of enforcement agencies should be to harness these electronic data for the purpose of detecting evidence of tax evasion. For example, it is easy to obtain sorted tables within an industry of the firms having the lowest excise payments per unit revenues. Further, since excise evasion is usually done through illegal removal of finished goods from factories, and it is easy to obtain sorted tables within an industry of firms, agencies could audit those that have the lowest excise payments per unit raw material expenses.

In a transparent environment, many strands of information about a firm combine to constrain the ability of a firm to engage in illegal activities on any one front. It is important to coordinate a single, integrated effort among income, customs, and excise taxes that seeks to collect information from multiple aspects of the functioning of the taxed entity.

The institutional infrastructure of the country should be redesigned so as to improve transparency and give better information to tax authorities about the activities of economic agents. Examples of such initiatives include (a) mandatory submission of payroll databases to tax authorities; (b) tagging of tax identification numbers on all financial securities transactions; (c) removal of existing impediments for public access to information filed by firms to the Registrar of Companies—where filing of the balance sheet is mandatory, but filing and dissemination of the profit-and-loss statement is not; and (d) prohibiting cash transactions in any purchase above a certain threshold (such as Rs 10,000). A comprehensive VAT would play a powerful role in this by generating information about multiple firms in production chains.

There are situations where innovative new information sources can be brought to bear on tax compliance problems by utilizing alternative institutional mechanisms. For example, in the area of customs, preshipment inspection in the country of supply of imports, on behalf of the government of the importing country, can be done in order to verify the value and classification of goods for customs purposes.

Currently, there is a narrow focus in tax collection on the largest firms. The CMIE Prowess database of approximately 6000 large firms accounted for 58 percent of income tax and 83 percent of excise payments (CMIE 2002). It is possible to obtain a sound tax compliance regime for all 150,000 nontrivial firms in the country by improving the transparency of the environment about the activities of these firms on the lines described above.

Through these approaches, the modern technologies of information processing and transmission open up remarkable opportunities for obtaining tax compliance without bringing about an oppressive policing culture.[4]

7. *The Destination for Tax Reforms: A Numerical Blueprint*

In this section, I explore the contours of tax collections in 2000–2001 under a sound, well-designed tax regime. These are obviously highly approximate calculations. However, they do serve to bring out the orders of magnitude involved and focus our attention on the key issues that need to be addressed.

These calculations use numerical values from 2000–2001. The process of tax reform will take several years, and the economy will be very different at that time when compared with the situation of 2000–2001. However, focusing on 2000–2001 is useful since it allows us to grapple with numerical values that were realized in 2000–2001.

Currently, the tax-to-GDP ratio is 9 percent, and the central government gross fiscal deficit is 6 percent of GDP. We will assume that the goal of tax policy should be to obtain central tax revenues of 15 percent of GDP.

As discussed above, one major element of tax reforms will be to phase out customs duties, so as to enable India to fully embrace international trade and benefit from it. This process implies that revenues of Rs 475 billion, or 2.3 percent of GDP, will be lost.

The central elements of taxation in our idealized tax regime would be a VAT and income tax. We first obtain broad estimates for direct taxes.

7.1 Personal Income Tax

Private final consumption expenditure is currently 65 percent of GDP. We may assume that the tax base here is made up of the richest 10 percent of the population, who have 24 percent of the income. This would imply that roughly 20 million households would file taxes, which is consistent with existing data on filers. If we assume an average tax incidence of 20 percent, applied to a tax base of 15.6 percent of GDP, this yields tax revenues of 3.1 percent of GDP.

7.2 Corporate Income Tax

The largest 6333 firms in India are directly observed in the CMIE Prowess database. If we focus on the profitable firms among these, the aggregate profit was Rs 970 billion, or 4.6 percent of GDP. These large firms account for approximately 60 percent of the profit by firms in India. We will assume that improvements in tax compliance are able to bring up the tax incidence from the region of 20 percent (for all CMIE Prowess firms) to the region of 30 percent (which is the level currently seen with foreign firms). Hence, if we assume an average tax incidence of 30 percent applied to a tax base of 7.5 percent of GDP, this yields tax revenues of 2.25 percent of GDP.

This reasoning suggests that direct taxes could deliver 8.75 percent of GDP.

7.3 Value-Added Tax

The tax base in the case of manufacturing, measured by value added from registered manufacturing as a percentage of GDP, was 11.5 percent. In addition, we

TABLE 6.4

Tax Revenues in 2000–2001, Reality vs. Blueprint

	Reality		Blueprint	
Source	Amount Collected	% of GDP	Amount Collected	% of GDP
Personal income taxes	317.64	1.52	647.28	3.1
Corporate income taxes	356.96	1.71	469.80	2.3
Customs taxes	475.42	2.27	313.20	1.5
Excise taxes	685.26	3.28	0.00	0.0
Service taxes	26.13	0.13	0.00	0.0
Single VAT	0.00	0.00	1,645.34	7.9
Total	1,886.04	9.03	2,982.15	14.3

SOURCE: Government of India and author's calculations.

may assume that 20 percent of GDP comes from services, which can be brought into the tax base without substantial costs of collection or noncompliance. This gives us an aggregate tax base for the VAT of 31.5 percent of GDP. A VAT that obtained average tax incidence of 25 percent would yield 7.9 percent of GDP. This assumes a *lower* tax incidence for manufacturing than the value of 32.2 percent currently seen for excise payments made by the CMIE Prowess firms.

Table 6.4 summarizes the status as of 2000–2001 and the hypothetical scenario as envisioned in these calculations. It suggests that we need to build a single VAT of 25 percent on both manufacturing and services, which would yield 7.9 percent of GDP as tax revenues. We need a major effort to apply an average personal income tax of 20 percent to the richest 30 percent of the country, which would yield 6.5 percent of GDP. This would give us tax collections amounting to 16.6 percent of GDP and a roughly zero fiscal deficit assuming the current level of spending is held intact.

8. Conclusion

Tax collection is widely acknowledged to be one of the most important problems for economic policy in India. The lack of improvement in the tax-to-GDP ratio has led to pessimism about tax reforms. While these concerns about the final outcome are well placed, there have been important successes in terms of structural change in the tax regime.

In the case of income, excise, and customs taxes, substantial reforms have taken place to simplify and rationalize the tax structure. Direct tax collections grew by 600 percent over an 11-year period. At the same time, customs revenues grew sluggishly due to tariff reforms. The net result was low growth in the tax-to-GDP ratio.

Looking forward, some outstanding issues remain to be addressed in terms of structural changes to the tax regime. However, the fundamental focus of tax policy must now be on improving compliance. We argue that this will best be achieved by obtaining a paradigm shift in transparency, and access to comprehensive information about all aspects of the taxed entity. The tax authorities should invest in information systems that detect inconsistencies and thus locate tax evaders. The focus should be on creating an information-rich environment, rather than hiring more inspectors.

Notes

1. The state electricity boards (SEBs) consistently suffered losses in the 1990s, rising from 12.7 percent of invested capital in 1991–92 to 21.1 percent in 1998–99 (Government of India 2000).

2. For example, compared to an average cost of generation and distribution of power of Rs 1.86 per kilowatt in 1996–97, the average price charged to farmers was only Rs 0.21, and that to all domestic consumers was only Rs 0.90. While industrial users paid a higher unit price, the average revenues earned by SEBs covered only 80 percent of the cost.

3. The details of this approach have been modified in the following years.

4. Information technology is central to the functioning of the tax authorities at a more mundane level also. As of March 2000, there were 12.8 million assessments pending with the Income Tax Department, reflecting the highly limited utilization of information technology in the process engineering of the department.

References

Buiter, W. H., and U. R. Patel. 1992. Debt, deficits, and inflation: An application to the public finances of India. *Journal of Public Economics* 47:172–205.

Chelliah, R. J., and R. K. Rao. 2001. *Rational ways of increasing tax revenues in India.* Technical Report. New Delhi: Madras School of Economics and NIPFP.

CMIE. 2002. *Corporate sector.* Economic Intelligence Service Report. Bombay: CMIE.

Government of India. 2000. *Economic survey, 1999–2000.* New Delhi: Ministry of Finance.

Lahiri, A., and R. Kannan. 2001. *India's fiscal deficits and their sustainability in perspective.* Technical Report. New Delhi: NIPFP.

Rajaraman, I., and T. Koshy. 1996. *A minimum alternative asset-based corporate tax for India. Economic and Political Weekly* 31 (29): 1941–52.

Rao, M. G. 2000. Tax reform in India: Achievements and challenges. *Asia-Pacific Development Journal* 7 (2): 59–74.

———. 2001. *Taxing services: Issues and strategy.* Technical Report. Bangalore: Institute for Social and Economic Change.

Shah, A. 1996. Minimum asset-based tax: A critique. *Economic and Political Weekly* 21 (30): 2046–48.

———. 2002. Understanding the slow growth of excise revenues. Technical Report. Mumbai: IGIDR and Ministry of Finance.

Shome, P. 2000. *India: Primary aspects of a medium term fiscal strategy.* Technical Report. New Delhi: ICRIER.

Srinivasan, T. N. 2000. *India's fiscal situation: Is a crisis ahead?* Technical Report. New Haven, Conn.: Yale University.

INDEX